THE
Wildest of the West

THE
Wildest of the West

FORBES PARKHILL

NEW YORK : HENRY HOLT AND COMPANY

COPYRIGHT, 1951, BY FORBES PARKHILL

Designed by Maurice Serle Kaplan

PRINTED IN THE UNITED STATES OF AMERICA

Biog 264 50

To the
DENVER POSSE
of
THE WESTERNERS

ACKNOWLEDGMENTS

THE AUTHOR gratefully acknowledges the generous assistance of Miss Ina T. Aulls, Head of the Western History Department of the Denver Public Library, and of her assistant, Mrs. Alys H. Freeze; of Acting Director and State Historian, Agnes Wright Spring of the Colorado State Historical Society, and her assistant, Miss Frances Shea; of members of the staffs of the Library of Congress, the Chicago Public Library, and the library of the Denver *Post*; and of deputies in the offices of the Clerks of the District and County Courts, Denver, Colorado.

Individuals to whom he is indebted for information included in these pages are: Herbert O. Brayer, Coleman Bell, Andrew L. Dillon, Hattie Green, John W. Fishback, Miss Mary F. Lathrop, James Maxwell, Fred M. Mazzulla, Charles Nolan, Miss Bertha Stockdorf, W. S. Thompson, Philip S. Van Cise, and L. S. Watson, all of Denver; Thomas M. Ashton, Jr., Tom Gant, William Rife, Will F. Toner, and C. M. Webster, all of Wray, Colorado; G. P. Shafer of Laird, Max W. Vawter of Leadville, Joseph Emerson Smith of Georgetown, J. J. Lipsey of Colorado Springs, Russell Thorp of Cheyenne, Wyoming, and Omer Holman of Peru, Indiana.

CONTENTS

ACKNOWLEDGMENTS   vii

BOOK ONE
HELL'S BELLES

1. Madame Vestal   3
2. Street of the Sinners   13
3. Brides of the Multitude   21
4. Oscar Wilde and the Gay Ladies   33
5. House of a Thousand Scandals   40
6. Riches Make Strange Bedfellows   50

BOOK TWO
GOLDEN FLEECE

7. Wooers of Lady Luck   63
8. Hot Decks and Cold   75

9. King of the Thimbleriggers   87
10. Overlord of the Underworld   97
11. Hop Alley   108
12. Headlines and Deadlines   117

BOOK THREE
DENIZENS OF THE OVERWORLD

13. Noblest Roamer of Them All   129
14. Queen Victoria's Colorado Cousin   141
15. Barren Gain and Bitter Loss   151
16. Memories that Bless and Burn   166
17. The Happy Dutchman   175
18. The Last of the Penroses   190

BOOK FOUR
SCARLET LADY

19. Mattie Get Your Gun   207
20. Scarlet Sister Mattie   214
21. Knight in Tarnished Armor   226
22. Wide, Wide Open Spaces   237
23. Pigs' Feet and Whisky   247
24. Sentimental Journey   255
25. Red Northern Lights   267
26. The Tumult and the Shouting   278

NOTES   287
BIBLIOGRAPHY   289
INDEX   295

BOOK ONE

Hell's·Belles

(1)

Madame Vestal

DENVER was a lusty, wide-open, free-spending young frontier city in 1876. Born of the Pikes Peak gold rush, nurtured on the wealth pouring from the mines of the richest square mile on earth at Central City, it had been transformed from a boom town to a boom city by the coming of the Kansas Pacific Railroad six years earlier. The resultant real estate and building boom yielded a golden harvest equal to anything produced up to that time by the nearby gold diggings.

This brave, new, Western world boasted some of America's most extraordinary characters, bad and not so bad. Of the most colorful many were denizens of the frontier's bold and brash new underworld.

Bad and better alike, they had plenty of money and no lack of ways to spend it. If one tired of spending it for real estate or mining stocks, there was always whisky. Or one could go down amid the red lights of Holladay Street, the wickedest street in the West's most sinful city, and spend his money on women.

And then, of course, there was Madame Vestal.

Soft-spoken Ed Chase, steely of eye and prematurely gray, was king of the gamblers, and Madame Vestal, dainty, dark of eye, and black of hair, was the Goddess of Chance. She held forth

3

in a huge tent on Blake Street and it was a positive delight to lose one's money to her, for she was accounted the most adept twenty-one dealer west of the Mississippi.

"Cards, gentlemen?" she would inquire gently in a cultivated voice sweetened by a soft Southern accent that seemed to breathe of the atmosphere of a plantation drawing room.

And when a bearded player would examine his hand and call, "Hit me, ma'am," she'd flip him another card with skill born of long practice—and smile. Smile faintly, a Mona Lisa wisp of a smile, a smile hinting of intriguing mystery.

It was this enigmatic smile that set her apart from all other professional gamblers, whose stock-in-trade is the frozen face. It set her apart from her own permanent employees, the impassive Fancy Dans who kept case at the faro bank, dealt stud, threw monte, spun the wheel, or tipped the keno goose. They were her trusted aides, the ones she had brought with her from yon side of the River. Her cappers and shills and ropers-in were local folk.

The young madame's flashing brown eyes were as unreadable as her wisp of a smile. Many an uncouth miner, fresh from the diggings, would have given all the dust in his poke to fathom their mystery.

None tried. In pioneer Denver one never questioned another about his—or her—past. Those who violated this quaint Western custom sometimes died abruptly, for many boomers, male and female, had had compelling reasons to leave their real names on the east bank of the Missouri. There, in her early thirties, Madame Vestal had left her real name, a famous name, a name every player in the gambling hell would have recognized. In fact, the good madame was in habit of changing her name every time she changed towns.

Madame Vestal's establishment included, as a matter of course, a bar, a temporary affair of rough planking; for to follow the booms she was prepared to fold her tent and move her equipment on a moment's notice. But in one respect her place was unlike any of the Blake Street gambling hells; it was a place for men without women.

She employed no feminine ropers-in, with their sweet talk, low necks, short skirts, and spangles. She was not like Katie Fulton and Minnie Clifford and Lizzie Preston and other madames of Holladay Street for, as perhaps her name was intended to indicate, Madame Vestal had nothing to sell but the chance to win something for nothing, plus the customary refreshments. Moreover, her games were reputed to be on the square.

All manner of men thronged through the madame's gaming establishment, so it is remotely possible that someone might have recognized her—someone from Jefferson City, Missouri, who had been a guest at the society debut, shortly after her graduation from the Female University at Lexington, of the charming young kinswoman of Missouri's last governor before the Civil War. Or one of the dashing young junior officers attached to the headquarters of Union generals H. W. Halleck and Newton M. Curtis; the young men who had escorted her to box parties at De Bar's Opera House at St. Louis and had lost their hearts and some of the Union's most vital military secrets.

For the name that Madame Vestal had left behind her on the eastern bank of the Missouri was the name of the celebrated Confederate spy, Belle Siddons.

At the outbreak of the Civil War the population of Missouri was almost equally divided in its sympathies between the North and the South. Governor Claiborne Fox Jackson was a rebel sympathizer, but the state assembly voted in the spring of '61 to adhere to the Union. Politically the state was Democratic, St. Louis Republican.

On November 18, 1861, Major General Halleck relieved General John C. Fremont as commander of the Union Department of the Mississippi, with headquarters at St. Louis. The city teemed with Confederate sympathizers, including some women of social distinction. General Halleck issued a manifesto against these "rebel rousers," who even "carried rebel flags on their persons and waved them at their rebel friends in the Gratiot Street prison." One prominent feminine church worker was found guilty of conveying important information to the enemy and was banished from the state. Other women of high position, who had lived outside the city, fled to St. Louis for safety. Some hatched schemes to aid the Confederacy. Some were removed to other states.

Fetching Belle Siddons was a belle of St. Louis prewar society. She was intensely Southern in her sympathies, but during the early years of the war her admirers were officers attached to Union Headquarters. These junior officers were her escorts from time to time at various social functions, and many were the military secrets that wound up in the possession of the charming Belle.

In December, 1862, General Curtis ordered her arrest as a spy. She fled on horseback but was captured near Ste. Genevieve. Documentary evidence of her activities was found on her person, and she was taken back to St. Louis. The petite prisoner confessed her guilt to General John M. Schofield, boasting that she had kept Confederate generals Nathan B. Forrest and Sterling Price informed of every movement planned at Union headquarters.

"I was the one," she proclaimed defiantly, "who provided the information enabling Forrest to cut off Grant's troops by his raid on the Memphis & Mobile railroad."

Sentenced to the Grant Street rebel prison, she speedily exerted her charms on the provost marshal. After keeping her prisoner for four months, he released her on condition she leave the state.

After the war she returned to Jefferson City, where she made use of her charms by becoming a lobbyist. There she met and married Dr. Newt Hallett of Kansas City, an army surgeon. The couple went to Texas, where he instructed her in the study of medicine and taught her dissection. When he died of yellow fever, she became for a time a tutor at the Red Cloud Indian

Agency, and subsequently a skilled twenty-one dealer in a gambling house at Wichita. Later she operated her own gambling establishments at Ellsworth, Fort Hays, and Cheyenne. The winter of '75-76 found her in Denver, operating her tented gambling hell under the name of Madame Vestal.

Meanwhile, in 1874, gold had been discovered in the Black Hills of South Dakota. The Indians objected to the appropriation of their lands by gold-seekers but, as usual, they finally were ejected, and their lands were thrown open to the whites.

By the winter of '75-76, Denver was almost depopulated of its boomers. The click of the roulette wheel in Madame Vestal's canvas Palace of Chance became more and more infrequent, and the twenty-one table no longer resounded to the sucker's cry of "Hit me again, ma'am." One by one her cappers and shills deserted her, victims of the gold fever.

The enterprising madame was prepared for just such an emergency. She bought a freight wagon to transport her tent, her gambling paraphernalia, her spindlemen, her dealers, and her case keepers. For herself she acquired—of all things—an omnibus, which she furnished like a boudoir, with dainty lace curtains and satin cushions.

Ensconced in this strange vehicle which resembled, as much as anything, a modern automobile trailer, she set out in regal seclusion and splendor for the new boom town of Deadwood, followed by her entourage in the freight wagon.

She might have traveled as far as Cheyenne by rail, but beyond the Wyoming capital she had no choice but to follow the dusty route of the soon-to-be famous Cheyenne-Deadwood stagecoach trail.

Already, as gold was beginning to be shipped out from the new diggings, the trail was the scene of frequent stagecoach holdups. Before long it was to witness a tragedy destined to reshape the destiny of the attractive young widow and ex-spy.

Somewhere along the line she changed her name again. When

her fancied-up omnibus rolled down the muddy main street of Deadwood, she called herself Lurline Monte Verde.

Her arrival was hailed with rejoicing, for many of the gold-seekers had been patrons of her Denver establishment. They staged an "old home week" welcoming celebration, which was described by a correspondent of the New York *Tribune* as follows:

> Then there is Monte Verde, with her dark eyes and tresses, who on her arrival in Deadwood stood on a board and was borne through the town on the shoulders of four strapping miners, and who now deals "Twenty-one" and dances a jig with a far-off look in her left eye.

Another writer described her as a "flawlessly groomed beauty, artfully jeweled and gowned," and wrote that at the time she was a total abstainer.

The lovely newcomer set up a gambling establishment in her tent on Main Street near Wall, in the heart of what was known as Deadwood's "Bad Lands" district. Among her patrons were outlaws, gunmen, prospectors, businessmen, law officers, soldiers; all the boomers and riffraff and adventurers and legitimate fortune-seekers who had been lured to the latest boomtown by the hope of gaining quick and easy riches.

Among them was the famed marshal and gunman, Wild Bill Hickok, who was shot from behind in another gaming house by Jack McCall on August 2, 1876, while holding what came to be known as the "dead man's hand."

Always, until this time, the petite lady gambler had kept her admirers strictly at arm's length, for she was convinced that romance and the cold business of gambling would not mix. And then, late one night, into her place strolled a burly young ruffian who walked with a swagger, stared at her long and boldly, and lost his last cent because he was unable to keep his mind on his cards.

Perhaps it was because he lost with a laugh instead of an oath, but something about him touched the sensibilities of the lady.

"Can I stake you to breakfast money?" she asked him, her feelings masked by her ever-present Mona Lisa smile.

"Thank you, ma'am, but no woman pays for Archie Cummings' grub," he replied, with a good-natured grin that revealed the absence of a front tooth. "But, if you don't mind, I'm coming back when my luck turns, and take you out to breakfast. Is it a go?"

A week later he was back, with a pocket full of gold. Perhaps she was unaware that he had acquired it by holding up a stagecoach, or perhaps she knew and just didn't care.

Everyone else knew that the young ruffian's real name was Archie McLaughlin and that he had fought as one of Quantrell's guerrilla raiders on the Kansas border during the last year of the Civil War. Now, as an enterprising road agent, he was accumulating sufficient wealth to make quite a splurge in Deadwood's various gambling hells.

She learned about his record soon enough, but by this time she was desperately in love with Archie. Whether he returned her affection is uncertain, but it is quite certain that he took advantage of her facilities for acquiring important information.

Heavy winners often were robbed of their take within a few minutes of leaving a gambling establishment. Some of these robberies were engineered by the gambling house proprietors themselves as a means of recouping their losses. Others resulted from tips provided by dealers and croupiers, who came in for a cut of the proceeds.

But Archie was shooting for bigger game. He was no penny-ante back-alley holdup. His specialty was the treasure chests containing gold shipped by stagecoach from the Deadwood mines. Drivers and guards and company employees with a drink too many under their belts were inclined to talk too much if wheedled a bit by a charming young lady with a Mona Lisa smile. Most of Archie's tips came through his sweetheart.

But criminals were not the only ones who made use of underworld clearinghouses of information. Boone May, a former stagecoach driver who became a famous peace officer, became acquainted with Belle Siddons-Vestal-Monte Verde and from her learned of plans for a stagecoach holdup in Whoop-up Canon between Deadwood and Rapid City.

On the night of July 2, 1878, the stagecoach carrying the treasure box was filled with special deputies armed with an arsenal of rifles and revolvers.

Archie, along with young Billy Mansfield and other members of his band of road agents, expected to turn an easy trick. When the coach was forced to halt by a cottonwood tree felled across the road, the highwaymen closed in. Alexander Casswell yelled "Up with 'em!" and grabbed for the bits of the coach horses. Archie and the others surrounded the vehicle.

As soon as they were all in the open, the deputies cut loose with a volley. Casswell dropped dead, a slug through his head. Bandit John H. Brown was shot through the abdomen, the bullet lodging near his spine. Archie was slightly wounded. Billy Mansfield and Jack Smith were unhurt. The surviving road agents fled, with the wounded Brown clinging desperately to the horn of his saddle. They holed up in a shanty in the timber near Deadwood.

For ten days Brown suffered as his wound festered, for his friends feared to call a doctor. It was Archie who finally solved the problem, for Belle had told him she had studied dissection under her army surgeon former husband. He sent Billy Mansfield to arrange a meeting with her in a Deadwood opium den.

"Can you dig a lead slug out of a man's carcass?" he asked her.

"I can try," was her response. "But why should I?"

"Because Archie wants you to," said Billy. That settled it so far as she was concerned. She followed the highwayman to the shanty where Brown lay, gritting his teeth in agony. With no other equipment than a short length of wire she probed the wound and succeeded in extracting the bullet.

According to one version of the story, one of the road agents wanted to kill her to make certain their secret was safe, and Archie was forced to draw a gun on him while she left the cabin and returned safely to Deadwood.

Could she have foreseen the consequences of her act of mercy, in all likelihood she would have let Brown die. For shortly after he recovered he was arrested and confessed, implicating Smith, Mansfield, and her sweetheart Archie.

Traveling by night, the three fled from the Black Hills country but a few months later were arrested and jailed at Cheyenne. Belle had planned to join him at San Francisco. On the night of November 3, 1878, on their way back to Deadwood in irons to stand trial for grand larceny, their stagecoach was halted by five masked Vigilantes at Little Cottonwood Creek, a mile north of Fort Laramie. The guards were overpowered and the prisoners were taken to a cottonwood grove near Watson's saloon, where ropes were looped about their necks. Billy Mansfield, the youngest, wept and begged for mercy. But Archie remained defiant to the last.

"Go ahead and hang me and to the hell with you," he challenged as he cursed his captors. "But you'll never find the $8,000 in loot that I stashed away in the hills."

They lynched him, along with his pals, and they never found the loot.

According to another version, the Vigilantes promised to spare his life and permit him to stand trial on the robbery charge if he would reveal the hiding place of the loot. He agreed to the proposal and led them to the spot where the gold was buried, but after they had recovered the money they broke their pledge and hanged him.

Brokenhearted at the death of her sweetheart, Belle swallowed poison. Failing to kill herself, she set about drinking herself to death and became addicted to the use of opium. She could bear the associations of Deadwood no longer. She dismissed her employees, sold her paraphernalia, and went to Cheyenne, but stayed only a short time.

She drifted to Leadville in 1879, and for a few months operated a dance hall on State Street. Then, her interest in life gone, she went to Las Vegas, New Mexico, to Tombstone, Arizona, and finally to San Francisco.

As one of the most skillful twenty-one dealers in the West, she never lacked for money, but spent most of it attempting to assuage her sorrow with whisky.

In October, 1881, she was arrested and jailed at San Francisco. The newspaper account of her arrest reported that she was far from destitute but was at the point of death from dissipation. She was transferred from her cell to the hospital ward where, after the chaplain had urged her to confess her sins, she revealed the story of her life substantially as here set forth.

There the record of Belle Siddons-Mrs. Hallet-Madame Vestal-Lurline Monte Verde ends. Perhaps she died in jail, dreaming of the days of her youth when she was daring death as one of the nation's leading spies—or, more likely, dreaming of the sweetheart who died at the end of a hempen rope under a cottonwood limb.

(2)

Street of the Sinners

DENVER'S Holladay Street, the most wicked street in the wild, wild West in the seventies and eighties, was the street of nobody's women and everybody's women. There, approximately one thousand "brides of the multitude" were inmates of the imposing "parlor houses" and lowly "cribs" which lined both sides of the street for a distance of three city blocks. This, the lusty frontier city's red-light district, was commonly known as "The Row" or "The Line."

Denver's first tenderloin comprised a cluster of log cabins on the south bank of Cherry Creek, just west of Larimer Street, in the district then known as Auraria. In the sixties it jumped the creek and moved some six blocks to the north, centering on Holladay Street.

Originally this thoroughfare had been named McGaa Street, after one of Denver's earliest settlers. Later it was named for Ben Holladay, operator of the Central Overland, California, and Pikes Peak Express Company stagecoach lines.

Denver's Chinatown, better known as "Hop Alley," occupied an alley adjoining Holladay Street. Opium dens and Chinese gambling establishments had entrances on Holladay, filling the street with the faintly sweet odor of opium smoke.

13

In the sixties and seventies the principal gambling hells operated by Ed Chase and his various partners, including his brother John, Hub Heatley, Bob Austin, Barney Boyce, John J. Hughes, and Ed Gaylord, were to be found two blocks distant, on Blake Street. Later the gaming establishments moved to Larimer Street, adjoining and paralleling Holladay, and still later many moved "uptown" to Curtis Street.

Because of the unsavory reputation of Holladay Street, the heirs of upright Ben Holladay in 1889 petitioned the board of aldermen to change its name. Thereafter it has been known as Market Street, except for an interval when a section was called Walnut Street.

The West's outstanding madame, blond and beautiful Mattie Silks, who reigned for more than two decades as Queen of the Red Light, at one time owned three imposing parlor houses on The Row. In March 1884, she paid A. H. Waters & Co. $14,000 cash for the premises on Holladay Street. She was to occupy this house for a quarter of a century, until she was dethroned as queen by the dashing brunette, Jennie Rogers, in as weird a plot of blackmail and possible murder as ever adorned the pages of the most lurid fiction.

Lizzie Preston, who, all unaware, found herself a "sporting lady," held out at 433 Holladay Street for some years. A police raid on her place, led by the amazingly beautiful girl later known as Baby Doe Tabor, touched off the most hectic romance in all Western history and led to the beauty's marriage to the West's wealthiest bonanza king, Senator H. A. W. Tabor.

Other noted madames of the early days included May Smith, Belle Jewell, Emma Nelson, Gussie Grant, Emma Lewis, Anna Guy, Marie Putnam, Clara Hayden, Lola Livingston, and Helen McEvoy.

Latter-day madames, operating after the street name was changed to Market, included Annie Ryan, Belle Bernard, Jennie Caylor, Clara and Emily Dumont, Lillian Dumont, Leona de Camp, Eva Lewis, Faye Stanley, Minnie Hall, Jennie Holmes,

Annie Londeau, Annie Wilson. The Fashion, at 2005 Market Street, originally was operated by Blanche Brown, later by Rose Lovejoy, and still later by Belle London. Nearby was a sporting house known as Paradise Alley.

The house at 2020 Market was operated for some years by sloe-eyed, statuesque Verona Baldwin, who figured in a scandal that filled the headlines of California newspapers for three years. She claimed to be a kinswoman of the noted California millionaire and turfman, "Lucky" Baldwin, and shot him through the arm after charging that he seduced her.

Of the two principal parlor houses not located on The Row, one was conducted at 2301 Lawrence Street by Madame Anna "Gouldie" Gould. When open prostitution was outlawed in Denver she moved outside the city limits, catering to the "silk stocking" trade at a bungalow court resort not far from a country club. Her place was commonly known as the "club annex."

The house of Rosa Lee on Arapahoe Street was noted for its magnificent carved furniture and woodwork. In 1887 neighbors demanded the removal of the house. At the court hearing Rosa was described as an attractive, demure young brunette, "attired in a dark brown dress, fur-trimmed walking jacket and hat to match." She won her court battle and continued to operate her Arapahoe Street house for many years.

A Denver resident describes as follows a visit to Rosa Lee's house in the nineties when he was an A.D.T. messenger boy.

"A man in a private dining room on the second floor of Tortoni's restaurant at 1541 Arapahoe Street called me to deliver a note to a girl at Rosa Lee's house, directing that it must be delivered without fail to the girl in person. I delivered the message afoot, for I owned no bicycle.

"At first, because of my youth, the Negro porter wouldn't admit me. When I refused to deliver the message except to the girl herself, he reluctantly called her to the door. When she read the note she looked scared, and whispered to me: 'Go back and tell him I can't meet him now.'

"I started to walk back, but when I was a hundred yards away two men burst from the door of Rosa Lee's place. One of them pulled a gun and yelled at me to halt. I ran, finally hooking a ride on the back of a delivery wagon. I thought I had eluded them, but they had taken a cab and were following me in an effort to find out who had sent the message.

"They were right behind me when I went up the stairs of Tortoni's. The man who had given me the note to deliver stepped into the hall, and another man was right behind him. Before I could deliver the girl's message both men behind drew their guns and began to shoot. I dodged behind a marble statue of Eros as the other two returned the fire.

"As if at a signal the four men stopped shooting. Two ran out the front door and the other two out the back. I never learned what it was all about. Even though the pistol battle was almost next door to the offices of the Denver *Republican*, neither that paper nor any other printed the story."

Lack of ventilation was characteristic of all the parlor houses. It is doubtful if the windows were ever opened, and the places reeked of stale drinks, stale smoke, and stale perfume.

The madames liked to call their places "young ladies' boardinghouses."

The "boarders" split their earnings fifty-fifty with the madames, but out of their share they were required to pay for their board. Two meals were served—breakfast at about eleven-thirty in the morning, and dinner at about five in the afternoon. All the boarders were required to dress attractively and expensively. The girls were encouraged to charge clothing to the madames' accounts at local stores as a deliberate means to keep them constantly in debt, thus giving the "boardinghouse proprietors" an additional hold upon them.

Denver stores vied for the profitable business of the fancy

ladies of The Row. The credit of the madames was excellent; that of the girls, worthless. Many stores made a practice of adding an additional twenty per cent to the bills of the Ladies of the Line and it was paid without protest, although not always cheerfully.

Most parlor houses employed a male piano player, but occasionally "the professor" was a Negro. Mostly they played for a small wage plus tips and drinks. It was customary for guests to tip "the professor" and to include him in a round of drinks. To encourage tips one "professor" placed beside his piano a box surmounted by a phonograph horn to receive tossed coins. The box bore a sign, "Feed the Kitty."

Among the leading "professors" were Clyde Rogers, Harry Loss, and a temperamental genius known only as "Mac." Mac would work only long enough to finance a prolonged debauch. A master of ragtime he was always in demand, and all the madames vied for his intermittent services.

"Hickey" McAndrews, accomplished pianist at the Haunted House resort, served a prison sentence for killing a man with a blow of his fist. One ambitious young student earned his way through the University of Denver law school by playing the piano in a parlor house. Later he became a noted jurist.

A young man who played the piano and sang at the Arcade was in love with a Market Street girl. Possessing some ability as a rough-and-tumble barroom fighter, he determined to become a professional boxer. But in his first match at the suburb of Littleton he took such a thrashing that he was ashamed to face his Denver sweetheart. He hopped a freight train and never saw the girl again. Presently he tried his hand at composing and sold his first song for ten dollars. Other song hits followed, and he won fame and fortune as a composer of popular songs. One of the sweetest of his love songs, a nostalgic composition that has been sung by millions, was written about the Market Street girl he left behind him in Denver, the sweetheart he never saw again.

A few sporting houses employed girls to play the piano. A famed vaudeville artist, temporarily down on her luck, played for three weeks in a Denver parlor house. After the turn of the century a girl played the piano at Mattie Silks's place for a few months. No male guest was permitted to have anything to do with her, giving rise to the rumor that she was "the madame's daughter."

In 1886 madames Mattie Silks, Jennie Rogers, Rosa Lee, and twelve others described in the *News* as "the giddy girls of Holladay Street" were arrested on charges of conducting lewd houses. Bitterly indignant at what they considered an unwarranted invasion of their constitutional rights, the "giddy girls" formed a defense pool, employed an outstanding lawyer, and announced they would fight the case right up to the Supreme Court.

When Jennie Rogers was brought to trial it developed that the only evidence against her was that of "stool pigeons." The case was dismissed and the newspapers quoted spectators as saying "the present means adopted to prosecute the Holladay Street women was little short of blackmail."

The jury hearing evidence against Minnie Clifford disagreed, and the case was dismissed. Jessie Sampson was found not guilty.

Winnie Purdy, Laura Stevens, and Eva Lewis were found guilty and appealed their cases to the Supreme Court. When the Supreme Court failed to take immediate action the trial court judge dismissed the cases.

Contrary to popular opinion, few of the parlor-house proprietors procured their boarders through international white slave rings. An exception was Maquereau Jack Maynard, proprietor of a notorious café and of a string of cribs, who did his own recruiting, making an annual trip to French North Africa to acquire girls. He achieved fleeting notoriety in the nation's headlines when he introduced the cash register system in the oldest profession.

The divorce courts provided a lucrative field for procurers. Alimony was less frequently asked and granted than today. A penniless young divorcee was almost certain to be propositioned by a procurer. His fee for each new girl ranged from five dollars to ten dollars, depending upon her age and general attractiveness.

Records of the Pinkerton Detective Agency give the case history of one notorious procuress, who worked into the business in 1894 by buying used clothing from society women and selling them to girls of the tenderloin.

The report, in part:

> An inmate of Jennie Rogers' house on Market Street, Denver, some twelve years ago. She got into trouble with the Rogers woman for bribing all of her girls to leave her and go to a house in Omaha—for which she was paid a procuress' fee of $5 to $10 apiece for the girls.
>
> She was a confidential servant in Rose Lovejoy's private house on Market Street, Denver, and with her several years.
>
> Was well known to Annie Wilson, another Denver woman who ran a place on Market Street, afterward had a place in Cripple Creek, and now lives in Kansas City.
>
> Known to Lola Livingston, with whom she went to San Francisco. Lived in Eva Lewis' house on Market Street at the time the Coxey army passed through here, and took a prominent part in the Denver preparations for their care.
>
> Is Known to Harry Loss, a piano player at 1925 Market Street, who says he knew her first in Omaha in 1894, where she lived in a house at Tenth and Douglas. She was then selling clothes to the girls.
>
> A sewing woman for the sporting class—name withheld—knew her twelve or fifteen years ago when she

lived with Minnie Hall, and afterward with Jennie
Rogers; says it was commonly reported that she was
a procuress by trade.

The subject of the Pinkerton report became favorably known
nationally as one of the outstanding leaders of a social reform
movement.

One of the most attractive of Jennie Rogers' latter-day
boarders went to Hollywood and achieved fleeting stardom
in the movies.

Louis Klipfel operated the Alcazar burlesque theater and
saloon on Market Street, where several noted actors, including
Eddie Foy, appeared. When Klipfel died two common-law
wives claimed his estate.

"Cooney The Fox" operated one of the most notorious saloons
on the street where customers rash enough to "show a roll" were
sometimes given a "mickey," rolled, and tossed out into the alley.

A stage-struck New York youth worked as a waiter in a restaurant across the alley from the Alcazar, so he could be near
the theater. He organized a troupe of his own and started East,
intent on reaching Broadway and showing up the Hammersteins
and Ziegfelds. His troupe went broke in the central West. Highly
respected for his integrity and business ability, he later became
the prosperous head of a chain of restaurants.

Denver's "gold dust" era lasted through the sixties, to be
succeeded by three decades of "hard money," when gold coin
was virtually the only medium of exchange recognized in the
parlor houses. But the silver dollar was always welcome in Holladay Street cribs, which were operated on the principle of huge
volume and quick turnover.

(3)

Brides of the Multitude

THE Holladay Street cribs were just wide enough for a door and two narrow windows. Each contained two tiny rooms; parlor in front, boudoir in back. The rent, from fifteen to twenty-five dollars a week, was collected daily in cash. In the white section the cribs were known as "dollar houses." In the black belt they were called "two-bit houses."

The parlor houses were conducted with at least the outward appearance of decorum and dignity, but in the earlier years the cribs operated just about as they pleased. In costumes usually consisting of low-neck, knee-length spangled dress and black silk stockings, the girls stood in doorways and solicited openly as the critical throngs of male shoppers sauntered down the sidewalks inspecting the wares.

"Come on in, dearie," was the customary invitation. If the prospect failed to respond, a young lady solicitor might resort to hat-snatching, high-pressure salesmanship.

Some of the cribs displayed advertising signs that shocked the none-too-shockable residents of pioneer Denver. Finally the harassed board of aldermen adopted an ordinance providing censorship regulations for the too-zealous Holladay Street advertisers. A sign complying with the censorship law read:

21

Rocky Mountain *News* of August 21, 1880, reported that the failure of a quorum to be present at a city council meeting was because most of the members were attending the opening of "a newer and fashionable den of prostitution on Holladay Street. "

Moreover, The Row afforded a rich source of municipal revenue. Whenever the city treasury was in the red, what could be simpler than wholesale raids and fines to balance the books? At one time Denver was described as possessing "as corrupt a gang of office-holding crooks as ever infested an American city."

The constituents of one rugged, bearded he-man alderman gave him a testimonial dinner and presented him with a diamond ring. Noting its absence after a few days, a friend questioned him about it.

"Aw, nobody wears diamonds except gamblers and whores," he explained, "so I gave it to my wife."

When the unhappy board of aldermen finally adopted an ordinance requiring every "soiled dove" on Holladay Street to wear a yellow ribbon on her arm as a badge of her profession, madames Mattie Silks, Jennie Rogers, *et al* schemed out a way to beat the game.

Denver's many hundreds of "public women" didn't stop with mere compliance with the ordinance. Dressed in yellow from slippers to bonnet, they paraded the streets and swarmed in the restaurants and other public places.

To a stranger it must have appeared as if there was scarcely a chaste woman left in Denver. The baffled aldermen speedily repealed the ordinance.

A Larimer Street wigmaking establishment was patronized exclusively by the ladies of Holladay Street. Many girls considered it expedient to possess wigs of sundry colors.

Nightly some excited rounder would rush up to the tough cop at the police box at the corner of Nineteenth Street, crying, "I been robbed! That redheaded wench at Foxy Lil's stole my wallet!"

"All right," the patrolman would reply wearily. "Point her

out to me and I'll get your money back or toss her in the tank."

But in the interval between the "rolling" of the guest and the arrival of the police the redhead would have donned a black or blond wig, perhaps switching to a different dress. When the bewildered victim failed to identify the girl who had rolled him, he was fortunate if the patrolman didn't jail him for drunkenness or disturbance.

Contemporary newspaper accounts help fill out the picture of hectic Holladay.

Immodest Annie Griffin, Daisy Smith and Belle Jones staged a nude "Dance of the Houris" on the sidewalk at Nineteenth and Larimer streets, and were fined in police court for "naughty capers."

Anna Tully of Holladay Street hired a buggy to keep a rendezvous at the Golden Eagle Hotel in West Denver. At the time it seemed a good idea to drive the buggy through the hotel door into the lobby. Anna never made it into the hotel but landed instead in jail.

The fast ladies of Holladay Street went in for fast horses. Two "female boarders" at Jennie Rogers' house, racing down Larimer Street at a headlong gallop, collided with another vehicle at the Sixteenth Street intersection. They escaped serious injury, but their buggy was smashed to pieces.

Some of the damsels went in for dogs, but the only dogs on the street were white poodles. Fire Chief John Healy, responding to an alarm, wrecked the fire department's first automobile trying to avoid running down a Market Street poodle. This breed became so closely identified with the *filles de joie* that no woman who valued her reputation dared own such a pet.

Blanche Farley had a man, Synne Kerr, but he "done her wrong." Trailing Synne and the "other woman" to the Tabor Grand Opera House, she bought a half-dozen overripe bananas and lay in wait in the foyer. When the show let out and Synne and his new girl friend appeared, Blanche peeled a banana and flung it in his face. Her scornful gesture cost her five dollars in police court.

In 1900 six well-heeled men dropped out of sight while visiting houses on The Row. The same year a Butte miner attending the American Federation of Labor convention in Denver was robbed of a roll of bills in a hookshop on Market Street, the former Holladay Street. Ashamed to make a report to police, he returned to Butte. The loss preyed on his mind, however, and six months later he returned determined to get back his money. This time the same girls "rolled" him again.

Insult added to injury prompted the visitor to notify the police. Captain Hamilton Armstrong ordered the arrest of Effie Ellsler, Klondike Liz, and Ruth Stanton.

The miner failed to recover his money and returned to Butte, where the ladies of Venus Alley never robbed a man but once. Among the outstanding Butte madames were Lou Harpel, Belle Rhodes, Mabel Lay, Mollie de Murska, Beryl Hastings, Pansy Brasier, and Mae Malloy.

Clasped in the arms of their gentlemen friends, the crib girls of Holladay Street were wont to rob their paying guests by biting studs from their shirt fronts, or scarf pins from their cravats. In 1884 Minnie Darley was arrested for biting a scarf pin off Frank Le Fevre. A Denver dentist won a widespread underworld reputation for making steel biters to clamp to the rear of the girls' front teeth.

Parlor-house madames refused to tolerate jewel-biting on the part of their boarders, for fear it would give their houses a bad name.

Two or three times a week some of Denver's 1,000 girls on The Line would swallow poison. It was not always because of remorse or disease.

In 1914 a young university student, scion of a well-to-do Colorado family, fell desperately in love with Sophie, a lovely young boarder in a parlor house. He gave her his fraternity pin, bought her an engagement ring, and announced his wedding plans to his parents.

Horrified, the father came to Denver and offered the girl a sizable sum to break the engagement and leave the state. But this was not, as he supposed, the customary blackmail scheme.

"I love him, I intend to marry him, and no amount of money can buy me off," she flatly told the youth's father.

World War I had just broken out, and at first the young man had been aflame with the desire to join the Canadian army. His love affair and the strenuous objections of his parents had led him to change his mind. But now his parents saw a way to break off the unfortunate love affair.

"Go ahead and enlist, son," they told him, "and if you still want to marry Sophie when the war's over, we'll withdraw our objections."

So the young man went to Canada and joined the army. Later, when the United States entered the conflict, he transferred to the American forces. Two years later the daily casualty list in the Denver newspapers published his name among those killed in action. The next day Sophie took poison and died.

Denver had no monopoly on colorful "scarlet ladies." In the early sixties, when the Leadville area was known as California Gulch, the outstanding courtesan was a girl known only as "Red Stockings." She was a petite young thing, with flashing black eyes and a ready come-hither smile. She always wore red ribbons in her hair and, of course, red stockings.

By the end of '61 Red Stockings had cleaned up $100,000. She went to Nevada, married, and lived in happy respectability forever after.

Principal Leadville dance halls of the late seventies were the Little Casino, Bon Ton, Pioneer, Odeon, and Red Light. They were described in the Colorado *Miner* as "breathing holes of hell, where the customers imbibe 'blue ruin' Torchlight whisky and indulge in the quadrille and the 'whirling sinuosities of the waltz.' "

The outstanding Leadville parlor houses were operated by Mollie May and Sallie Purple. Other madames were Frankie Page, Carrie Linnell, Minnie Purdy, and Mollie Price. Hundreds of girls operated from cribs in the tenderloin district, which included Coon Row and French Row.

Madames Mollie May and Sallie Purple were deadly rivals. Their feud once flamed into armed warfare, and for more than an hour the two, each barricaded in her own house, exchanged shots. There were no casualties.

Mollie May broke into the headlines in May, 1882, when she bought a baby from a destitute couple named Moore. Newspaper editorial opinion was divided. One faction saw sinister motives in the purchase. Another praised her highly for providing a home for the infant. She finally married a liveryman known as "Scotty."

Winnie Purdy, madame of a house at 115 West Fifth Avenue, and who later removed to Denver, was said to be a sister of Sallie Purple. Madame Fannie Moeller also moved to Denver.

Madame Mattie Cook had a son, Alpha, who married "sporting woman" Etta Clark, who was so skinny she was known as "Grasshopper." Etta later opened a sporting house at El Paso, Texas, where she was killed.

Gambler George Silks lived at 113 East Eighth Avenue in 1881 and 1882.

One of Leadville's minor madames was known as "Great Eastern."

Notable among the feminine contingent at Dodge City were "Dutch Jake" and Belle Starr. The former was a madame who provided riding horses for her girl "boarders," cooked delicious cookies, and owned a white poodle. When Belle Starr's husband, Sam, lost $2,000 in a faro game, Belle held up the gambling house and acquired $7,000 at the point of a gun, proving that a pair of six-shooters beats a pair of sixes.

Georgetown's Brownell Street once boasted five parlor houses. Mattie Estes, whose real name was Elizabeth C. Deyo, was a pioneer madame. She supported a "solid man" named King, and later operated an establishment at New Orleans.

Mollie Dean, whose real name was Mary Ann Nephue, was another leading madame. Among her "boarders" were Lillie Thomas, Sady Wells, and Hattie Grant, alias Nelson. Arden Shea, a miner, fell violently in love with Mollie and, catching her stepping out with another man, killed her, and then blew out his own brains.

Many others made the headlines in Georgetown.

Madame Jenny Aiken was burned to death in 1878, after a man was shot to death in her establishment. Madame Ada La Monte, also known as Mrs. Sheridan, at one time had been a circus rider.

Most popular girl in the camp was Lottie White's "star boarder," a girl known as Tid-bit. In 1877 an older sister took her back to her St. Louis home and a life of respectability.

Anna Moynahan called her house "Star Aiden." Other madames were Mollie Walker, Belle Keyes, Josephine White, and Liz Greer.

Blue-eyed Liz was only twenty when young Ben Wade, goldseeker, fell victim to her charms. When she accepted the attentions of a miner named Hayes, Ben killed him. A posse took after him, and he literally hid behind the skirts of Liz. She hopped aside and the posse riddled him. It was too much trouble to dig two graves in the frozen ground, so they tumbled both corpses into a single grave. When Liz's house was destroyed by fire she moved from Georgetown to Denver, where she died in the early eighties.

In Cripple Creek during the mining boom of the nineties beer was as cheap as water, since both had to be hauled in barrels. The camp's leading madame was Blanche Burton.

Laura Bell was a leading madame at Colorado City, near Colorado Springs. The principal parlor house was known as "The Mansion," owned by Mayme Majors and operated by her sister.

The Colorado City red-light district was destroyed by fire January 8, 1909.

For many years the queen of Pueblo's tenderloin was a madame known as "Spud" Murphy.

Calamity Jane Canary was a contemporary of Belle Siddons-Madame Vestal-Lurline Monte Verde at Deadwood. Previously she had been a boarder in houses conducted by the notorious Madame Moustache at various towns along the Union Pacific Railroad.

Upon her release from the Cheyenne jail, Jane once hired a rig, stocked it with several quarts of frontier "bug juice," and set out to visit gentlemen friends at nearby Fort D. A. Russell, now known as Fort Francis E. Warren.

The army post was only three miles distant, but Jane's excess spirits warped her sense of direction. She took the wrong turn and kept right on driving and drinking and drinking and driving until she finally wound up at Fort Laramie, ninety-seven miles away.

Isolated frontier army posts bought their beef from neighboring cattle ranches, but since pork was unavailable on the cattle range, each post maintained its own hog ranch. Also a fixture near each army post was a cluster of buildings where the soldiers might purchase liquid refreshment and feminine companionship.

Since many cattle ranches were hundreds of miles from the nearest town, enterprising madames found it profitable to establish resorts in the wilds, somewhat like modern roadhouses, to serve their cowboy clientele. As these resorts served the same purpose as those adjoining the army posts, in the course of time they, too, became known as "hog ranches."

In his story, *How Lin McLean Went East*, Owen Wister relates that his hero, Lin, incurred a broken leg "at a hog ranch across the bridge." The reference must have been confusing to innocent Eastern readers, who, unfamiliar with Western nomenclature, doubtless were led to picture vast herds of hogs roaming the Western ranges, like cattle.

Cattle Kate of the Powder River country was one of the most noted hog ranchers. Because of her skill with a rifle, she was occasionally known as the Duchess of Winchester. When a cowboy customer lacked cash she could be persuaded to accept a calf in trade. According to what might be an apocryphal story, by hard work and devotion to business she built up a valuable herd of cattle. She finally came to grief at the end of a cottonwood limb, hanged alongside her man, Jim Averil. Westerners say she was the only woman ever hanged for cattle rustling.

In the days of the Black Hills gold excitement a character known as "Madame Featherlegs" opened a log-cabin palace of sin on Demmon Hill between Rawhide Butte and Running Water on the Cheyenne-Deadwood stagecoach route. She was the mother of Tom and Bill Shepard, Louisiana outlaws after the Civil War. Living with her was "Dangerous Dick" Davis.

Although Calamity Jane wore pants, the ethics of Madame Featherlegs' profession precluded anything so unfeminine. Riding astride, she galloped blithely along the Deadwood trail with her skirts rolled up about her waist, displaying, perhaps not unintentionally nor unconsciously, her glamorous and alluring red flannel drawers. Cut loosely and fastened at the ankles with drawstrings, they flapped in the wind like feathers and earned her the *nom d'amour* of Madame Featherlegs.

An unkind fate finally laid the madame low in 1879. One morning after a wild party her bullet-riddled body was found near her doorstep. She was buried in the back yard of her hog ranch.

Dangerous Dick vanished. So did $1,500 belonging to the madame. In Louisiana a few years later, just before he was lynched, Dick confessed the murder of Madame Featherlegs.

As a youth Russell Thorp, until recently secretary and chief inspector of the Wyoming Stock Growers' Association, Cheyenne, lived near Rawhide Butte. His father operated the stagecoach line between Cheyenne and Deadwood. Of course young Russell learned the story of Madame Featherlegs. One dark night twenty years after her death, he and several youthful companions, in the interest of historical research, exhumed the body while the coyotes howled on the nearby butte. They agreed that in all their young lives they had never beheld a lovelier twenty-year-dead corpse.

But this is beside the point, for Russell and his friends were motivated by a serious and worth-while purpose, and their discovery is of considerable historical import.

Yes, Madame Featherlegs actually did wear red flannel drawers.

(4)

Oscar Wilde and the Gay Ladies

FROM Capitol Hill to Holladay Street all Denver was atwitter with the news. Oscar Wilde was coming! The apostle of aestheticism was booked to bring culture to the uncouth Queen City of the Mountains and Plains in two easy lectures at the gorgeous new Tabor Grand Opera House on June 13 and 15, 1882.

Newly rich social leaders of the lorgnette set hastened to bone up on the writings of the distinguished Irish poet-playwright-author-lecturer. So did their frail sisters-under-the-skin in the cribs and parlor houses of The Row. Their reactions were strangely unalike.

The public prints had pictured the long-haired Oscar in velvet coat, knee breeches, and silk stockings, gazing raptly at a lily. During his lectures in Eastern states a lone lily had adorned the speaking platform. In the minds of the public the lily had become identified with Oscar Wilde.

Among those who pondered the problem of aestheticism were Madame Minnie Clifford and her boarders. Her establishment occupied the site of the original stagecoach stables of the Leavenworth City & Pikes Peak Express Co. Minnie had bought it December 23, 1880, and had converted it into a maison de joie.

Before many years it was destined to figure in the West's most fantastic story of blackmail, scandal, and possible murder and was to become Mattie Silks's famous House of Mirrors.

Minnie Clifford and Emma Nelson and the rest of the girls had no use for effeminate lily-lovers. They much preferred Western he-men, who might better be symbolized by the tough, gaudy, rugged sunflower, whose acrid emanations lacked something of the fragrance of the lily.

On the afternoon of April 5 Minnie and a group described by the newspapers as "a number of her subjects" set out to promenade the length of Larimer Street, then Denver's principal business thoroughfare. Minnie's bonnet was adorned with an enormous sunflower the size of a dinner plate. Emma sported a "very intense lily."

Police Officer Thomas O'Connor was pacing his beat in front of the Windsor Hotel. Prancing up to him with mincing steps Emma Nelson, cribbing an expression attributed to Oscar, observed in a shrill feminine falsetto:

"Oh, Officer O'Connor, in that new helmet you look too, too divine! Yes, indeed—too, too!"

The sunflower-sporting Minnie bellowed, "I know what makes the wildcat wild. But who makes Oscar?" The query bore all the earmarks of a tart remark.

Emma fluttered a lace handkerchief under the patrolman's nose. "Oh!" she giggled. "Isn't Minnie too utterly utter?"

Officer O'Connor flushed to the roots of his red hair.

"Sure, and you can't make a monkey out of Oscar Wilde, and him a product of the ould sod!" He called the dooly wagon and carted Minnie and her blossoming "subjects" to the city jail. The account of the episode in the *News* bore the headline:

ARRESTED FOR ESTHETICISM

Officer O'Connor was somewhat confused as to the charge to lodge against his prisoners. After consulting with Chief of

Police James J. Lomery he booked them for "meretricious display."

The next morning the defendants were hauled before the justice of the peace. Failing to discover in the statute books any law prohibiting "meretricious display," his honor dismissed the case after lecturing the girls on ethics rather than aesthetics. Denver's fair name was at stake. Her distinguished guests must not be insulted.

Chief of Police Lomery, himself a product of the Emerald Isle, was enraged by the court's failure to avenge the insult to the noted Irish lecturer. He promptly issued an order calling for the arrest of any female "who appears on the street in a promenade costume which shall by its odd or brilliant display, attract public attention."

Immediately the case became a *cause célèbre*. Society leaders wrote letters to the editors demanding to know whether they must dress wholly in black to avoid being jailed.

An anonymous poet penned an account in the April 9 *News* of the case entitled *Ascerbated Esthetics*. Excerpts from the *News* follows:

>Then the one most esthetical
>Turned to the Chief
>And in language not brief
>But quite exegetical
>Said, why will you make it,
>Make all this bother
>About a big sunflower?
>Now isn't one flower
>As good as another?
>Suppose I should carry
>A shamrock or daisy
>Would that drive you crazy
>To play the old Harry
>With me, a true esthete?

Oh, Oscar! Oh, Oscar!
Pray take a hoss car
And hasten to aid us;
Aid or we're busted.
No daffydowndilly,
No sunflower or lily
In Denver is trusted!

Following are excerpts from a lengthy, anonymous "Ode to Oscar" published on the morning of the distinguished visitor's arrival:

Nor do we much admire thy mystic
Poesy, for we have here Professor Haskell,
And the only W. E. Pabor who can knock
The silk socks off of
Thee in winding up the Lyric Muse
And grinding out sweet words of pleasant rhyme,
Whereby to noble heights is lifted up the soul,
And men are nerved to do great deeds and leave
The State. We do not languish for thy high-
Cut pants, for from our snow-clad peaks there comes
A cutting breeze which is not tempered to
The trouserless.

Our admiration for the
Pure, pale lily and the more gaudy bloom
Of sunflower is abated since our great
Chief guardian of the public peace, and high
Curator of the moral weal has said
They were obscene, and that he holds them as
The superfluity of naughtiness.
When thou talkest of being utter
We show up "Windy" Clark who, we will bet
Can utter more in the brief circumscribing
Of a minute than thou canst in a week.

If thou dost boast of being too, we will
Produce Charles Baggs, M.D., who is as too
As thou art, and a durned sight tooer.

The Denverites named in the "Ode to Oscar" were Thomas N. Haskell, author of a book of poems, occupation listed in the 1882 city directory as "literature"; W. E. Pabor, editor of the Colorado *Farmer*, and "Doc" Baggs, notorious confidence man and at the time a capper for "Soapy" Smith, king of the bunco men.

Reporters who boarded Wilde's train at Greeley were surprised to discover that he wore long pants. They were unfavorably impressed by his black velvet coat. But he wore a broad-brim slouch hat that, although blue, gave him somewhat the appearance of a Westerner, and his flowing locks reminded them of "our own bad men of Bitter Creek."

William F. "Buffalo Bill" Cody, who wore just such flowing locks, a few days previously had been robbed on Larimer Street of $2,000 worth of jewelry, including a diamond-set golden buffalo-head ring given the noted scout by the Grand Duke Alexis of Russia for his services as guide on a buffalo hunt. Because of his show-off qualities, Cody was known in the West as "See Me Bill." Unhappily, he may go down in history as the Hopalong Cassidy of the nineteenth century.

Newsmen told Wilde of the jugging of Minnie and of Chief Lomery's order concerning unaesthetic feminine apparel. The *Republican* reported: "With indignation, blazing with greenery, gallery glare in his eyes, Wilde said, 'He considered a sunflower meretricious? What kind of a man is this Chief?' "

Informed that the feminine aesthetes might be found at a resort known as "The Heights," the distinguished visitor remarked that he "would be glad to see them."

For his lecture on "Interior and Exterior House Decoration," Wilde appeared at the Tabor Opera House in short pants and silk stockings. Both audience and critics received his lecture with something less than enthusiasm. One bold damsel appeared in the audience wearing a sunflower in her hair. She was identified as Minnie Clifford.

At Leadville the next night Oscar received a much warmer reception. Someone fomented a plot to get him tight before the lecture. It seemed a good idea at the time, but Oscar drank the fomenters under the table. Leadville's surviving two-fisted drinkers still speak with awe and respect of the Irishman's mighty capacity.

In his *Impressions of America* Wilde later wrote that the Leadvillians gave him "whisky and more whisky and still more whisky." He liked them. They liked him.

The lecturer was booked for a return engagement in Denver Saturday night, April 15. O. H. Rothacker, president of the Denver *Tribune*, had planned to take him for a tour of the city in Rothacker's "six-horse drag," or tallyho. After the lecture he was to be guest of honor at a dinner of leading citizens at the Denver Club.

At the suggestion of Charles E. Locke, Wilde's advance man and press agent, Rothacker had assigned his most brilliant reporter to cover the story of the Irishman's arrival. The reporter was none other than Gene Field, who recently had joined the *Tribune* all-star staff.

Wilde's train was late. The welcoming committee adjourned to a Larimer Street saloon. Between drinks press agent Locke remarked that it was a shame to deprive the waiting throngs of a spectacle. Field agreed to impersonate Wilde, and the nearby hairdresser who supplied the Holladay Street trade provided him with a wig resembling Oscar's flowing locks.

Wearing a wide-brim hat and an overcoat and sporting a lace handkerchief in his sleeve, Field was driven triumphantly through the streets of Denver by the press agent. For the benefit of the crowd the pseudo-aesthete languidly fluttered his fingers in his best lackadaisical la-de-da manner at the gaping throngs.

There was no applause. One disgusted newsboy shouted, "Shoot Oscar!"

A huge crowd awaited the arrival of the celebrity at the *Tribune* office. On the steps stood dignified F. J. V. Skiff, the *Tribune* business manager, later to become director of the World Columbian Exposition and the St. Louis World's Fair.

Suddenly the crowd was paralyzed with horror when Skiff, instead of shaking hands, angrily threw a broom at the city's distinguished guest. The broom knocked off the wig, exposing the hoax. Skiff had, of course, recognized the masquerading *Tribune* reporter.

Apparently Oscar failed to relish Field's prank. The records show that he departed on the ten-thirty train, indicating that he passed up the Denver Club dinner.

The *Tribune's* rival, the scooped *Republican*, opined that the whole affair was a "low trick."

Many accounts of the famous hoax have been written—mostly garbled. Many a story has been told of the weird pranks of poet-reporter-editor Eugene Field, that roistering, eccentric genius of the old *Tribune*—mostly true.

The story that he wrote one of the loveliest of his touching poems of childhood while recovering from a hangover at Mattie Silks's house is untrue.

(5)

House of a Thousand Scandals

MANY other madames envied Mattie Silks. None ever successfully challenged her supremacy as Queen of the Red Light except Jennie Rogers.

Vivacious, brunet Sara Jane "Jennie" Rogers was far and away the most beautiful of Denver's Holladay Street madames. She was several years younger than plump, blond Mattie Silks.

Jennie came to Denver in 1880 from Pittsburgh by way of St. Louis, where she was noted for her beauty and lively manner. In St. Louis her principal "gentleman friend" was the chief of police, who paid her frequent visits after she moved to Denver. For some years an oil painting of the chief hung in her Denver parlor house. She bought her first Holladay Street house from Mattie Silks for $4,600.

At the time of her arrival Denver boasted a population of 35,629, and wealth was pouring into the city from the Leadville mines. The ore production slackened off in 1882, and for three years Denver experienced a period of depression. On July 29, 1884, Jennie was arrested on a charge of operating a lewd house and told the arresting officers her name was Calvington. Later she was known as Mrs. Leah J. Fries.

By 1887 Denver had recovered from the depression and entered upon a period of wild speculation, and its population had reached 96,000. The Colorado Midland Railroad had just tapped the riches of the new mining town of Aspen. The Missouri Pacific Railroad began running trains into Denver over the tracks of the Denver & Rio Grande. The Rock Island Railroad was nearing Colorado Springs, to provide Denver with another rail outlet. The narrow gauge lines of the Rio Grande had been built into many mining districts. In 1888 the Denver, Texas, and Fort Worth Railroad was completed. Denver's history had been made up of a series of booms and busts with each boom following a new mining discovery. The boom of the late eighties was aided by the extension of rail transportation facilities. By 1890 the city's population had grown to 106,713. Good times prevailed until the panic of '93 brought about the biggest bust in Denver's history.

"Everybody with money to spare or credit to mortgage, plunged into the buying pool," reports Hall's *History of Colorado*. "Some, nearly all, suffered for it later on, but meanwhile, before the crash came in '93, Denver boasted the largest army of landed millionaires to be found west of the Missouri River. At this writing [1895] it has been reduced to a mere corporal's guard."

It was said that the newly rich speculators, who couldn't stand prosperity, spent their money on the Holladay Street damsels, who couldn't stand posterity.

Holladay Street shared the prosperity, if not the posterity. By this time Jennie Rogers owned the sporting house at 527 Holladay Street. She was a familiar figure driving her high two-wheeled trap, or cart, behind her tandem of matched bays. She always wore emerald earrings.

Jennie later acquired three adjoining Holladay Street establishments. These three houses were encumbered by a $6,500 mortgage. A real estate agent had been in the habit of calling on her to collect the quarterly interest payments. When, early in 1888, he failed to make his customary call, Jennie thought nothing of it until she was served with an eviction notice and learned that the property had been put up at public sale and had been bid on for only $4,000 by the daughter-in-law of the morgage owner.

Scenting a plot to trick her out of her property, Jennie brought suit against the mortgage holder to have the public sale declared invalid.

Filed just at the time the street name was being changed from Holladay to Market, the suit designated the property as 1957, 1959, and 1961 Holladay. Jennie brought with her $6,500 in cash, which she turned over to the court with an offer to pay off the entire remainder of the mortgage. The court ruled in Jennie's favor, setting aside the public sale on condition she pay the purchaser her $4,000, plus interest, or a total of $4,636.

Jennie still envied Mattie Silks her dominant position as madame of Holladay Street's leading house.

"I'd sell my soul, if any, for a house finer than Mattie's," she confided to her boy friend, the St. Louis police chief, on one of his periodical visits to Denver.

"Don't worry, honey," he assured her confidently. "It's as good as yours, right now."

He had heard rumors concerning the private life of one of Denver's leading millionaires who was ambitious to seek high public office. Following is the substance of the whispering campaign conducted against the tycoon.

While still in his teens this individual had married in Ohio and had become the father of a daughter. Joining the gold rush to the Pikes Peak region, he had worked as a freighter and later found a minor job with a firm of contractors. He sent for his bride and their infant daughter to join him.

The principal owner of the concern had an attractive wife many years his junior who owned a considerable amount of real estate in her own name, including acreage on the edge of soon-to-boom Denver.

Presently the bride of the young employee dropped out of sight, leaving the infant daughter with the young father.

The young wife of the boss procured a divorce on the ground of desertion, based on the testimony of the employee who swore that the husband had departed permanently from Colorado Territory, although the city directory continued to list him as a Denver resident then and for several years thereafter.

At that time there was no six-month interval before a final divorce decree could be entered in Colorado. Immediately after the decree was granted the divorced wife of the boss married the young employee, and the new husband stepped up from a humble position to take the place of the boss as head of the firm. The erstwhile husband and boss was kicked out and was compelled to earn a living as a common laborer. At one stroke the younger man acquired a rich wife and control of the business.

The succeeding real estate boom multiplied by from five to ten times the value of Denver building lots. The new wife's acreage became immensely valuable. The new husband proved to be a shrewd businessman and a canny investor. Judicious investments in mines, railroads, and real estate pyramided the wife's stake into one of Colorado's greatest fortunes.

Within a few years the rising young businessman was ranked among Denver's most bountiful civic benefactors. He built one of the city's most imposing mansions, with the gold-plated door knobs and silver-plated lighting fixtures that constituted the symbols of financial success for so many of the community's newly rich. He and his second wife were numbered among Denver's foremost social leaders.

Had he not aspired to become governor, Jennie Rogers might never have achieved her ambition to outrank Mattie Silks, but as soon as his ambition became known, his political enemies began spreading ugly rumors.

What had become of his first wife? Had he disposed of her so he might be free to wed the wealthy wife of his employer? If she had merely deserted or divorced him, why had she deserted her infant daughter, who remained in the father's care?

The bride had last been seen entering a cab after attending a performance, alone, at a Denver theater. She had been heard to direct the cab driver to take her home. What had happened to her when—or if—she had reached her home? Was it true she had been murdered and her body buried in her own back yard?

These were the ugly stories Jennie Rogers' unscrupulous lover had heard.

It was the custom of the Plains Indians to dispose of their dead by leaving the bodies on pole platforms built in trees. From one of these burial places the police chief procured the skull of an Indian woman. When the tycoon was absent on a business trip the skull was buried in his back yard in the dead of night.

The night after his return he was visited by the St. Louis officer and two aides wearing police badges. Representing themselves to be investigators from the district attorney's office, they served him with a forged search warrant. They dug up the skull, confronted him with it, and served him with a forged information charging him with the murder of his first wife.

Covering him with a gun, the leading blackmailer told him menacingly, "The only way you can keep from being hanged is by confessing."

The civic leader, terrified, had no way of knowing the three blackmailers were impostors nor of knowing the search warrant and the murder warrant were forgeries.

There is not the slightest evidence that his first wife was murdered. In all probability she simply tired of the rigors of life in pioneer Denver and returned home, there to die a natural death or possibly to free her young husband by means of a divorce. There is no record of her death or divorce in Denver.

Knowing himself to be innocent but believing the blackmailers to be legitimate officers, the millionaire still had every reason to be terrified. Convinced that he was facing trial for murder, he doubtless reasoned that even though he were acquitted of the charge his career would be ruined and political hopes blasted. No one knows what passed through his mind before he said:

"Isn't there some way we can fix this up, boys?"

"Why, yes," generously agreed the leader of the blackmailers. "Jennie Rogers needs $17,000 to build a new house. If you can take care of her, I reckon we can forget the murder charge."

Such is the story of the fantastic blackmail scheme by which the money was forthcoming for the magnificent new parlor house later known as 1942 Market Street, which enabled Jennie to dethrone Mattie temporarily as Queen of the Red Light. The abstract of title shows that Jennie, under her real name, Leah J. Fries, on September 20, 1888, acquired the Minnie Clifford property for $12,000. She refused to make the final payment to the contractor who rebuilt the place, and when he threatened to bring suit, defied him by saying, "You know as well as I do that no judge or jury in Denver would ever find me guilty of anything." Believing her, he never brought suit and never collected his final payment.

Jennie employed architect William Quayle to remodel the building. Quayle was a distinguished architect of the day, having designed the First Congregational Church, the West Denver high school, several office buildings, and a number of Denver mansions.

Whether Jennie Rogers' impish sense of humor inspired the telling of the fantastic blackmail story in stone, or whether Quayle, aware of the whispering campaign, took it upon himself, no one knows. However, above the second floor level, the façade of the imposing remodeled gray stone house bore five faces carved in rose stone, said to represent the five principals involved in the strange case.

Seductive Jennie supposedly was represented by the full-bosomed Circe with the magnificent cleavage in the triangle at the peak of the façade. At a lower level appeared the leering face of a man with muttonchop whiskers, one eye closed in a know-

ing wink: supposedly the blackmailed civic leader. Next was
the plump countenance of his second wife, the wealthy grass
widow. Then the unsmiling, lovely lineaments of the supposedly murdered bride and, last of all, the sorrowful features of a
man with long handlebar mustaches—the boss who lost both his
wife and business to his young employee.

The doorpost was ornamented with a design carved in the
same rose stone—a horseshoe in a bed of lotus leaves. At the first
floor level were carved friezes bearing varying designs, possibly
phallic symbols.

Years later, when the building again was remodeled during
the summer of 1948, the 300-pound block of stone bearing the
likeness of the blackmailed civic benefactor came into possession
of the author, and was presented to the Denver posse of The
Westerners, a group interested in the preservation of Western
Americana.

As is generally the case, the actual cost of remodeling exceeded
the estimates, and the blackmail victim was tapped for an additional $780. He lost his fortune in the panic of '93, but his mem-
ory was preserved for more than half a century by the likeness
on the front of Denver's leading sporting house.

The interior of the house was even more magnificent than
the exterior. The reception hall was paneled in a relief design of
painted cattails.

The famous parlor of mirrors opened from the right of the
reception hall. Walls and ceiling were covered with plate-glass
mirrors framed in golden bird's-eye maple. From an eight-foot
circular ceiling mirror hung a crystal chandelier. Oriental rugs
covered the parquetry floors. The room was tastefully furnished
with furniture of the Biedermeier period.

In front of the huge plate-glass front picture window was a
marble-top bird's-eye maple table. A bird's-eye maple love seat
stood in the center of the room, directly beneath the chandelier.
In one corner was a grand piano of bird's-eye maple. What appeared to be a tiled fireplace was built into one wall, but it was

a sham. When the heavy ornamental cast-iron fire screen was removed it revealed no fireplace, but a blank brick wall.

Sliding plate-glass doors led from the mirrored parlor into the ballroom, furnished with another grand piano and a number of golden chairs ranged along the walls.

Behind the parlor was the dining room, where the boarders ate their two daily meals, prepared in a small kitchen in the rear. In the basement beneath the kitchen was the wine cellar, where years later a mysterious coffin was discovered.

A narrow walnut-banistered staircase led from the reception hall to the second floor, devoted entirely to the rooms of the boarders. Except for the plate-glass front window, all windows were grilled with half-inch iron bars.

The barred windows served a double purpose, one of which was to guard against robbers. Every madame always kept a considerable amount of cash and jewelry in her safe, and Mattie Silks's safe already had been looted of $25,000 in money and gems. The second purpose was to prevent the boarders from cheating the madame of her fifty per cent cut by receiving gentlemen callers who might be disposed to crawl across rooftops and clamber through windows.

Jennie immediately leased from Jacob Lang the adjoining building at 1946 Market Street and cut a doorway between the two. The leased quarters, as shown by the inventory of Jennie's estate, were furnished to represent a Turkish harem.

Jennie's blackmailing sweetheart presently passed out of the picture. In August, 1889, she married a bartender employed at the Brown Palace Hotel and financed him in the saloon business in Salt Lake City. Some time later, paying an unannounced call, she discovered him in the arms of another woman, whipped out her pistol, and shot him through the arm.

When Salt Lake police asked why she had tried to kill him, she cried out in words that since have become an underworld classic, "I shot him because I love him, damn him!"

After the shooting he also passed out of Jennie's life. In April,

1904, she was married secretly at Hot Springs, Arkansas, to Archie T. Fitzgerald, Chicago politician.

In October, 1909, Dr. Hugh L. Taylor was summoned to 1942 Market Street and found Jennie at the point of death from Bright's disease. When he informed her she had but a few days to live she made out her will, bequeathing her sizable estate to kinsmen in Pennsylvania and Ohio. The will was witnessed by the attending physician and by a madame said to be the sister of a noted actress.

No trained nurse would risk attending a patient on Market Street, since her reputation would be blasted if she were seen entering or leaving an establishment on The Row. So Jennie was removed to Mercy Hospital, where she died on October 29, 1909.

When the will was probated Dr. Taylor was called to attest his signature.

"Please tell the court, doctor," said the lawyer, "where you were at one o'clock on the morning of October 10."

"At Jennie Rogers' house at 1942 Market Street," he testified, but hastened to add, "in a professional capacity, of course."

Archie Fitzgerald appeared, produced proof of the Hot Springs secret marriage, and, as Jennie's husband, claimed half of the estate, which included business property and a residence in North Denver. Among the claims against her estate was a bill from Harry E. Burlew, private detective, for services in shadowing Archie at Kansas City in February, 1907.

In settlement of Archie's claim against the estate, the other heirs agreed that he should have $5,000, a diamond ring, and all the letters he had sent to Jennie. The abstract of title shows that on September 20, 1910, the premises at 1942 Market Street passed into the hands of Archie Fitzgerald, executor of Jennie's estate.

In 1907 Mattie Silks had moved to larger quarters at 1922 Market Street and had leased her old house at 1916 to another madame.

On January 16, 1911, Mattie bought the House of Mirrors at 1942, subject to a lease to Etta Kelly, from Jennie's estate for $14,000.

Mattie caused the name "M. Silks" to be inlaid in tile on the doorstep. Once more she was Queen of the Red Light.

(6)

Riches Make Strange Bedfellows

DESCRIBED in the newspapers as "the most beautiful girl on the Pacific coast," Verona Baldwin, later one of Denver's leading madames, crashed the nation's headlines frequently and explosively from 1883 to 1887. When she shot her cousin, multimillionaire E. J. "Lucky" Baldwin, turfman, speculator, and hotel owner, claiming he had seduced her, she provided California newspapers with the most sensational scandal of the lusty eighties.

Lucky Baldwin founded his immense fortune speculating in mining stocks during the days when the Comstock lode at Virginia City was pouring forth its riches. He built the huge and costly Baldwin Hotel at San Francisco, assembled one of the greatest racing stables America has ever known, and became one of the greatest landowners in California.

In the El Dorado gambling saloon at San Francisco, he once won $200,000 on the turn of a card. He gambled for heavy stakes at the Bella Union and the Verandah at San Francisco, at the Casino at Saratoga and at John Daly's New York establishment.

Baldwin had four known wives, numerous sweethearts. No man, the newspapers reported, ever was named defendant in more seduction and breach-of-promise suits.

In his book, *As I Remember Them*, C. C. Goodwin describes him as: "The only man we ever heard of who pleaded in answer to a complaint filed against him that his public reputation was such that every woman who came near him must have been warned against him in advance."

His cousin, Verona, was tall, slender, and possessed huge, sloe-like hazel eyes. She spoke with a cultured English accent and claimed to be "a member of British royalty." When she was twenty Lucky Baldwin brought her to California, where she taught school and lived at his ranch.

The headlines flared their scandal first on January 5, 1883. Following is a story published in the San Francisco *Call* of that date:

A WOMAN'S REVENGE
Lucky Baldwin Shot by His Young Cousin, Verona

Yesterday at 10:10 o'clock a young woman who calls herself Verona Baldwin, a cousin, shot E. J. Baldwin through the left arm at the level of the heart as he was leaving his private dining room on the second floor of the Baldwin Hotel. She fired from behind him at a distance of six feet, without warning. She was immediately disarmed and arrested.

Baldwin walked to his rooms, bandaged his arm with towels and awaited a doctor. The girl, in jail, said: "He ruined me in body and mind. That is why I shot him."

The wound is not very dangerous. Reuben H. Lloyd, Baldwin's attorney, was summoned at once. The girl, about 23, known as Fannie, is a tall brunette, of slight build, large hazel eyes, and good looking. She told a *Call* reporter:

"I ought to have killed him. Yes, I ought to have killed him at the ranch."

She says she was employed by Baldwin on the ranch as a school teacher and he assaulted her and then had charges of improper conduct brought against her and had her fired. "He was afraid that I knew something that might be damaging to him, and he made these charges so as to impeach my testimony should I ever appear as a witness against him. . . . I did not try to kill him. I hit him just where I wanted to, for I am a good shot and never miss anything I aim at. But it would have been better far if I had killed him."

Baldwin's attorney said: "What I know about the case is this. Mr. Baldwin placed her in the school on the ranch; and all the people on the ranch live in a large house there. At the time this woman was dismissed there was on the ranch a certain doctor, the guest of Mr. Baldwin.

"One evening a servant named Silas reported to Mr. Baldwin that he had accidentally entered one of the rooms and had surprised the doctor and Miss Baldwin there. Upon this Mr. Baldwin ordered the doctor to leave the ranch, and Miss Baldwin was dismissed. Miss Baldwin while on the ranch was on friendly terms with a man named Garvey who had made a claim to some of Mr. Baldwin's land in Los Angeles County . . .

"Some time ago Miss Baldwin came to my office and said she would kill Mr. Baldwin unless he gave her some money. She wanted to pay a premium for $50,000 life insurance. (Lloyd suspected a suicide plan.) She also sent letters to Mr. Baldwin asking for money, and once he gave her $20 to pay her fare to Oregon. At another time she wanted to obtain $100 from him. At that time she threatened to kill Mr. Baldwin."

When Verona was brought to trial Baldwin declined to testify against her, and she was acquitted. Her immediate removal to what then was Washington territory might have been interpreted as indicating a settlement out of court. But the scandal was not to be suppressed.

Three years later Verona reappeared with a threat to sue Baldwin for the maintenance of the child whom, she insisted, he had fathered. That threat was hushed quickly. Again Verona vanished. She made the headlines a third time when she was found to be insane and was committed to the state asylum at Napa by Judge Lucien Shaw.

When the court ordered her sent to the institution she screamed "that she was of British royalty on British soil, and they could not send her to an asylum."

Horace Bell, a Los Angeles lawyer and publisher of *The Porcupine*, wrote: "Our hellish statutes protected him (Baldwin) and enabled him to send his victim to an insane asylum."

Verona displayed no evidence of insanity when she appeared in Denver in the late nineties as mistress of a parlor house. From 1903 until the law dimmed the red lights of the tenderloin she operated a house at 2020 Market Street.

Although there is no evidence to support her claim that she was "of British royalty," in appearance she was every inch a queen. Nearly six feet tall, she wore a royal purple velvet de Medici costume trimmed with white lace. She became prematurely gray, and the tall de Medici collar framed a face of patrician lines, surmounted by a piled-up mass of white hair upon which she wore a jeweled tiara. She carried a shoulder-high staff and moved with a stately, dignified tread. When it came to regal appearance, buxom Mattie Silks, who was accorded the title of Queen of the Tenderloin, could never approach the mien of distinguished-looking Verona Baldwin.

After the authorities closed The Row, Verona lived in an apartment on Denver's fashionable Capitol Hill and operated a tavern called "The Baldwin Inn." She is said to have been a shrewd, intelligent businesswoman who left a considerable estate when she died a few years ago.

Lucky Baldwin later lost most of his fortune. The Baldwin Hotel in San Francisco had burned to the ground. The luck of his earlier days seemed to have deserted him. He still owned huge tracts of land, but they produced income barely sufficient to meet taxes, leaving him "land poor."

An old man, he determined to make a new start in the Alaska gold fields in 1898. When he departed from Seattle he was surrounded by a bevy of girls, leading to the report that he planned to establish a bordello. Actually he expected to open a saloon and gambling house at Nome. He failed to find a suitable site, and his stock of liquors and his gambling paraphernalia lay on the beach for months. He was victimized to the extent of several thousand dollars for supposed taxes and returned to California some months later, still further in debt as a result of his Alaskan venture.

Verona's house at 2020 Market Street once had been occupied by Lillis Lovell, who possessed a personality of a distinctly different type. Lillis had been the leading madame at Creede, but when the Amethyst vein began to play out she came to Denver.

Lillis had a younger sister, Lois, who fell desperately in love with a rising young Denver businessman, who was just as deeply in love with her. On the eve of a business trip in 1907 he begged her to marry him.

"I love you too much to marry you, darling," she told him, heartbroken. "You can't marry a Market Street girl. It would ruin you socially. It would wreck your business career. I love you too much to wreck your life. It wouldn't be fair to you. No, it's just not in the cards."

"Mattie Silks married gambler Cort Thomson," he pointed out impetuously. "Jennie Rogers married Jack Woods."

"But they had nothing to lose by marrying Market Street girls," she argued, weeping a little. "They didn't marry out of their class. No, darling, I won't marry you, and the reason I won't marry you is because I love you so."

Dry-eyed, she watched her heartbroken suitor stumble down the steps. Dry-eyed, she went back to her room and removed the chatelaine watch pinned to her shirt-waist. Dry-eyed, she sat with the watch cupped in the palm of her hand, waiting, waiting for the hour her lover was to leave on his business trip. His train was to depart at twelve ten in the morning, and at twelve ten Lois swallowed poison and died.

A week later he returned to Denver and called at the Market Street house to renew his pleading. He had worked out a blueprint for happiness. He and Lois were to be married, leave Denver, bury her past and start life anew in a California city. Eagerly he bounded up the steps.

His ring was answered by the Negro porter, known to all Market Street rounders as Stuyvesant Van Rensselaer Cohen.

"Please, sir," said the porter uncomfortably, "Miss Lois, she ain't here no mo'."

"Where is she?" demanded the eager lover impatiently. "Speak up, Van—I've got to see her, tonight!"

Bluntly, the porter told him, "Miss Lois, she's out at Riverside cemetery—dead."

The lover made no scene. For a long time he sat on the staircase, while the thumping notes of ragtime and gay voices came from the ballroom in the rear. After a while he said, without any trace of emotion, "I'd like to know where she's buried, but the cemetery office isn't open at night. Call a hack, Van, and I'll give you a dollar to show me her grave."

At the cemetery the porter pointed out the fresh heap of earth. For a long time the lover stood staring down at the mound, until finally the porter, impatient and a bit nervous, asked:

"Please sir, don't you reckon it's about time to go, now?"

The lover handed him a silver dollar. "No, Van. I've got to see Lois—tonight."

He drew a pistol, blew out his brains, fell dead across the new grave of the girl who loved him too much to marry him.

The other Lovell, Lillis, died March 21, 1906, leaving, according to court records, an estate of $40,500.

"Amy Bassett" was the professional name of a madame who came to Denver from Kansas City in 1888. For some years she operated a house at 2015 Market Street. When she died January

2, 1904, from burns incurred in a gasoline explosion, it was revealed that she was a member of a respected Kentucky family and was the mother of two children—a daughter reared in the East and a son who had graduated from Yale.

Annie Ryan was a six-foot madame whose brother, Jim, ran a saloon on Market Street. This saloon was the scene of a double murder on August 13, 1899, when Wellington C. Llewellen, a soldier, killed patrolmen Tom Clifford and William Griffiths. Annie's solid man was Maurice Lyons, a former policeman employed by Jim Ryan as a bartender. In 1909 Annie became vexed with Maurice and took a shot at him, and missed. She had better luck on August 9, 1930, and killed him. A jury found her guilty of manslaughter and a judge set her free.

Madame Etta Kelly accumulated a small fortune which she invested in northern Colorado farm lands. She lost most of her money in the failure of Denver's Globe National Bank, set up a still on her ranch near Grover, and during the prohibition era went into the moonshining business. Federal officers raided her plant and enterprising Etta was sentenced to serve from two to three years in the penitentiary.

At New Orleans in the late sixties respectable Lizzie Preston married a young veteran of the Civil War who was suffering from tuberculosis as the result of a bullet wound incurred in action. Lizzie longed for children. After a few years, becoming convinced she could have none of her own, on October 19, 1874, she visited St. Anne's Infant Asylum at Washington, D.C., and picked out a fourteen-month-old girl whose parentage was unknown. Before the infant, whose name was Inez May, was turned over to her, she was asked to promise that she would not reveal the secret of her birth until the girl was twenty-one years old. She neglected to go through the formality of adoption proceedings.

She changed the child's name to Essie May. Shortly afterward the family came to Denver in the hope that the climate would benefit the husband's health, but he died a few days after their arrival.

The young widow with the adopted infant looked about for some means to support herself, finally decided to mortgage her home to make the down payment on a boardinghouse. A real estate agent showed her a place at Twenty-third and Lawrence streets. She made the down payment before she learned the "young ladies' boardinghouse" actually was a brothel.

Faced with the prospect of losing the money she had invested, she continued to operate the establishment and found herself an unwilling madame of a bordello. Finally, unable to dispose of the place and convinced she had lost her reputation anyway, she made up her mind to continue in the business. In later years, under the name of Lizzie Preston—which was her professional and not her real name—she became known as one of Denver's outstanding madames.

Meanwhile she bought a home at 3051 Stout Street, where she reared the adopted infant as her own, calling the child by the pet name of "Dollie." As she grew older, the girl was led to believe she was Lizzie's own daughter, and was never permitted to learn the nature of her foster mother's business.

When the child was thirteen Lizzie felt it would be difficult to conceal the nature of her occupation much longer, so she sent Essie May to a convent in Chicago and later to a convent in Indiana.

Completing her convent education at eighteen, Essie May returned to Denver, determined to surprise the woman she believed to be her mother. Failing to recognize the beautiful young lady as the child of a few years before, Stout Street neighbors told her she could find the older woman at the house Lizzie Preston then operated at 1943 Market Street. Essie May was inside the parlor house before she realized the true nature of the business conducted by the woman she believed to be her mother.

The emotional shock to the convent-bred girl was terrific. She became hysterical.

"You've ruined my life!" she screamed at Lizzie. "Now I can

never marry a decent man, because everyone will know I'm the daughter of a Market Street madame!"

Brokenhearted Lizzie tried her utmost to calm the girl she loved so deeply. "I'll send you away to college, where no one will ever know," she told her, sobbing. Still she held to her promise that she would not reveal the secret of the child's birth until Essie May was twenty-one. Had she violated her promise and disclosed that she was not the girl's real mother, tragic consequences might have been averted.

"I've gone to hell," screamed the hysterical girl. "All I can do is follow in your footsteps. I'm going to be one of your boarders."

Horrified, Lizzie naturally refused to consider the hysterical proposal. Essie May marched out of the house and across the street to another brothel and became a bride of the multitude. Although she became a boarder at the house across the street, she never spoke to Lizzie again, but still took it for granted the woman was her natural mother. Lizzie failed in numerous efforts to induce Essie May to abandon her life as a Market Street girl.

The madame who called herself Lizzie Preston died on April 29, 1904. She left a large estate, but no will. Still believing herself to be Lizzie's daughter, Essie May claimed the estate. Immediately twenty-one other kinsmen, including brothers, sisters, cousins, nieces, and nephews, contested Essie May's claim. They produced records and witnesses from St. Anne's Asylum showing beyond a doubt that Essie May was not Lizzie's own daughter, that she never had been legally adopted. The court disallowed the girl's claim, and the estate was divided among the numerous kinsmen.

Production of the records gave Essie May the first knowledge that she was not, as she believed, Lizzie Preston's own child. There is no record of what became of Essie May, who might have lived a respectable life had Lizzie revealed the secret of her birth in time and who might have inherited a small fortune if the older woman had not neglected to adopt her legally. The court's ruling was based, in part, on a pathetic letter written by Lizzie to one of the kinsmen, admitting Essie May was not her own daughter and relating the difficulties she had experienced up to that time in preventing her from learning the nature of the supposed mother's occupation.

On the night of March 2, 1880, twenty-year-old Baby Doe Tabor led a police raid on Lizzie Preston's parlor house. This raid touched off the most hectic romance in all Colorado history. It led to a series of court actions and secret marriages, one of which took place in Washington with a president of the United States as a witness and quite possibly altered the course of Colorado political history.

The girl was Elizabeth "Baby" Doe, then the wife of Harvey Doe and later the wife of Colorado's fabulous silver king multimillionaire and U. S. Senator H. A. W. Tabor.

BOOK TWO

Golden Fleece

(7)

Wooers of Lady Luck

THERE's a sucker born every minute, and someone to take his money. A good share of the riches produced by Colorado mines eventually found its way into the hands of the professional gamblers.

Writing in 1866, historian J. E. Wharton offers the following graphic description of "The Gambling Hells of Denver."

> The pernicious practice of gambling was conducted in the most open and shameless manner . . .
>
> At night everything that could add attraction was resorted to in order to seduce miners and strangers into the toils of the scores of blacklegs who were the habitues of these resorts. Wine, liquors and cigars of the rarest vintage and the most costly brands garnished the splendidly furnished bars, while the best musical talent of the country was employed in entertaining with vocal and instrumental melody, the crowds of customers drawn together by these allurements.
>
> Around the walls of the room were ranged the tables of the gamblers, each temptingly displaying its piles of new and shining bank notes, besides the implements of

the nefarious trade, and presided over by a smiling demon, under whose blandishments there lurked a heart that considered all men his prey, and which measured humanity only by the capacity of a pocketbook and the means of getting possession of its contents.

Besides these houses, of which two were located on Blake Street, the city had half a dozen or more private club rooms, where large sums changed hands nightly at the games of "faro" and "monte."

When the original Legislative Council in 1860 passed an ordinance legalizing three-card monte in Denver, G. W. Clayton, council member, indignantly resigned. In January, 1866, meeting at the then capital, Golden, the Territorial Legislature passed an act forbidding gambling. Half a century passed before it was effectively enforced.

Ed Chase was the ace of all Denver gamblers. He arrived with the first gold-seekers and long after the turn of the century was still going strong. The Heatleys and the Gaylords, Soapy Smiths and the Blongers, and the Chucoviches came and went, but Ed Chase stayed on forever, almost.

Chase was tall, his eyes were ice blue, his hair was prematurely white, and he was always immaculately tailored. In the early days he sat on a high stool with a shotgun across his arm and watched the boys as they played Lasconette, Over and Under Seven, High Dice, Van Tuama, roulette, and Spanish lottery. He never used the shotgun. The menace in his iceberg eyes was enough to keep the jacklegs and sharpers in line. He always ran a square game.

Chase was born December 20, 1838, at Saratoga, New York, where his parents operated a fashionable hotel. His mother was a Quaker. His father owned a stable of fine horses. Young Chase attended Zenobia Seminary, was a classmate of Leland Stanford, and during the summers worked at his parents' hotel. At this noted resort he learned the inside of the gambling racket. Among the guests who took a fancy to the slender young man who met the trains with the hotel bus were Daniel Webster and Henry Clay. They wrote to him occasionally in later years. He left Saratoga years before Richard Canfield, famed gambling house proprietor, took over the Casino.

When he was twenty adventurous young Chase took off for the wild West with a friend, Sam Wood. They spent a winter in Montana and in the spring of '59 joined the rush to the gold fields of the Pikes Peak country.

Chase was twenty-two years old when he arrived in Colorado, June 6, 1860. For a time he clerked at Ford Brothers' store at Golden. He managed a prizefighter, without success.

At that time Denver's principal gambling establishment was a sixty-by-ninety-foot log cabin with a canvas roof and dirt floor. It was known as Denver Hall, and its reputation was none of the best.

Learning that young Chase knew how to operate pool, billiard, and card tables, a group of leading citizens induced him to open a "recreation game" room. One of his sponsors was Jerome B. Chaffee, later United States senator. Denver's first billiard table was brought across the plains by ox team for Chase's recreation game room.

During his many years in the gambling business in Denver, broken only by a brief venture at Deadwood, South Dakota, during the Black Hills gold stampede of '78, Chase had many partners. The first was Elias McIntosh who, unable to write his own name, "made his mark" in signing documents on behalf of the partnership in '63.

Francis P. "Hub" Heatley was his partner in the ownership and operation of the Progressive Club, a frame building on Blake Street. The part-owner of a theatrical troupe, gambling in the establishment, lost the troupe's $300 payroll and then put up his half-interest in the venture and lost that, too. Chase found himself in the theatrical business with Sam D. Hunter, the other owner, under the firm name of Chase & Hunter.

Heatley subsequently bought Hunter's interest, and the theatrical company was merged with the gambling establishment. At one time the Progressive Club property was recorded in the names of the wives of Chase and Heatley, a circumstance which led to extended litigation following Hub's death in 1870. Chase became administrator of the Heatley estate and, two years after the death of his partner, sued Heatley's widow to partition the estate.

Chase served as captain of Company F, Third Colorado Cavalry, which was made up of the "hundred-day volunteers" who, under the leadership of Colonel J. M. Chivington, took part in the Sand Creek massacre of the inhabitants, including women and children, of an Indian village. From 1865 to 1869 Chase served as a member of the Denver board of aldermen.

The tall and handsome young gambler married a Denver girl on February 25, 1871, but within two years his wife, Margaret Jane Chase, sued him for divorce on the ground of adultery, charging that he was keeping Nellie Bellmont, also known as Nellie Mohant, in a "love nest" at the Progressive Club. She set forth in her complaint that he owned $75,000 worth of Denver real estate, $30,000 in real estate at Saratoga, New York, and $100,000 in cash and personal effects. The court granted her a divorce but no alimony, since she owned Denver real estate of considerable value.

By 1877 Chase married again. In answer to a suit by Dwight D. Mallory over the Progressive Club property, he claimed the real estate was and for some time past had been recorded in the name of his then wife, Helen Chase.

In the sixties Chase and Heatley built the Palace, a two-story brick structure on the opposite side of Blake Street, housing a variety theater and gambling rooms. In the winter of 1869-70 Chase, in partnership with his brother, John, opened the Cricket Club, a gambling house with a variety show to attract the customers. It was known also as the Blake Street Opera House.

For years the Palace was Denver's principal gambling establishment. Among the entertainers were the beautiful and talented

Barbour sisters. In 1880 one of the sisters, Frances Minerva, became Chase's third wife. Two years later his head bartender, Ed Gaylord, married the other sister, Addie, and was promoted to manager. Later he became one of Chase's partners, but subsequently branched out into the livery stable business. He was a sportsman interested in fast horses and bicycle racers. He won $500 betting on Hackenberry, a long shot in a bicycle race. He frequently went on Chase's bond when the latter was in trouble with the law.

With Robert A. "Bob" Austin and Barney Boyce, Chase opened a saloon, dance hall, and gaming establishment in the old Daniels mansion at 1422 Curtis Street known as the Inter-ocean Club. It was furnished with rich oriental rugs and fine paintings and was the swankiest gambling casino between Kansas City and San Francisco.

Drinks were free to all patrons of the gaming tables. Forty employees were required to operate the place. A lawsuit filed in 1901 named W. S. Hunt, James Thornton, and George O. Hunter as copartners with Chase and Austin, but it was more likely they were employees working on a percentage basis.

Thornton was shot and killed by Alton E. "Big Al" Hoffses, another gambler, in Chase's office at the Inter-ocean October 11, 1906. Big Al was found guilty of voluntary manslaughter and was sentenced to serve from six to seven years in the penitentiary.

Previously David Stubblefield, gambler, shot and killed John Martin at Chase's Palace February 27, 1879, and was sentenced to serve ten years in the penitentiary. He died July 2, 1880, three days after receiving a pardon.

Daniel Burke was killed at the Palace June 4, 1888, but the killer was acquitted.

Most losers accepted their losses philosophically, if not always cheerfully. Only occasionally did one go to law in an attempt to recover his losses.

George Marion brought suit against Ed Chase for $2,852. He

charged that the gambler made a practice of "enticing men into his house and robbing them of their money or property by means of games of chance." He said he had endorsed over to Chase three $1,000 notes issued by the National Bank of Laramie, Wyoming, in payment of a gambling debt. The case was dismissed May 29, 1883.

Oddly enough, wives took a dim view of the sacredness of their husbands' gambling debts. Nellie M. McDaniel brought suit against Chase and Austin, claiming they had fleeced Orville A. McDaniel of $500 of her money given to him for safekeeping, by means of a roulette wheel in their Cottage Club gambling resort on Curtis Street. The case was dismissed the following year.

Ida M. Harlow was equally unsuccessful in an attempt to recover from Chase and Austin $200 she had given W. J. Harlow to deposit in the Central Savings Bank but which he had lost at roulette. Out of luck also was Ella Turner, who sued the two gamblers for $91.25 William C. Turner had lost at faro and poker.

Of necessity the proprietors of gambling houses were shrewd judges of human nature, for they were without legal recourse if a patron gambling "on tick" welshed on making good his losses. On July 5, 1863, John Hughes, Jr., brought suit in the Colorado Territorial Supreme Court against Charles A. Cook for $3,000, representing unpaid losses "in a certain game called Seven Up." Despite the fact that Hughes was represented by Attorney Moses Hallett, later a distinguished judge of the United States District Court, the jury returned a verdict in favor of Cook.

Hughes became a partner of Chase in a Larimer Street gambling establishment. Gambler Jim Moon, whose real name was John E. Wilcoxon, was shot and killed at this place June 16, 1881, by Clay Wilson, who was found not guilty by reason of self-defense.

The top spindlemen for Chase and Hughes at this place were C. W. Hunsicker and Robert D. "Bob" Stockton, who later went into business for themselves, leasing the building formerly occupied by Brinker's Collegiate Institute, a school for girls. They operated it as a gambling house under the name of the Richelieu Hotel. They failed to make a go of it, and the place was taken over by Chase and Vaso Chucovich, who called it the Navarre.

When city authorities made a gesture toward outlawing open gambling, they moved their gaming tables upstairs and devoted the ground floor to a saloon and restaurant. Private dining and gaming rooms were available upstairs. The restaurant displayed a sign, "If Madame is with you and you desire privacy, enter by the north door."

The gambling rooms at the Navarre finally were ordered closed as the result of a newspaper campaign conducted by an editor of the *News*, who played there frequently. A few hours before the establishment was closed for the last time the editor returned for a final fling and won $200.

"That's adding insult to injury," remarked Ed Chase with a wry smile. "You not only close me up, but you top it off by winning my money."

Chase and his third wife occupied a Capitol Hill mansion at 1492 Race Street, now the site of the Aladdin Theater.

Criterion Hall, built in '59 by Ed Jump was, according to one authority, "probably one of the vilest places ever operated in this city, the resort of criminals and desperadoes of all grades."

"Count" Henry Murat, who claimed to be a nephew of Joachim Murat, Napoleon's king of Naples, took over the Criterion and with his wife, the "Countess" Katerine, attempted to operate it as a high-class saloon and gambling casino modeled after European standards. They were unable to overcome its evil reputation and, after extended difficulties with their creditors, lost it through a mortgage foreclosure in 1873.

The "count" and his "countess" were among the earliest residents of Denver. He operated a barbershop in a log cabin and the countess took in washing.

Denver's first American flag flew from the roof of the log

cabin barbershop-laundry. The countess made it from her red flannel petticoat and blue cloak.

Among the barber's best customers were newly arrived emigrants who had spent many weeks unshaven while crossing the plains. When a cloud of dust signaled the approach of an emigrant train the tall and dignified count, who always dressed in sober black and smoked a huge meerschaum pipe, would hop astride his horse and, coattails flapping, ride out to meet the wagons and extol the virtues of his barbershop and the countess' laundry. When Horace Greeley visited Denver Murat charged him five dollars for a shave and the countess charged a commensurate amount for laundering his shirts.

Count Murat was a restless soul and made several trips to California and Nevada in an effort to better himself. He finally struck it rich in the latter state and returned to Denver with $50,000 in dust and nuggets in many buckskin bags sewed in the lining of the countess' skirts as a precaution against road agents.

By 1880 he lost his fortune. He settled at Palmer Lake, between Denver and Colorado Springs, where he planned to establish an American Monte Carlo. His ambitious plan failed to materialize, and he died a pauper.

Cibola Hall, one of the earliest of Denver's gambling establishments, was built and operated by James Reid, a former Mississippi River pilot. All the early saloons dispensed "Taos lightning" in blue bottles. By the drink it cost one dollar. When Albert A. Cass was shot and killed in Jack White's saloon, police records show the killer died in jail the following day "of the jim jams."

In 1885, 200 persons were employed in Denver gambling houses. There were six square games in operation, the rest being crooked, or brace games. Faro dealers were paid five dollars a day and were employed for a six-day week.

Clifton Bell operated private gambling rooms in the Tabor Opera House block, where H. A. W. Tabor played for high stakes, and usually lost. Bell operated another place at 1218 Sixteenth Street known as the Clifton House. It was managed by

James K. Ellis. Later, with D. M. Pomeroy and C. F. Samson as partners, he operated at 268 Sixteenth Street and at 1653 Lawrence Street.

Gambler Robert Ronan was shot and killed at the Missouri gambling house October 24, 1890, by another gambler, who was never brought to trial.

James Young was killed by the blow of a fist at Gavin & Austin's gambling house on March 12, 1894. His assailant was freed when the jury disagreed.

Henry Schoonover and James Morgan conducted a "skinning house" at 1007 Fifteenth Street. Curtis Street boasted three gambling places beside Chase & Austin's Inter-ocean and Cottage Club. They were the Pony Club, the Pavilion Club, and Leadville Club, which was located above the Watrous Café. It was in the latter place that Joe Lowe was shot and killed on February 11, 1899. The killer was acquitted.

The Chicken Coop, on Seventeenth between Larimer and Lawrence streets, was one of the most notorious "skinning houses." Jim Marshall operated gambling establishments at various localities.

Dapper little "Con" Featherly, a Louisianan who had come to Denver from Leadville, conducted a game in the Brown Palace Hotel. The hotel at one time was operated by W. H. "Billy" Bush, whose financial backer was Augusta Tabor, divorced wife of H. A. W. Tabor.

The Welsh brothers operated a game in the Albany Hotel.

Guiney Murray and Dan Hickey were among the second-rate gambling-house proprietors.

In later years the Quincy Club and the Dry Climate Club were among the leading gaming houses.

Except for Belle Siddons, the noted Civil War spy, Denver boasted only one feminine gambling-house operator. At about the turn of the century Anna Guth was the city's "gambling queen."

In 1900 Jim Tracey, consort of Helen McEvoy of Market Street, was run out of town for operating a brace game.

Soapy Smith's shell man, Tom Cady, also known as Tom Keady, ran a shell-game pitch at Orchard Place, just outside the city limits.

Newspaper files reveal that innumerable crusades were conducted against the men of guile. Time after time headlines proclaimed that gambling had been stamped out, or was about to be stamped out, but the games continued to operate.

Ed Chase's places were raided on innumerable occasions. Customarily he faced separate charges of operating a gaming room, a roulette wheel, a faro bank, and a stud poker table. Usually the cases dragged through the county court for two or three years and were dropped after he paid ten dollars' costs on each count.

His Inter-ocean Club contained so many rooms that the evidence usually vanished before the raiders could find their way through the maze to the actual gaming rooms. If one of his places was padlocked, he opened for business at another location.

The story is told of a penniless young Easterner who came to Colorado in 1880 to seek his fortune. Within six months by hard work and diligent application to business he accumulated $800, a riding horse, pack mule, watch, chain, rifle, two revolvers, and a meerschaum pipe.

The young man had never gambled, but one night friends induced him to try his luck at roulette. At first he won a few dollars, and then his luck turned. He lost his $800, his horse, mule, watch, chain, rifle, and revolvers.

Despondent, he shuffled from the gambling house, determined to kill himself. Reaching in the pocket where he usually carried a gun, his hand closed upon the meerschaum.

Dashing back into the gambling house, he succeeded in borrowing twenty dollars on the pipe. He staked it all on a turn of the wheel and won. In a few hours he won back his two revolvers, his rifle, watch, chain, mule, and horse. He won back his $800, but kept right on playing. When daylight came he quit with $4,800 winnings. He never gambled again.

As played in the sixties and seventies, poker differed somewhat from the modern game. Straights and flushes were unknown, and there were two unbeatable hands—four aces, and four kings with an ace. These hands were equivalent to today's ace-high straight flush.

One morning when the cashier of a pioneer Denver bank came to work, he found three men sitting on the steps of the bank. One said he had come to the bank for a $5,000 loan.

"I've been sitting in a poker game across the street, and there's more than $4,000 in the pot," he explained impatiently. "There are three or four pretty strong hands out, and as I've every cent I own in the center, the boys gave me thirty minutes to raise a stake on my hand."

He produced a sealed envelope and handed it to the cashier.

"My hand's in this envelope," he explained. "Just look at it, but don't give it away to these gentlemen. They're in the game, and came along to make sure I don't monkey with the cards."

The cashier opened the envelope and found one of the two unbeatable hands—four kings and an ace.

"But this is highly irregular," he said stiffly. "We don't lend money on cards."

"But you ain't going to see me raised on a hand like that?" protested the poker player incredulously. "These fellows think I'm bluffing, and I can clean out the whole gang."

The cashier refused the loan, and the player, accompanied by the two watchers, drifted away. On the corner they met the bank president, who had just come himself from a quiet little all-night game.

When they explained the case the president dashed into the bank, seized a bag of money, and followed the trio. Ten minutes later he returned with the bag and an extra handful of twenties.

"Here—credit this $500 to the interest account," he told the cashier. "I thought you had more business snap. Ever play poker?"

"No," acknowledged the cashier.

"Thought not," snapped the president. "If you did, you'd know what good collateral is. Remember that in the future four kings and an ace are always good in this institution for our entire assets, sir—our entire assets."

(8)

Hot Decks and Cold

FARO was the most popular game in Western gambling houses up to the turn of the century. Supposedly it offered the player his greatest chance of winning, since the percentage in favor of the house was only one and three-fourths, while the house cut in other games ranged upward from six per cent.

The "wise" players preferred faro because it commonly was believed to be impossible to operate as a crooked or brace game. The belief was an illusion, for any "banking" game operated by a house player is subject to cheating. A clever dealer at faro or twenty-one could make his own odds in favor of the house.

"Readers"—marked cards—could be used in faro as easily as in any other game. So could cards trimmed slightly along the ends or edges, known as "strippers." Sometimes cards were "sanded" to cause them to stick together. Even a new or "clean" deck could be marked during a few deals, by means of a tiny needle set in the dealer's ring. A horsehair in the dealer's box could be used to hold back any desired card until the moment came for a killing.

Roulette was popular in the larger gambling houses. In a square game the house percentage ranged between five and six per cent, but few roulette games were operated honestly. Stud poker was more popular than draw. Keno, a dice game operated by means of a "goose," appealed to those who customarily played for small stakes, and in another form exists today under the name of bingo.

In the San Luis Valley of Colorado and in the Mexican border states where Mexicans predominated, Spanish monte, a game similar to short faro, was favored above all others. The Mexicans called the gringos "'los God dammes."

Spanish monte should not be confused with three-card monte, which is a variation of the old shell game in which cards are used in place of walnut shells. While Spanish monte is a gambling game, three-card monte is essentially a bunco game in which the operator of the "pitch" deceives the sucker by his dexterity in manipulating the three cards.

The operator of the three-card game is never called a dealer. Since he throws his three cards face down on the table, he is known as a monte "thrower." While nearly all card and dice games are played indoors, the monte thrower frequently set up his pitch out-of-doors on a street corner. He takes three cards, called "the tickets," bent slightly lengthwise, shows one—usually the ace of hearts—to the players. He makes a few passes, throws them face down, and asks the players to bet which was the one they had seen.

Sometimes a capper pretends to start an argument with the thrower and, while his attention apparently is distracted, turns down the corner of a card to make the sucker think he is betting on a sure thing. The thrower turns down the corner of another card while throwing and trims the sucker.

Here is a sample of the monte thrower's come-on spiel:

"Here you are, gentlemen; this ace of hearts is the winning card. Follow it with your eyes as I shuffle. Here it is, and now here, now here, and now—where? You win if you point it out the first time; but if you miss, you lose. Here it is, you see; now watch it again. This ace of hearts, gentlemen, is the winning card. I take no bets from paupers, cripples, or orphan children.

The ace of hearts. It is my regular trade, gentlemen, to move my hands quicker than your eyes. I always have two chances to your one. The ace of hearts. If your sight is quick enough, you beat me and I pay; if not, I beat you and take your money. The ace of hearts—who will go me twenty? It is very plain and simple, but you can't always tell. Here you are, gentlemen; the ace, and the ace. Who will go me twenty dollars?"

Hieronymous, a dice game similar to chuck-a-luck, at one time was widely popular in the West. It is played with three dice and two wooden bowls, the smaller ends of which are connected by a tube. Bets are made on a numbered layout. The dice are placed in the upper bowl and fall through the tube upon a tambourine upon which the lower bowl is inverted. The operator pays even, two and three to one, according to how many figures on the dice correspond to those on which bets have been made. The percentage in favor of the house is enormous.

A gambling house at Pueblo, Colorado, operating in the eighties and nineties, was famous for its Hieronymous bowl. It also operated six faro banks, four roulette wheels, four tables for hazard and craps, two for stud poker and two for draw poker, one for short faro, and one for twenty-one.

Keno games and policy drawings were held daily in two back rooms. The place was open twenty-four hours a day and employed fifty men working in three eight-hour shifts. Instead of giving money to a "busted" loser, it gave him a brass check which could not be played at the gaming tables, but which was good for drinks at the bar, for a night's lodging, or for a meal.

The game of twenty-one was known in France as *vingt-et-un*, and is said to have been Napoleon's favorite game. In England it was called Van John. It became popular in Mobile and New Orleans early in the eighteenth century. Today it is called blackjack.

At Leadville faro was the favorite game at Coleman's Place, one of the earlier gambling hells and rival of the Little Casino. The twenty-one tables were always crowded. English hazard attracted only a few. Also popular was keno. It was played with grains of corn, and three grains in a row elicited the call of "keno!"

At Cheyenne, the Greer brothers' Gold Room Saloon got the biggest play. There George Devol, famous Mississippi sharper, dealt faro for several months about 1872. The game was run by a gambler named Bowlby, who prospered until Wild Bill Hickok visited Cheyenne in 1874. Bowlby's dealer attempted to swindle Wild Bill, who knocked him down with a cane, wrecked the faro table, and walked out with the contents of the cash drawer.

The West gave birth to a number of poker superstitions. It was believed to be bad luck to count one's chips or to play with a kibitzer looking over one's shoulder. Everyone took it for granted that a player who drew a pat hand of jacks full on red sevens would not leave the game alive. The easiest way to change one's luck was to walk three times around one's chair.

It was bad luck forever to play with a one-eyed gambler. This superstition gave rise to the expression, "There's a one-eyed man in the game," meaning, "look out for a cheat."

The belief arose from an incident in an early-day game in which a one-eyed player was suspected of cheating. Another player whipped out his gun, demanded a new deal, and said, "I'm not making any insinuations, but if I catch any son-of-a-bitch cheating I'll shoot his other eye out."

Women gamblers were not uncommon. A four-foot-five French firebrand, Eleanore Dumont, better known as Minnie, the Gambler, was the sweetheart of "Colorado Charley" Utter.

Colorado Charley was a guide and hunter in Colorado's Middle Park in 1861. During Georgetown's mining boom he ran a livery stable at that camp and engaged in freighting and jackass-packing.

He was a man of light build, and very much of a dandy, dressing in fringed buckskin. He wore his hair long and sported a longhorn mustache. He possessed one eccentricity which set him apart from all other frontiersmen—he bathed daily, summer and winter. As the icy mountain streams provided the only bathing facilities, most of his contemporaries thought him a bit touched in the head.

He married Matilda Nash at Empire in 1866, but the marriage failed to "take," although he was an excellent cook. In 1876 he led a party of Georgetown miners to Deadwood.

Up to this time he had been considered an unobtrusive little man of mild manners, but he immediately formed a friendship with Wild Bill Hickok and thereby somehow gained the reputation of being a "bad man." Calamity Jane Canary is said to have admired him immensely, but was unsuccessful in her efforts to win his favor, and he married Minnie, the Gambler. She dealt stud for Charley at El Paso until 1904. The two then organized a medicine show which toured Mexico and Central America. Charley died on the tour, and Minnie retired to southern California with a modest fortune.

Madame Moustache was one of the famous feminine gamblers of the West. She operated games at San Francisco, Nevada City, Cheyenne, Boise, Bannock, and Eureka, Nevada. She followed the boom towns as the Union Pacific was built through Wyoming, and at one time employed Calamity Jane Canary. In September, 1879, at Bodie, California, after a professional gambler broke the bank in her faro game, she killed herself with poison.

In those days, when a cattleman desired to end his life, he usually blew out his brains with a .45. A miner preferred to hold a half-stick of dynamite in his teeth and touch a match to the fuse. A woman never used such violent means of suicide. She invariably took poison or drowned herself because, it is said, she always wanted to make a lovely, unmutilated corpse.

"Policy" was the poor man's gambling game. Like its offspring, the numbers racket of today, it made the poor poorer and the operators richer. Western cities of the seventies, eighties, and nineties abounded with policy shops.

Originally the winning numbers were taken from the drawings of the Colorado State Lottery, established in 1867, and later from the Kentucky State Lottery, or the Frankfort Lottery.

A "day number" paid five to one if any number up to seventy-eight chanced to be one of the first fifteen numbers drawn. A "station number" paid sixty to one if a selected number appeared in a specified position on the lottery list. A "saddle" paid thirty-two to one if two selected numbers appeared anywhere on the list. Lou Blonger was kingpin of the policy shop racket in Denver.

In 1890 gambler Ed Chase was president of the Colorado Policy Association with offices on Larimer Street. At one time twelve policy shops were listed in the Denver city directory, as was also the Denver headquarters of the Louisiana Lottery.

The West drew many of its professional gamblers from the Mississippi steamboats, from New Orleans swamp district, from Natchez-under-the-hill, from the Landing area at Vicksburg, and from Chicago's Sands district.

For years paper money was viewed with suspicion in Denver. In the earliest days gold dust was the prevailing medium of exchange. Every saloon, gambling hall, and sporting house contained a pair of gold scales. The scales always rested on a small square of carpeting. A cashier with an unsteady hand could always manage to let a few grains fall into the nap of the carpeting. The value of the dust shaken from this square of fabric at the end of the night's business ranged from ten to twenty dollars.

For a time the twenty-five-cent piece was the smallest coin in circulation. Two bits was the price of the morning paper, of a loaf of bread, or of a shot of Taos lightning.

Gold dust no longer was current in the eighties, but Denver liked the feel of "hard money." As much as anything, this preference was due to a desire to patronize home industry, since gold and silver were the region's principal products.

Gambler Ed Chase's only real rival, Vaso Chucovich, was born in the little town of Risan, in Dalmatia, then a part of Austria-Hungary. Risan, on the coast of the Adriatic, numbered only 800 souls. A chunky Slav, with red hair and large, melting, brown eyes, Vaso was one of nine children. Besides the Dalmatian dialect, he spoke Italian, Greek, and Russian fluently. His parents sent him to a school for commercial travelers. When he came of age his father gave him one hundred dollars and bade him good-by and good luck.

Vaso grew a fierce red mustache and set out to walk across Europe. Hearing tales of the riches to be gained in America, he shipped as a sailor on a vessel bound for San Francisco. He was penniless when he jumped ship, and could speak not a word of English.

His first job was that of night watchman guarding a huge pile of watermelons on a San Francisco wharf. When a docking vessel jolted most of the melons into the bay, the frightened Dalmatian lad sought refuge in a Slav monastery at San Francisco.

Within a few months he learned to speak passable English. No longer frightened, he decided the monastic life was not for him. He found a job as a swamper in a Slav poolroom. He was an excellent pool and billiard player and picked up quite a bit of side money through his skill, but his ambition was to become a bartender.

Friends lured him to Carson City, Nevada, with tales of the riches pouring from the mines. Vaso found a job in a stamp mill. The mill used mercury in separating the gold from the ore, and presently young Vaso lost all his teeth from mercury poisoning.

He became a bartender in a Carson City saloon, but hearing that the dealers in the gambling hall upstairs earned considerably more than bartenders, he set out to learn the trade. He was successful at gambling, and within a year or so accumulated $46,000. Investing his stake in a mine, he lost it all. He went to Omaha and through his gambling operations soon acquired a stake of $74,000.

As a gambler he still considered himself a tyro. Throughout the West Ed Chase of Denver was known as the master gambler. In 1886 Vaso went to Denver, taking with him his $74,000 in gold coin. He served an apprenticeship tending bar in Chase's place, then being operated by Chase's partners, Pete and Charles

Persson and Johnny Hughes. A year later, with "Square-shooter" Johnny Hughes, he set up business at the Arcade, which was listed in the city directory as a saloon and as a restaurant. Indignant Chase announced he would run "Chuck" Chucovich out of town.

Usually the Slav operator wore a pink shirt adorned with a huge diamond. He was affable and likable, but his weakness was a nervous disposition that caused him to lose his temper easily. He possessed an uncanny financial instinct and was an adroit politician—which Chase was not.

Chucovich cultivated the friendship of Robert W. Speer, president of the Board of Police Commissioners and later mayor. They became lifelong friends. Court records show many gambling charges were filed against Chucovich, but not so many as against Chase, although both enjoyed the reputation of running nothing but square games. Chase swallowed his pride and made his peace with his former employee. Although never friends, Chase and Chucovich became partners many years later in operating the Navarre.

Both invested heavily in real estate, and retained the same real estate lawyer, Denver's first woman attorney, Mary F. Lathrop, a pint-size Quaker lass. She was the first woman ever admitted to membership in the American Bar Association, and for years has been recognized as one of Denver's foremost title experts.

She was recommended to Chase by the lawyer who handled his defense in criminal cases. Chase doubted the ability of a woman attorney but determined to give the gentle, tiny she-lawyer a trial. When he called upon her, she was unaware he was Denver's leading gambler. Commissioning her to check the title of a parcel of real estate he planned to buy, he asked her to telephone him when her investigation was completed. She never dreamed the phone number he gave her was the Arcade gambling joint.

When she asked to speak to Chase, a man's voice replied, "He ain't in, honey, but I am. You got a mighty sweet voice, darling, and I'd sure like to know you better. How about us stepping out tonight?"

"I am Mr. Chase's lawyer," said Miss Lathrop icily.

"Yeah, and I'm the Prince of Wales," was the reply.

"What is this place?" she asked, bewildered. The reply gave her the first intimation who her new client was.

When she mentioned the incident to Chase, he threatened to fire the employee.

"Please don't," she begged, laughing. "The joke is on me. I'm a Quaker, and I never get angry at anyone."

She represented Chase in his real estate operations for the remainder of his life, and when he died at the age of ninety-one, she settled his estate. Chase always addressed her as "My dear attorney." She never sent him a bill, and he always paid her approximately twice the amount she would have charged him.

Few residents of Denver had ever heard of Dalmatia, where Chucovich was born. When Chuck learned that Mary Lathrop in the course of her world travels had visited his home town of Risan, he, too, employed her to handle his real estate dealings.

Unlike Chase, Chucovich was a haggler. After she had handled his work for many years, she once sent him a bill for twenty-five dollars for legal services. He called at her office, handed her a ten-dollar bill, and said, "That young lawyer on the first floor would only charge ten dollars."

She marked her statement "Paid in Full" and passed it to him with his bank note. "It seems you need this money more than I do, Mr. Chucovich," she told him sweetly. "Get another lawyer. I want no more dealings with you."

The gambler was flabbergasted. He pretended it was a joke, promised he'd never question her charges again. "You aren't mad at me, are you?" he asked.

"I am a Quaker, and I never get angry," said the half-pint lady lawyer. "I just don't care to have you as a client." The next day he sent her a huge box of candy, which she returned. She never represented him again.

"Chucovich bitterly resented his lack of education," said Miss Lathrop. "He used to curse the fate that made him a gambler. Under different circumstances he would have made a brilliant banker, for he possessed keen financial acumen."

Chucovich's integrity was never questioned, and he was highly respected.

Chase, who died in 1921, left his third wife, Frances Minerva, his entire estate of $650,000 in real estate, telephone stock, and government bonds. Chucovich's estate totaled $1,250,000. He left $750,000 to build a hospital in his native village of Risan, then in Yugoslavia. During World War II the magnificent hospital was reduced to ruins by German bombers.

He left a quarter of a million to build a monument to his friend, Mayor Speer, in Denver's Civic Center. The courts construed his will to permit the construction of the present Speer Memorial Hospital as an adjunct of the Denver General Hospital.

Pete Persson, one of Chase's partners, left an estate of $700,000.

Most of the gambling house proprietors died rich. Most of their customers died poor. Colorado's wealthiest citizen, H. A. W. Tabor, lost immense sums in Clifton Bell's private gambling rooms in the Tabor Opera House block. Bell profited only to the extent of the house cut, and the bulk of Tabor's losings went to other wealthy poker players.

Of course, Tabor did not always lose. "Colonel" Billy Thompson, who at the time was tending bar at Jones's Place, adjoining the Tabor building on Curtis Street, says:

"One evening the boys up in the private rooms sent down for a two-gallon jug of Old Crow whisky and a box of 'Can't Be Beat' cigars. I took the order up to the room, and arrived just as Tabor was getting up from the poker table.

"He said, 'I'm sorry to quit the game so early, boys, but I have a dinner engagement at home. How do I stand? Am I winner or loser?'

"Clifton Bell figured it out on a piece of paper and said, 'You're ahead by $5,200 tonight, Governor.' "

For a short time when he served as lieutenant governor, Tabor was addressed as governor.

At the best none too bright, and often befuddled by too much whisky, Tabor was no match for the wealthy, big-time poker players who frequented Clifton Bell's place. Shrewdest and boldest poker player in the entire West was United States Senator Edward O. Wolcott of Colorado, notable for his huge, drooping mustache. He was one of Colorado's most able and distinguished statesmen.

In 1888, when he was a candidate for the United States Senate, Wolcott's enemies charged that he had lost $22,000 playing faro. According to Alexander Gardiner in his book, *Canfield, True Story of the Greatest Gambler*, he scorned to deny the charge.

"It's nobody's business but my own," he said. "Besides, I had just won the money the previous day at the races."

His candor won him the election. He served in the Senate from 1889 to 1901 and helped make history in big-time poker-playing circles in Washington.

Most of Washington's private poker games were held in private rooms at Chamberlin's Restaurant, which deducted no kitty for the house. At some of these sessions, writes Asbury in his book, *Sucker's Progress*, especially those in which Wolcott was concerned, the stakes were very high, and frequently as much as $100,000 changed hands in an evening.

During his term as senator, Ed Wolcott was regarded as the ablest poker player in the capital and, with the possible exception of Robert C. Schenk, was probably the greatest Washington ever produced.

Wolcott was rated the most compelling orator in the Senate, and was keynoter of the Republican National Convention that nominated McKinley for his second term. Strangely enough, as a young lawyer starting his practice at Georgetown, Colorado, he was too shy to appear in a courtroom—but he was an accomplished pool player. He was the best-dressed member of the U. S. Senate, and wore striped trousers, a fawn waistcoat, and a boutonniere.

Wolcott played poker in Washington, but when he went to New York he liked to "buck the tiger" at Richard Canfield's famous gambling establishment. The bulk of Canfield's business, writes Asbury, was a group of famous plungers who flourished in the nineties.

They included Colonel Isaac Ellwood; John A. Drake, son of an Iowa governor and owner of a racing stable; Wolcott, whose special limit at faro was $2,000 on cases and $4,000 on doubles, and who frequently "bucked the tiger" for two days and two nights at a stretch; state Senator Patrick McCarren of Brooklyn, who in one day lost $100,000 at faro; Phil Dyer, race-track king, who once lost $100,000 at roulette; Reginald Vanderbilt, who gave Canfield an IOU for $300,000 and finally settled for $130,000; Theodore Hostetter of Chicago, who gambled away a million dollars in a few months and who liked to match pennies at $1,000 a turn; and finally, the kingpin plunger of them all, John W. "Bet-a-Million" Gates. Gates's faro limit of $2,500 and $5,000 was only slightly higher than Ed Wolcott's.

When Canfield retired he held approximately $250,000 in IOU's he was never able to collect. When his lawyer, John Delahunty, sued Canfield in 1906, it was brought out that one item he had collected was Wolcott's IOU for $60,000. The account was settled for one hundred cents on the dollar. Wolcott died at Monte Carlo in March, 1905.

(9)

King of the Thimbleriggers

JEFFERSON Randolph "Soapy" Smith, born in Georgia in 1860, originated a variation of the old shell game that brought him a fortune and the title, "King of the Thimbleriggers."

As a cowboy he had been "trimmed" by a shell-game operator while attending a circus at San Antonio. Scenting a means of making easy money, he joined the circus grifters and learned how to manipulate the profitable walnut shells. At San Antonio he learned the fine points of the shell game from "Clubfoot" Hall, a veteran pitch man, and developed the "soap game" at Leadville before coming to Denver.

Dark-eyed, dapper, slender, genteel, glib, bearded Soapy would set up his pitch on a busy street corner, using a sample case "keister" on a tripod to display his wares—a pile of soap cubes and some squares of blue wrapping paper. Doc Baggs was his chief capper, but there were always several come-on men planted in the crowd. The only man ever permitted to pinch-hit for Soapy himself was "Sure-shot" Tom Cady, a top-flight shell man.

"Use this soap and wash your sins away!" twenty-eight-year-old Soapy would call, spilling a handful of loose banknotes beside the pile of soap. "Cleanliness is next to godliness, but the feel of good, crisp greenbacks in the pocket is paradise itself. Step up, friends, and watch me closely."

He would then offer to sell those interested in cleanliness alone a soap cube for twenty-five cents. As this was some five times the market price, there were few takers. So he would hold up a hundred-dollar bill from the pile before him.

"But if you want to take a chance on winning one of these little green papers with the big numbers on them, I'll sell you a wrapped bar at the ridiculous price of five dollars."

The watchers saw him apparently twist the hundred-dollar bill around a cube of soap and then wrap it in a square of blue paper, tossing it carelessly alongside the unwrapped pile. Swiftly his dexterous fingers would wrap additional cubes, apparently enclosing one-, ten-, or twenty-dollar bills with each.

Someone would step up, pay his five dollars, and carefully select a wrapped cube. Unwrapping it, he would shout gleefully as he displayed the hundred-dollar bill he found inside. The first buyer was, of course, Doc Baggs or another capper.

Eagerly the suckers would swarm in to take advantage of this get-rich-quick offer. But surprisingly they would find no banknotes wrapped with their soap. When business slackened off then another capper "found" a hundred-dollar bill.

A variation of the old shell game and of three-card monte, Soapy's racket depended for its success on the dexterity of the nimble-fingered pitch man, who simply palmed the bank notes as he wrapped the soap. The gullible sucker stood just about as much chance of winning as he did of guessing which walnut shell concealed the vanishing pea, or which of the three monte cards was the ace of hearts. However, the soap game differed from the shell game and three-card monte in that the sucker always got something for his money—a five-cent cake of soap for five dollars.

It has been written of Soapy, "He took 'em as fast as they laid their money on the layout. His boosters dragged the suckers in, and Soapy put the ax to them where Nellie wore the beads . . .

Soapy was beyond doubt the slipperiest of the slippery with his line of bull con and the simple little walnut shell game."

Long before the arrival of Soapy Smith, Doc Baggs was trimming suckers in Denver. The 1882 city directory lists him as a "traveling agent." Doc, who wore a glossy stovepipe hat and carried a silk umbrella, experienced more difficulties with the press than with the law. He always succeeded in persuading the authorities to listen to reason, but the newspapers irked him by occasionally publishing the "squawks" of his victims.

"I am conducting a fair, legitimate business," he told a reporter for the Rocky Mountain *News*. "My mission is to skin suckers. I defy the newspapers to put their hands on a single man I ever beat that was not financially able to stand it.

"I am emotionally insane. When I see anyone looking in a jewelry store window thinking how they would like to get away with the diamonds, an irresistible desire comes over me to skin them. I don't drink, smoke, chew, or cheat poor people. I pay my debts."

Doc Baggs was growing old at the time bearded, young Soapy Smith blew into Denver from Leadville. There is some evidence to indicate he was pressured into joining forces with the "Soap Gang," for he could never understand why anyone should waste his talents skinning a sucker out of five dollars when it was almost as easy to take him for five thousand. Soapy Smith's adherents were known as the Soap Gang to distinguish them from a rival underworld faction known as the "California Gang."

Soapy preferred small and fast profits in mass volume. Although his henchmen included several professional bunco men, Soapy himself never adopted Doc Baggs's racket. It remained for Lou Blonger to develop the Doc's con-game technique into a multimillion-dollar operation, employing scores of assistants.

One of Doc Baggs's bunco steerers was Clifton Sparks, a former gambler from St. Joseph, Missouri, who always wore a $2,500 diamond stud on the front of his boiled shirt.

Soapy Smith's chief henchman was "Troublesome Tom"

Cady, who trimmed thousands of suckers at Denver's old Manhattan Beach resort. He was noted for his woebegone expression as he informed the sucker who had bet that the little pea was under a certain walnut shell, "No, it's not under that one." For protection he carried a swordcane.

Prospecting near Wagon Wheel Gap in southwestern Colorado, N. C. Creede drove his pick into a pay streak in 1890 and shouted deliriously, "Holy Moses! I've struck it rich!"

Thus was the famous Holy Moses mine christened and the short-lived but hectic boom town of Creede born. It was as wild and tough as the worst, attracting boomers, speculators, gamblers, con men, desperadoes, and virtueless women. It is best described in the oft-quoted lines of poet-editor Cy Warman:

> It's day all day in the daytime,
> And there is no night in Creede.

Here came Soapy Smith and his crew of thimbleriggers, short-card artists, and shell men, and promptly took over the town. Writer Richard Harding Davis—who would have been a sucker for modern one-arm-bandit slot machines—learned to his sorrow that Tom Cady's hand was quicker than Richard's eye. He was fascinated by Troublesome Tom's dexterity with the walnut shells, and his expense account was expanded mightily to meet his losses.

Already beautiful blond Lillis Lovell had established herself as red-light queen of Creede. Other madames included Slanting Annie, Lulu Slain, the Mormon Queen, and six-foot-two Rose Vastine, known as "Timberline" because of her elevation above sea level.

Until the arrival of Soapy Smith and his gang, Bob Ford was the boss of the newborn camp. This was the same Bob Ford who ten years earlier had killed the bandit Jesse James in cold blood while a guest at the home of James, who sometimes used the alias "Mr. Howard." The killer operated a saloon and gambling joint known as Ford's Exchange.

Bob Ford was the villain of the popular dirge of the day:

> O! The dirty little coward
> Who shot Mr. Howard
> And laid Jesse James in his grave!

Gunman and former peace officer Bat Masterson was manager of the Denver Exchange.

Soapy Smith established the Orleans Club and speedily deposed Ford as camp dictator. Soapy ran Creede with an iron hand. No grifter could operate in the camp without his approval and without cutting him in for a fifty-fifty share of the take. Cy Warman's newspaper called Soapy Smith, "Sapolio Smythe."

To Creede on a June day in '92 came Ed O. Kelley, whose wife was a sister of Cole and Bud Younger, members of the James boys' old outlaw band. Five minutes after Bob Ford had commented that his opal scarf pin was an omen of ill luck, Kelley marched into the Exchange and blasted his life away with a shotgun.

Ford's body was "planted" in Shotgun Hill cemetery, later was transplanted by his common-law wife to the less rocky soil of Missouri. Kelley was tried, convicted, imprisoned, pardoned.

Creede soon went into a decline and Soapy returned to Denver to establish his notorious Tivoli Club saloon and skinning joint.

As a fair warning to customers, Soapy posted a sign at the top of the stairway leading to the gambling rooms: *Caveat emptor*. Few knew its meaning. None heeded it.

Soapy detested nickel-in-the-slot music boxes, forerunners of the modern juke box. He learned that a nickel, hammered to expand its diameter slightly, would jam a music box so it would play indefinitely. He delighted in jamming every available music box. One at the Denver Union Station, so jammed, played "Maggie Murphy" over and over for six straight hours before mechanics succeeded in removing Soapy's oversized nickel.

Other Denver gambling resorts of the period included Murphy's Exchange, Clifton Bell's two establishments, one a select "club" in the Tabor Opera House building where H. A. W. Tabor lost a part of his fortune, the Morgue, the Chicken Coop, the Bucket of Blood, and the Missouri Club.

Operated by Jeff Argyle, the notorious Missouri Club but recently had been the scene of the murder of a sucker by a gambler known as the Black Prince. On the night of October 11, 1892, Troublesome Tom Cady used his cane to belabor gambler Jim Jordan, alias Henry Gilmore, in the Missouri Club, and was arrested.

Jordan repaired to Murphy's Exchange—the Slaughterhouse— at 1617 Larimer Street. Here three murders had been committed within two years. Only a few months earlier Frank Marshall had killed Johnny Clough, a prizefighter, as he stood at Murphy's bar.

Here Jordan found Cort Thomson, Mattie Silks's solid man; Doc Baggs's ex-steerer, Cliff Sparks, wearing his $2,500 "headlight" diamond stud; and Sparks's closest friend, Bill Crooks, a penny-ante, tinhorn, chicken-feed gambler. Behind the bar were saloonkeeper Johnny Murphy and his head bartender, Mark Watrous.

Meanwhile, Soapy Smith had given bail for his shell man, Troublesome Tom Cady, and the two strolled into the Slaughterhouse. Tom Cady made a menacing flourish with his swordcane. Jordan whipped out his gun.

Six-guns blazed. Bystanders scattered. When the gun smoke cleared away, Cliff Sparks lay gasping his life out alongside the brass rail.

Kneeling by his side, saloonkeeper Johnny Murphy lifted his head. In the following words he told Cliff he was dying: "Cliff, old man, they're off at Sheepshead, and you're last."

Cliff repeated, "I'm last," and died. His friend, Tinhorn Bill Crooks, rushed forward and pushed Johnny Murphy aside, dropping to his knees beside the body of the slain man.

"They've killed my dear old pal," he cried out in anguish. "They've killed my best friend, Cliff Sparks!"

He clasped the dead man tight against him and, sobbing, pressed his face close to Cliff's breast. And as he sobbed, he robbed his dead friend by biting the $2,500 diamond stud from the bosom of Cliff's boiled shirt.

Cort Thomson and Johnny Murphy were jailed. The next morning Soapy Smith gave himself up to police. Mattie Silks bailed Cort out. No one could—or would—tell who had killed Cliff Sparks. The case was dropped. As a sop to public sentiment police temporarily closed Soapy's skinning house, the Tivoli, and McEvoy and Dale's gambling establishment on the second floor above Murphy's Slaughterhouse.

In 1893 Populist Davis H. Waite was elected governor of Colorado on a woman's suffrage and reform ticket, pledging himself "to fight iniquity if I have to ride through blood to my bridles." But Denver wanted none of his reform. When the Denver fire and police board refused to obey his repeated orders to clean up the city, he called out the militia to take possession of the City Hall and enforce his orders.

City officials called on Soapy Smith for aid. Soapy filled the City Hall with armed henchmen and defied the militia, even though cannons were trained on the building. "Blood to the Bridles" Waite confessed defeat and withdrew the troops.

For a few months Soapy was riding high, but his luck ran out on him when his eccentric brother, Bascom, was jailed for an unprovoked assault on Johnny Hughes, a square gambler and Ed Chase's partner in the Arcade.

Soapy left Denver and drifted to Texas and thence to Mexico, where he failed in a bold attempt to organize a foreign legion under his own generalship.

Returning to Denver in '95, he found Lou Blonger an underworld czar. A French-Canadian underworld character who had operated in New Orleans and Salt Lake City, Lou, with his brother, Sam H., had opened a saloon, dance hall, and gambling joint in Denver in 1880. Soapy found himself compelled to pay half his "take" to the Blongers for police protection and permission to operate.

Word of the gold strike in the Klondike almost depopulated Denver's underworld. Soapy Smith led the stampede of Denver's underworld to the new gold regions of the North. With his thimbleriggers, bunco men, and gamblers he left Denver in the summer of 1897, and after a brief stop at Seattle to accumulate a stake, arrived at Skagway in October.

Skagway was a mushroom boom town, much like Creede had been during the days of Soapy's dictatorship, and it offered the same possibilities for a man of imagination, enterprise, and few scruples. Soapy set up his soap pitch on Broadway, and deliberately set out to become the community dictator.

Shortly after Soapy's arrival, John E. Fay, a bartender, killed Deputy U. S. Marshal Rowan and Andy McGrath, a bystander, when threatened with arrest. A mob set out to lynch him. Soapy intervened, made an impassioned plea for law and order, and persuaded the mob to turn over the killer to the authorities to await trial.

Immediately after the killing Rowan's wife gave birth to a baby. Soapy took up a collection for her. Fay subsequently was acquitted on the grounds of self-defense.

Soapy immediately proclaimed himself boss of Skagway and announced that from that moment he was running the town. With John Clancy as partner he opened a saloon known as Jeff's Place.

The better citizens met his proclamation of dictatorship by organizing the Vigilance Committee of One Hundred and One. Soapy countered by forming an underworld organization called the Committee of Three Hundred and Three and took up a collection of $600 to build a church.

Six-foot "Diamond Lil" Davenport of Chicago was madame of Skagway's principal parlor house and queen of the red-light. She accumulated a fortune in Klondike gold, squandered it, and at the time of her death was working as a scrubwoman in Seattle.

In May of 1898 construction of the railroad was begun, and presently thousands of gold-seekers were pouring through Skagway on their way to the interior. With the outbreak of the war with Spain Soapy recruited a company of militia known as the Skagway Guards. He was chosen grand marshal of the Fourth of July celebration. The peak of his career was reached when he led the parade on his gray horse, wearing a wide-brim white hat.

He was the absolute dictator of Skagway, as he had been the dictator of Creede. He was literally running the town, and running it to suit himself. The members of his gang were preying upon the tenderfoot "cheechakos," relieving them of the funds they had brought to finance their gold-seeking venture, and at the same time were "skinning" the successful miners who were returning to the states with their accumulation of gold dust. He found so little opposition that he abandoned his former methods in favor of outright robbery.

In the rear of his saloon he kept a huge captive eagle. A victim, persuaded to "see the eagle," was led into the back room, given a mickey, beaten, robbed, and tossed out into the alley. The money was pouring into Soapy's coffers, but he spent it as fast as he made it, financing the Skagway Guards, contributing to charities, and aiding the down-and-outers.

Among his gang's victims was J. D. Stewart, returning to his home in British Columbia with $2,700 worth of gold dust accumulated in the Klondike. After being "rolled" of his poke of dust when taken to "see the eagle," he told his story to city engineer Frank H. Reid, who called a meeting of the Committee of One Hundred and One to consider the case. Members of the committee crowded the street in front of Jeff's Place, but when Soapy appeared in the doorway carrying a rifle in the crook of his arm, the crowd melted away.

The committee called a meeting in a local hall, but finding it packed with Soapy's men, adjourned to the Juneau wharf, where guards were posted with orders to refuse admittance to Soapy's adherents.

Hearing of the meeting, Soapy took his rifle and started for the wharf, alone, confident that his glib tongue could once more persuade the crowd to disperse. As he approached the wharf in the darkness Reid recognized him and shouted out a command to halt. Instead of obeying, Soapy raised his rifle. Reid whipped out his pistol and fired at the same instant Soapy drew the trigger of his rifle. Soapy dropped dead, a bullet through his heart. Reid was seriously wounded and died twelve days later.

The Committee of One Hundred and One swept through the streets of Skagway, searching out the members of his gang. Forty were jailed, and were about to be lynched when martial law was declared and the United States troops took over the town. The forty were placed on the first ship bound for the states.

The King of the Thimbleriggers was only thirty-eight years old when he met his death on July 8, 1898, only four days after his greatest triumph. His nimble fingers, glib tongue, and audaciousness had brought him more than a million dollars. Most of his winnings had been spent or given away almost as fast as the money rolled in, and he died virtually penniless.

(10)

Overlord of the Underworld

SOAPY Smith was a piker compared with Lou Blonger. Soapy's favorite racket netted him about $100 a night, and during the brief periods he was dictator of Creede and of Skagway he levied tribute on all local underworld operators. But Lou Blonger, adopting methods used by Soapy, finally forced the king of the con men to pay him half his earnings for permission to operate in Denver, and some years later developed a multimillion-dollar racket of his own, with branches in Florida, California, and Havana.

From the late eighties until 1922 he held the Denver police department in his corrupt grasp. During a part of that time he maintained a direct telephone line from his office to that of the chief of police, and his orders were law. For years Denver was what is known in police and underworld parlance as a "protected city." In other words, criminals were never molested in Denver so long as they operated outside the city limits. Through this system, still common in some American cities, the administration can point with pride before each municipal election to an excellent record of law enforcement within its own limits.

Under Blonger's dominance of the underworld, the members of his million-dollar bunco ring preyed upon Denver visitors

but never victimized a Colorado resident. Lou was uninterested
in collecting tribute from yeggmen, holdups, and others who
specialized in crimes of violence, for their "take" was only a drop
in the bucket compared with the revenue from the operations of
his sixty-man confidence ring, which tapped its victims for from
$5,000 to more than $100,000 each.

To maintain protection from the law Blonger contributed
liberally to the campaign funds of both parties in municipal elections, and especially to the campaign funds of the candidates for
district attorney. Key members of the police department, of the
district attorney's staff, and even of the Denver office of the
United States Department of Justice were on his payroll. His
political influence was such that his hirelings were named to
almost any offices he wished to control.

Sam Blonger was a man of huge stature, fiery temper, and a
weakness for beating up those with whom he disagreed. He got
away with it with everyone except his wife, Sadie, who went to
court and after her second try won a divorce on the ground of
cruelty in 1893. Five months later Jessie Wheat sued Sam for
$25,000 for breach of promise but later dismissed her suit. Like
his judgment, Sam's eyes were none too good, and he coddled
them with blue-tinted glasses.

Brother Lou was short, rotund, affable. His eyes were gray
and drooping, his outstanding facial characteristics a huge, bulb-
ous nose and a protruding lower lip. He liked to appear in full
dress at the theater and other public gatherings.

In 1899 his wife, Nola, brought suit against him to foreclose a
$2,000 mortgage she held on the Forest Queen lode mining claim
at Cripple Creek. Lou confessed judgment.

From the saloon business Lou branched out into the policy-
shop racket for a short time before he crashed the big time with
his organized ring of confidence men. He operated the bunco
organization from what ostensibly was an insurance office in the
old German-American Trust Co. building.

His chief assistant was Adolph W. Duff, alias "Kid Duffy," a former pickpocket, opium smoker, and gambler, and once a member of the infamous Maybray gang. Duff was a thin, wiry little fellow with a deeply seamed face and bartender curls. A generation later he would have described himself as Blonger's "administrative assistant" and the other members of the mob as "technicians."

During the summer tourist season, the bunco steerers watched the newsstands closely. Spotting a prosperous-appearing man who bought an out-of-town newspaper, the steerer would follow him to his hotel. At the first opportunity he would take a seat beside him. Presently he would disappear, unobtrusively managing to leave a wallet on the chair he had just vacated.

Discovering a wallet by his side, the stranger examining it would find it contained a ten-dollar bill and a number of newspaper clippings and documents. The clippings would describe the operations of a stock-market manipulator who had recently made a "killing," and would include a picture of the "plunger." Among the documents would be a bond for $100,000, guaranteeing the good faith and faithful performance of the man whose photograph was attached—the same man described and pictured in the newspaper clipping. Clippings and documents were forgeries, of course—the bait to lure the intended victim into the clutches of the bunco ring.

Almost invariably the prospective "sucker" would turn over the wallet to the hotel clerk. The following day the bunco steerer, accompanied by a pal known as the "spieler," would reclaim the wallet and call upon the finder. The sucker would recognize one of the two as the stock-market operator whose pictures he had seen in the wallet.

"Without that bond I'd have been seriously hampered in my market operations," the steerer would say, "If I may reward you—"

Quickly the spieler would interrupt, "From his appearance, this gentleman obviously is not the type who would accept a cash reward. Why don't you show your appreciation by giving him a tip on the market? Give him a chance to make some money."

"It isn't supposed to be done," the steerer would say with apparent reluctance. "But he has really done me a great service by returning my bond."

If necessary to hook the sucker the steerer would depart and the spieler would take over, extolling the abilities of the supposed market operator. "He's made more than $100,000 in the last thirty days. As a result of the tip he gave me, I just cleaned up a couple of thousand. I'm sending home to raise some more money, because in the next few weeks he stands to make a real killing, and I want to get in on it."

By the following day the sucker is readied to visit a fake stock exchange with the two. The supposed plunger is told, in the hearing of the sucker, that his stock has gone up two points in a few days, leaving him a profit of many thousands. He declines to cash in his winnings, predicting that it will double in value in a few weeks.

Now the spieler begins high-pressuring the sucker. "This is too good a chance to lose. Let's get in on this together and make a killing."

The spieler pretends to buy a few thousand dollars worth of the stock, on margin. In a day or so he and the sucker are told the stock has gone up again. To the sucker it looks like a "sure thing." He, too, places a modest buying order but puts up no cash. Day after day he sees the stock go up. Finally, when it appears that he and his friend, the spieler, have tripled their money, they decide to sell out and take their winnings. The cashier actually places a huge bundle of bills in the sucker's hands. Then, discovering the customer has not "established his credit," he takes it back.

"Our customers must either establish a line of credit or put up the actual cash for our protection in case the stock declines," the businesslike cashier informs him. "It's merely a formality. As soon as you produce the cash as an evidence of good faith, we'll settle the account."

The spieler urges the sucker to go home and mortgage his home if necessary to raise the needed cash. To the sucker it appears that all he has to do is show a certain amount of cash to withdraw his winnings. He goes home, raises the money, comes back, accompanied by the spieler, turns it over to the cashier, who tells them both to return the following day for their money.

But when they return, the cashier informs them regretfully that the market has broken overnight, and they are both wiped out. The spieler becomes indignant, sometimes even punches the cashier in the nose. He takes the sucker back to the hotel to bemoan their loss.

Because the victim's friend apparently has suffered an equal loss, the sucker seldom suspects he has been the victim of a confidence game, but believes he has lost his money in a legitimate market transaction.

Now it is time for the spieler to get the sucker out of town. Sometimes he tells him he will repay the loss himself if given a few weeks to raise funds. Sometimes he says he will persuade the supposed operator (the original bunco steerer) to make repayment. He advises the victim to return home and await word. Often the ruined sucker never realizes that he has lost his money in an illegitimate transaction. If he finally becomes aware that he has been victimized, he may be ashamed to complain to authorities and thus admit publicly that he has been a sucker.

Swindles totaling $645,720 were traced to the Blonger gang, but many remained undisclosed and some victims, even when discovered, were reluctant to admit they had been bilked by confidence men.

Perhaps once in the course of a year's operation some sucker would return to Denver and complain to the police. He would be turned over to the bunco squad, members of which were on Blonger's payroll. As the fake stock exchange operated from several offices, the office where the sucker was trimmed would always be vacated before the detectives arrived with the victim. The officers would accuse the sucker of lying to them and wasting their time, and would tell him that if his story were true he himself was involved in an illegal operation, and would threaten to jail him unless he left town.

If he complained to the district attorney or to the United States Department of Justice, he received the same brush-off. In the rare instances when a complaint was actually filed, the steerer and the spieler usually had plenty of warning to leave town. In case of an actual arrest, Blonger posted a nominal bond which the defendant promptly jumped.

The bunco procedure could be varied to suit the circumstances. If the sucker proved to be a "sport" rather than an investor, he was taken to a fake betting establishment to place bets on fake horses.

In the early days, when the ring was unable to afford expensive office suites for fake stock exchanges, the suckers were given the "up and down" treatment. They were led past an imposing office building and were told it housed the "stock exchange." After looking the building up and down, the sucker was supposed to be, and often, was, impressed by the legitimacy of the transaction.

During the heyday of the ring the con men never attempted to "tie" a sucker who could raise less than $5,000. Individual victims were trimmed for amounts ranging up to more than one hundred thousand dollars. Although the bunco ring's "take" approximated a million dollars every tourist season, only one member of Blonger's gang was ever tried and convicted in Denver until 1922.

In 1920 politically inexperienced Philip S. Van Cise, a colonel in World War I, became a candidate for district attorney. Blonger offered to contribute $25,000 to his campaign fund on condition that Van Cise, if elected, would fix the bonds of any of his friends who might be arrested at $1,000.

Van Cise rejected the offer and, as soon as he was elected, began to lay plans to smash Blonger's underworld gang. He hired special investigators, planted dictaphones in Blonger's office, and collected information from all over the country on the gang and its victims.

Fifteen months passed before he was ready to spring his trap. At daylight on the morning of August 24, 1922, he assembled his deputies, along with fifteen friends sworn in as special deputies and fifteen members of the state ranger force for a series of raids designed to capture every one of the sixty-three members of Blonger's Denver gang. Van Cise planned to imprison them in the Universalist church until the raids had been completed. Had he taken them to the city or county jails, the first arrest immediately would have tipped off the rest of the gang, and they would have escaped.

At midnight a reporter for the Denver *Post* received word that a surprise raid was to be launched at the statehouse at dawn. He had no intimation that Blonger and his gang were involved or that the raids were to be directed by the district attorney. Since Colonel Patrick J. Hamrock, adjutant general and commanding officer of the state rangers, had been denouncing the Industrial Workers of the World, he assumed that the raiders would be rounding up members of the I.W.W.

At the statehouse he encountered a number of deputies from the district attorney's office. As a newspaperman he was poison to them, for premature publicity would tip Van Cise's hand and wreck his plans. They refused to speak to him, dashed outside, leaped into cars, and drove away.

The reporter hurried to one of the capital building offices to call a taxi. There he found deputy district attorney Lewis D. Mowry using the phone. An expression of dismay on his face, Mowry hung up the phone after saying, "I'll see you at the church."

At the moment the words meant nothing to the reporter, who took them to be the current slang expression, "I'll see you at church." As Mowry vanished, the reporter called for a taxi, and while he was waiting, Adjutant General Patrick Hamrock put in an appearance at his office. The reporter questioned him in vain.

"It's Van Cise's party," said Hamrock. "I know nothing about it except that I've lent him some of my rangers."

After a heated argument the reporter remembered Mowry's words as he hung up the phone. "All right," he said. "If you won't play ball with the *Post*, I'll have to go out to the church myself."

It was a shot in the dark, but it struck home. Hamrock was vastly agitated. "If you do that, Van Cise will think I tipped you. Tell you what I'll do. If you promise you won't tell Van Cise you talked to me, I'll take you out to the church myself."

The reporter couldn't have wished a better break. Hamrock called his car and took the newsman to within a block of the church, where he left him. A moment later a car drove into the alley behind the church, two deputies with drawn guns hopped out on either side of a prisoner whose face was streaked with blood. The reporter followed them to the basement door, where he was barred by Captain Orville L. Dennis of the rangers. He demanded to see the district attorney.

In his book, *Fighting the Underworld*, Van Cise later wrote that Captain Dennis came to him and said, "A *Post* reporter is outside, wants to see you, and says he has the story!"

This was sheer bluff, for the reporter still theorized that the I.W.W. were being raided. Van Cise came to the door, said, "God, I'm sorry to see you! Come inside. Sit down. I'm awfully busy. I'll talk to you presently."

Two or three prisoners were brought into the church, stripped, and searched. Among them the reporter recognized Blonger. Every Denver newspaperman knew of Blonger and his activities, and now the full meaning of the raids flashed upon the reporter.

The deadline for the *Post's* early street edition was approaching. The impatient reporter arose, intending to go across the street to phone in his story.

"Sit down, buddy," curtly ordered the ranger who had replaced Dennis at the door.

"I'm a newspaperman. I'm just going out to phone."

"No, you aren't," snapped the husky ranger. "My orders are that you're to stay right where you are!"

"You can't do this to me!" cried the indignant newsman. "Am I under arrest?"

"Try to get out, and you'll find out," remarked the ranger ominously. A moment later he was called out to take part in the raid, and another ranger was posted to guard the door. Apparently he had received no instructions regarding the reporter and took him to be one of the deputies, for presently he said, "Watch the door for me a minute while I go to the washroom, will you, buddy?"

"Sure," agreed the reporter. A moment later he was across the street phoning his story to the *Post*. Cockily he returned to the church, confident he had scored the greatest newspaper beat in years, for as yet the opposition newspaper had no inkling of the raids.

But when he announced to Van Cise that he had phoned the story to the newspaper, the district attorney grabbed a phone and called William G. Shepherd, managing editor and later publisher of the *Post*. Shepherd hurried out to the church. When he learned that publication might prevent arrest of the remaining members of the gang, he promised to withhold the story until the following day. His promise broke the heart of the reporter who had scored the greatest beat in years only to have it temporarily suppressed.

It was not until late in the afternoon that one of the opposition newspapers learned of the raids. Van Cise persuaded the editor to withhold the story, as had the *Post*. The story broke simultaneously in the early street editions of the newspapers the following day.

The day Duff was released on bond the reporter was sent to interview him at his office. Like Duff, he was unaware that a dictaphone had been planted in the chandelier and the messenger call box on the wall and that every spoken word was being taken down by a stenographer in a building half a block away.

Duff claimed he and Blonger were respectable real estate men, and that political animus had inspired the raids because they had refused to contribute to Van Cise's campaign fund.

"Things have come to a pretty pass when a businessman must be subjected to political persecution," he flared angrily. "Isn't that true?"

Unwilling to antagonize the man from whom he was attempting to gain the interview, the reporter said, "That's right."

The next morning the district attorney called the reporter into his office. Without cracking a smile, he said, "I understand you agree with Duff that he's been subjected to political persecution. Right?"

Still unaware of the planted dictaphone, the reporter was on the spot. He dared not deny the charge, so he simply stalled.

Blonger and Duff spent a fortune on their defense, employing a small army of lawyers who argued countless motions before the case went to trial the following February. Of the thirty-four bunco men captured in the raids, twenty actually went to trial in Denver. Six had jumped their bonds, one was declared insane, and the others were turned over to the authorities in other states. The reporter was listed among the state's witnesses, to be called on rebuttal, but since the defendants rested on the contention that the state had failed to prove its case, there was no rebuttal, and he was never called to the witness stand.

When the case finally went to the jury, Van Cise called the newsman into his office and handed him a typed transcript of his dictaphoned interview with Duff.

"I had you sweating blood." He laughed long and uproariously. The reporter still can't see the joke.

The bunco men were confident of acquittal. They sent out for a supply of prohibition whisky and began to celebrate. The courtroom was jammed with spectators waiting for a speedy verdict.

Deciding they needed entertainment while they waited, the small army of reporters staged a mock rape trial during the absence of the judge. Their most dignified member took the part of the judge, their ugliest became the defendant and was led handcuffed into the prisoner's dock. A lovely young sob sister was the complaining witness and testified from the witness stand in detail concerning the alleged offense. The reporter who took the part of the counsel for the defense later became a distinguished jurist and has since presided over the very courtroom where Denver's most famous mock trial was held.

The newsmen raided the judge's chambers and helped themselves to his charge to the jury in statutory rape cases. When the defendant was found guilty and sentenced to twenty-five years in the state penitentiary, he cursed the judge as he was led struggling from the courtroom. The fascinated courtroom spectators never doubted that they were witnessing an actual criminal trial.

The following day all the newsmen and court attachés were summoned before the grand jury. Strangely enough, none of the reporters could recall the source of the refreshments that inspired the mock rape trial. The deputy sheriff who had brought the liquor for the bunco-case defendants was fined one hundred dollars.

The bunco-case jury deliberated four days before reaching a verdict. All the defendants were found guilty. Blonger and Duff were sentenced to seven years in prison, the other defendants to three years. Blonger, seventy-three years old, died in the penitentiary.

Van Cise, one of Denver's finest public officials, had smashed organized crime, had brought to an end an era in which the underworld had dominated Denver's politics. At the next election he was defeated.

(11)

Hop Alley

WHEN the Kansas Pacific Railroad was completed to Denver in 1870, members of a gang of Chinese coolie track laborers were discharged, forming the first inhabitants of the city's Chinatown, later known as "Hop Alley."

Chin Lin Sou was foreman of a gang of Chinese coolies brought to California in 1859. In 1870 he brought his workers to Colorado to work in the mines of Gregory Gulch. He came to Denver a few years later, and by common accord was given the title of "Mayor of Chinatown." He brought his wife from China and, in describing her to newspaper reporters, said:

"Her countenance shone like the moon at midnight. Her lips were like lotus blossoms, and her fingertips were dripping with honey."

In 1873 she became the mother of the first Chinese child born in Denver. The daughter, Lily Chin, married Look Wing Yuen in 1894. The buttons on her wedding dress were five-dollar gold pieces, and she wore a necklace of gold nuggets. Guests at her wedding included Governor Albert W. McIntire and Mayor M. D. Van Horn. She was generally known under her English name of Lily Look and after the death of her father was accorded the title of "Queen of Chinatown."

With her husband she kept a store, with entrances on Market Street and on Hop Alley. In addition to American merchandise, she sold Chinese silks, clothing, Canton china, jewelry, and such edibles as birds' nests, Chinese ginger, lichee nuts, tea, and pickled bamboo shoots. The madames and their girls were among her customers, but Lily, whose own reputation was beyond reproach, looked upon them with scorn. When one of the leading madames asked her to direct customers to her establishment, Lily said:

"Get out of my store, please, and never come back. I am a respectable woman. You have a thousand men, but I"—she drew herself up proudly—"I have a husband."

Lily Look, who was a leading member of the Colorado Pioneer Society, died February 10, 1933, at the age of sixty. She left a son, George, a graduate of the Colorado School of Mines, and a daughter, Pearl. At her death her brothers, James and Willie Chin, became leaders of the Chinese colony. Willie became the mayor. He was a Presbyterian, a leader of the Bing Goo tong, and conducted a store at 2059 Market Street. He was a natural leader, a highly respected citizen, and always represented his countrymen when they fell afoul of the law. He died in 1939 at the age of fifty.

Except for their weakness for gambling and for the use of opium, the residents of Hop Alley were, with few exceptions, peaceful, law-abiding citizens. They were ambitious for their children, and many of the second- and third-generation Chinese were given college educations.

Favored gambling games were fan-tan, pi-gow, Chinese lottery, and American policy. It was customary for a non-Christian Chinese, before trying his luck, to burn a stick of punk before the altar of his joss. If the smoke drifted toward the joss it was a sign of good fortune. If it drifted away, the gambler would wait until another day. Horn Dock and Louis Chung were Denver's outstanding fan-tan gamblers of the nineties.

Opium dens consisted of a number of tiny, unventilated cubicles opening off a dark, narrow, main corridor. Each contained only a cot and a taboret upon which reposed the smoking layout. The layout included a lamp consisting of a glass globe with a hole at the top, where burned a sputtering flame; a horn or bone box, called a "toy," containing a twist of wire, or "yen hok," and the pipe or "stem" containing a tiny needle-hole opening in the bowl. Some layouts included a damp sponge called a "souey pow."

The wire was twisted in the molasses-like opium mixture until it had accumulated a few drops, when it was held over the lamp flame until it began to sputter greasily and acquired the consistency of soft candy. It was then removed from the wire and rolled between the fingers until it was formed into a pill. The pill was placed over the tiny opening in the pipe, and the addict then reclined upon the cot. Leaning over, he held the canted bowl against the flame of the lamp and inhaled the smoke, blowing it through his nostrils. As he became drowsy, he placed the pipe on the taboret and lay down to pleasant dreams. A single pill cost from fifty to seventy-five cents.

The 1896 *Visitors' Pocket Guide* to Denver contains the notation:

> Chinese quarters—Wazee, between Sixteenth and Seventeenth; Market, between Twentieth and Twenty-first. Visitors apply at Central Police Station for guides.

Under the conservative leadership of the Looks and the Chins, tong wars were unknown and crimes of violence were rare. In 1889 Yee Chung, laundryman, brought a bride, Matsu, from China. Matsu was kidnapped and Yee Chung persisted in trying to find her. His body was found in Hop Alley minus his head.

Lee Gon, also a laundryman, took subtle revenge on his enemy, Ah Sing, by committing suicide on his doorstep, causing him to lose much face.

Chinese prostitutes, numerous in San Francisco, were almost unknown in Denver.

In the days of the earliest mining booms, Gee Chow was a merchant in one of the leading gold camps. As the Chinese enjoyed the reputation of being incorruptibly honest, the miners deposited their accumulated gold dust with him for safekeeping.

Day after day a group operating a placer claim in a nearby gulch brought in rich deposits of dust, pledging Gee Chow to secrecy. He kept their secret, but cast about for a means to get in on what promised to be a bonanza discovery. When the miners refused his offer to buy an interest in the property, he employed an American agent, who managed to buy the property for $60,000. The miners withdrew their deposit of dust and departed.

Gee Chow employed a crew of Chinese to work the claim, but soon discovered it was worthless and realized he had been stuck with a "salted" claim. He said nothing, but kept his Chinese crew at work. Every day one of the Chinese brought a poke of gold dust to Gee Chow's store and left it for deposit. Covetous American miners who once had laughed at the trick played upon the Chinese, now came to the conclusion that Gee Chow actually had struck pay dirt on the supposedly worthless claim. They finally paid him $160,000 for the property, and Gee Chow promptly departed for China. Then the purchasers discovered the claim actually was worthless, and realized that the Chinese had used the same poke of gold dust over and over again in making the daily deposit.

Prejudice against the Chinese was exceedingly bitter, and race riots were frequent. In 1874 white miners at Gregory Gulch cut off the queues of all Chinese mine workers and ran them out of town. H. A. W. Tabor imported a gang of coolies to work one of his Leadville mines in 1878. The fact was used against him by his political enemies when he sought election to the United States Senate.

October 31, 1880, marked a night of terror for the girls of Holladay Street and the 2,000 residents of Denver's Chinatown. The preceding evening members of the two political parties had staged torchlight parades through the principal streets. The Democrats carried illuminated transparencies calling for the expulsion of the Chinese, who were said to be "taking the food from the mouths of the whites."

Hell broke loose as a result of the demonstration. Rioting started when a group of whites, led by a half-wit known as "Happy Jack," "cleaned out" a Chinese saloon on Wazee Street. Within a matter of minutes mobs were storming through the tenderloin, wrecking Chinese business houses, dragging forth the occupants and beating them. One was lassoed and dragged to death, and his body was strung up on a lamppost. Another was saved when white friends nailed him in a department-store packing box.

Jim Moon, notorious desperado and gambler, was the only white man with courage enough to defy the mob. With guns drawn he stood in front of the place operated by his Chinese laundryman, and dared the rioters to come on.

"I'll shoot the first so-and-so that touches Wong," he cried. "If you kill him, who in hell will do my laundry?" He saved sixteen Chinese by hiding them in the basement of the Arcade gambling hall.

The police department was without a head, since Chief Hickey had just been suspended, pending a hearing on graft charges. Mayor Richard Sopris ordered the saloons closed and tried to quell the rioting himself. Failing, he appointed General David J. Cook to take charge of the situation. Two units of militia were hurriedly assembled—the Governor's Guard and the Chaffee Light Artillery. A volunteer posse of 500 men was recruited. Most of the possemen were Republicans, who saw an opportunity to capitalize on the rioting inspired by the Democrats. Many Chinese were jailed "for protection," and the streets finally were cleared of rioters. As a result of the riots the Republicans were elected by a landslide a few days later.

Similar race riots occurred elsewhere throughout the Rocky Mountain region until passage of the Chinese exclusion act. In

1893 Montana labor unions at Butte, Anaconda, and Missoula boycotted all Chinese business firms and finally expelled all Celestials.

In 1900 all Chinese miners were run out of Rock Springs, Wyoming. In 1901 the Chamber of Commerce and the labor unions at Cripple Creek united in adopting a resolution urging Congress to adopt the exclusion act. In 1902 members of the cooks and waiters union at Silverton, Colorado, placed nooses about the necks of the Chinese, led them to the edge of the camp, and bade them begone.

Most of Denver's Chinese operated laundries, restaurants, or small mercantile establishments. On New Year's Day they presented their customers with gifts of Chinese lilies, lichee nuts, or Chinese ginger.

In February the Chinese New Year was observed to the popping of thousands of firecrackers, the explosion of bombs, and the beating of gongs and drums. The celebration began at sundown and lasted until midnight, when those who had not become Christians knelt before idols in the joss houses, one in the rear of Lou Quong's store and another at 1618 Wazee Street.

Those of the Chinese who embraced Christianity usually followed the lead of the Looks and Chins and became Presbyterians. One of the wealthiest Chinese was a gambler, Chin Gee Chow, who died in 1899. He was a member of the Masonic order and was given a Christian burial at Riverside cemetery, in one hand a fan and in the other a deck of cards.

Kong Ping, another leading Market Street gambler, was buried November 25, 1902, with colorful non-Christian rites. Red prayer papers were scattered from the top of his hearse, and roast duck and other foodstuffs were placed on his grave. Later his body was shipped to China.

In 1878 Yee Chow Jung died of leprosy. That night his combination laundry and home burned to the ground. Curiously enough, the fire department appeared on the scene before the

blaze broke out. Firemen poured water on the adjoining buildings, but made no effort to save the home of the leper.

In 1910 health authorities discovered Yee Kee to be suffering
from leprosy. On his promise to return to China he was not molested. When he reached China he found himself an outcast and
drowned himself.

Intermarriages between whites and Chinese were not infrequent. Chan Hon Fan, forty-three years old, a leading San Francisco merchant, and Mrs. Ida Hall, forty-two, a social worker of
that city, were married at Trinity Methodist Church, Denver,
February 25, 1901. Leo Lott Sing and Nellie Mershon, thirty-
one, both of Idaho Springs, were married at Orchard Place, a
Denver suburb, June 13, 1902. Ah Lee Pang, Chinese confec-
tioner of 2021 Market Street, and Lottie Gourney, a telephone
operator, were married July 1, 1909.

During the second week of January, 1903, the lyrical comedy,
San Toy, was playing at the Tabor Grand Opera House. Overnight all the billboards advertising the production were painted
over with a huge Chinese character. Chinese leaders denied responsibility, but were quoted as saying they were boycotting the
production because it presented an unfair picture of their race.
The incident bore all the earmarks of a shrewd press-agent publicity stunt.

Divorce was easy among the orthodox Chinese, until a wife
gave birth to a son, after which divorce was impossible. The wife
of a leading Denver Chinese merchant refused to accompany him
when he left China. Since she had given birth to a son, divorce
was out of the question. He sent $800 to China to buy a concu-
bine. After her arrival in Denver she was accepted by the whites
as his wife.

They became the parents of a daughter, who in the course of
time was graduated from the school of medicine at a leading university. She went to China, imbued with the ambition to bring
the benefits of scientific medicine to her own people.

A year later she was back in Denver, bitterly disillusioned and humiliated. The carefully preserved genealogy of her family showed her to be the daughter of a concubine, hence an outcast. No Chinese aware of her antecedents would permit her to treat him. She became an outstanding research specialist in an American hospital.

Perhaps the most widely known Denver Chinese was Jim Wong, for many years steward of the Denver Press Club. Originally Jim had been part-owner of a co-operative Chinese restaurant at Cripple Creek during the boom years. During the labor troubles at the camp "Big Bill" Haywood, leader of the I.W.W., informed him that all the restaurant employees must join his organization.

"We got no employees," said Jim. "We all bosses; all part-owners."

"Join or get out," was Haywood's ultimatum. Fearful of violence, the Chinese dissolved their partnership and got out. Jim returned to China with $20,000 in gold coin, which he buried in four earthenware jars under the floor of his home as a precaution against bandits. He floored the house with cement, instructing his wife to tap only one jar at a time when she needed money, and then he returned to the United States.

It was Jim's habit to return to China every few years in an attempt to father a son, but his visits resulted only in the birth of daughters. Before becoming steward of the Press Club, Jim had been an attendant at another Denver club, of which the author's father was a member. When the author became a member of the Press Club, Jim asked him, "You Doctor Pa'khill's little boy?"

Assured that he was, Jim proceeded to tell a story. Upon returning from one of his son-seeking trips to China, he went back to his job at the other club. The rest of his story is told in his own words:

"Some of club members not there any more. I ask, 'Where Smith?' They tell me, 'He die.' I ask, 'Where Jones?' They say, 'He die.' I ask, 'Where Doctor Pa'khill?' They say, 'He die.' "

Jim paused a moment to scowl at the youngster who had just joined the club. Then, with a grunt, he said:

"Huh! Me, you, big damn fools, we live. Good men die."

Today, Denver's Chinatown, still in Hop Alley, numbers only a few hundred souls. The Japanese population, however, has skyrocketed since the relocation measures of World War II.

(12)

Headlines and Deadlines

IN the days when any newspaperman could get a free railroad pass, Denver, with its five dailies, was the stopping-off place for innumerable "tramp" reporters, on their way to or from the Pacific coast. These "tramps," including some of the most accomplished newsmen in the country, would stop in Denver for a few weeks, or long enough to earn a small stake, and then drift on. Today the "tramp" reporter is a breed almost as extinct as the buffalo.

Denver had sent Damon Runyon, Gene Fowler, and other top-flight newsmen to New York, and Eugene Field to Chicago, so local members of the craft resented their Eastern brethren who "put on airs." An ex-New Yorker with a weakness for boasting and for making disparaging remarks about the local boys particularly irritated the police reporters.

At the time they occupied a semibasement room in the southeast corner of the old police station at Fourteenth and Larimer streets. Formerly the police surgeon's emergency room, it was floored with tile, with a depression and drain in the center for carrying away blood.

Each reporter possessed a private phone connected directly

with his office. In addition, the room contained a glass telephone booth for use in phoning confidential messages.

The New Yorker always used the booth phone. This was too much for the rival reporters to take, for it implied that all his stories were "beats." They felt it necessary to give him a taste of real Wild West journalism. As a build-up they primed him with an assortment of tall tales about competition in Denver.

"What happens when you big-shot New Yorkers get scooped?" they asked him with apparent innocence.

"Competition in New York is mighty tough," he responded loftily. "You come back from an assignment with an exclusive, or you don't come back."

"Huh! Nothing to lose but your job," was the local man's comment. "Out here it's different. You've got to settle with the boys you've scooped. They're right touchy about such things. What kind of a gun do you pack?"

The New Yorker paled slightly. "I've never found it necessary to carry firearms."

The local boys drew forth pistols and placed them alongside their typewriters. (The weapons had been borrowed for the occasion from friendly police officers.)

"What," one local reporter asked of another, "was the name of that guy from the East who slipped one over on the rest of us?"

"I've kind of forgotten," was the reply, "but you can find it on his headstone out at Riverside cemetery."

Perhaps it was force of habit that led the New Yorker to the glass booth to phone his next story. At a signal his four competitors rushed the booth and, with the victim inside, overturned it with a crash. As the terrified New Yorker crawled from the wreckage, they whipped out their pistols and began shooting into the ceiling. When last seen the newcomer was streaking it toward the Union Station, pausing not even to collect his pay.

Chief of Police Hamilton Armstrong stomped into the smoke-filled room. Neglecting to inquire if anyone were dead or

Daylight scene in Leadville's red-light district.
(*Denver Public Library Western Collection.*)

Professional card of
Madame Verona
Baldwin, who came
to Denver after the
name of Holladay
Street had been
changed to Market
Street. (*Daniels &
Fisher Stores Co.*)

VERONA BALDWIN

2020 MARKET STREET

PHONE MAIN 2250   DENVER, COLORADO

For the crib girls of Denver's tenderloin life was a ceaseless struggle to keep the wolf at the door. A daylight photograph of the 2100 block, Market Street, in 1905. (*Denver Public Library Western Collection.*)

Saloon in the mining camp of Montezuma, Colorado. Dance hall and gambling salon in rear. (*Denver Public Library Western Collection.*)

Myers Avenue, Cripple Creek's tenderloin. Since named Julian Street after the author, Julian Street, who wrote a magazine article revealing the wickedness of this street of sin. (*Photo by H. S. Poley, from Denver Public Library Western Collection.*)

Louis Dupuy, eccentric Frenchman whose real name was Adolphus Francis Gerard, built the Hotel de Paris at Georgetown, Colorado, before the coming of the railroad. The frontier hostelry became one of the most famous in the Rocky Mountain region. (*Photo from Library of Congress.*)

Mattie Silks, queen of the Denver tenderloin, in the de Medici gown made with special pockets for gold coins. Taken in the eighties, when she was about forty years old. (*Fred M. Mazzulla Photo.*)

Famous old sporting house operated by Mattie Silks, taken just before it was remodeled into a warehouse. The five sculptured heads on the façade represent the principals in a fantastic story of scandal, blackmail, and possible murder. (*Fred M. Mazzulla Photo.*)

The full-bosomed stone Circe at the peak of the House of a Thousand Scandals is supposed to represent lovely Madame Jennie Rogers, leading figure in a story of blackmail and possible murder. (*Fred M. Mazzulla Photo.*)

A fantastic story of black-mail is told in the faces sculptured on the façade of the House of a Thousand Scandals. These two faces supposedly represent (left) the murdered bride and (right) the boss who lost both his wife and his business. (*Fred M. Mazzulla Photo.*)

Soapy Smith, King of the Thimbleriggers (center, black beard) underworld dictator of Creede and Denver, Colorado, and of Skagway, Alaska, shown in his Skagway saloon shortly before he died with his boots on, July 8, 1898. (*Denver Public Library Western Collection.*)

Bunco man Lou Blonger, once the overlord of Denver's underworld, died in the penitentiary. (*Photo courtesy Philip S. Van Cise.*)

Ed Chase, proprietor of the Palace burlesque house and gambling resort, was a college classmate of Leland Stanford and a friend of Henry Clay and Daniel Webster. He married an actress in the Palace burlesque troupe. (*Denver Public Library Western Collection.*)

The celebrated beauty, Baby Doe Tabor, led a police raid on Lizzie Preston's sporting house in Denver, touching off the West's most torrid romance which culminated in her marriage to the multimillionaire, H. A. W. Tabor. (*Denver State Historical Society.*)

She loved him till the day of her death, but divorced him to further his political ambition. Augusta Tabor, first wife of Bonanza King H. A. W. Tabor. (*Denver Public Library Western Collection.*)

Bonanza King H. A. W. Tabor, one of the principals in Colorado's most hectic romance. (*Denver Public Library Western Collection.*)

wounded, he snapped angrily, "You boys make too damned much noise around here. Cut it out, see, or I'll toss you all in jail."

Police reporter Paris Montgomery was short and fat. His pal and competitor, Bill Collier, later to become co-author of Soapy Smith's biography, was tall and fat. Neither was a teetotaler. Each spent a great deal of time trying to induce the other to "climb on the wagon."

Among other duties, the police reporters of that day were supposed to check periodically at the coroner's office in Hofmann's undertaking parlors a block from the police station. With the connivance of members of the coroner's staff, Monty cooked up a scheme that promised to make a teetotaler of anyone.

At ten-thirty in the evening Collier received a phone call from Hofmann's.

"Prepare yourself for a shock, Bill. Poor Monty has been run down and killed by a runaway. Better come over right away."

To nerve himself for the ordeal, Bill took a last swig and raced to the coroner's office. A tiptoeing attendant led him to the embalming room, where six sheet-covered figures lay stretched out on slabs. Silently and solemnly the attendant drew back one of the sheets, revealing the naked Montgomery, his body a ghastly white from a liberal application of talcum powder. Collier bent over the still form and burst into tears.

"It's all my fault!" he sobbed remorsefully. "It c-couldn't have happened if he'd been s-sober. I could have made him quit drinking, but I didn't. I feel like a m-m-murderer!"

He wept unashamed. The dripping tears tickled the bare chest of the pseudo-corpse. Unable to restrain himself, the corpse burst into a raucous laugh.

Terror was Collier's first reaction, followed instantly by overpowering rage.

"By God, I'll make a real corpse out of you, you condemned little so-and-so!" he bellowed angrily. The erstwhile corpse catapulted to the floor. Pursued by the raging Collier, he made

three circuits of the corpse-laden slabs and then darted through
a door into the alley. Collier snatched up a wooden mallet used
as a doorstop and took after him.

The theater crowds were just emerging from the Tabor
Grand Opera House when the chalk-white, stark-naked, tubby
little Montgomery raced screaming down Sixteenth Street, only
a jump ahead of the cursing, mallet-armed Collier.

A police officer patrolling Curtis Street disarmed the raging
Collier and wrapped his overcoat about the shivering Montgomery, who was given a free ride in the dooly wagon to the
police station. To give Collier time to cool off and to prevent
the threatened homicide Chief Armstrong placed the naked
Monty in "protective custody" overnight.

Collier was not to be easily cheated of revenge. Under the
guise of friendship he retrieved Monty's clothing from the
coroner and threw it all into nearby Cherry Creek. Other newsmen procured clothing from Monty's rooms, and presently the
rift that threatened to end a touching friendship was closed, and
by payday Monty's untimely "death" was forgiven, if not entirely forgotten. One thing left Monty completely and forever
confused. When in his cups he was wont to mutter over and over
again, "A mallet in an undertaking shop! What do they use it
for? I don't get it. I just don't get it." A few years later Monty
killed himself in the Denver Press Club.

Ernest U. "Blondy" Lebfrom was a police reporter who delighted in being mistaken for a murderer. His jaw was under-
shot, his cheeks were deeply lined, and he bore no resemblance
to a Sunday School superintendent. He carried a pistol with the
grip wrapped in bicycle tape.

When the police ambulance responded to a call, a morbidly
curious crowd would always collect on the sidewalk. If the case
were a particularly bloody one, such as a tubercular hemorrhage,
Blondy would emerge from the doorway in advance of the at-

tendants carrying the stretcher. Cowering under a protectively
raised arm, he would whimper:

"I didn't mean to kill her, Mister Policeman. Honest, I didn't!
Do you think they'll hang me?"

"That's the murderer!" members of the sensation-hungry
crowd would cry, pointing, much to his delight, at Blondy.
"You could spot him as a killer, anywhere!"

When truce was declared in the newspaper war between the
Scripps-Howard papers and the Tammen-Bonfils *Post*, the
Scripps Evening *News* and the Morning *Post* were scrapped,
leaving a horde of newspapermen jobless. Blondy lost his $40-a-
week job, but not his confidence.

Assuming a dignified air, he called upon the late Sam Sherman,
general merchandise manager of the May Company department
store.

"My wife's health made it necessary for me to come to Denver
from Washington, where I was a merchandise manager for
women's wear at Woodward's," he bluffed. "While I'm com-
fortably fixed, I feel I'm too young to retire, so I'm looking
about for something to keep my mind occupied."

The store executive was duly impressed. "I'd like to have a
man of your capabilities identified with our business, Mr. Lebfrom, but of course all our department heads are employed on a
contract basis. I don't wish to insult you by offering a man of
your standing a $75-a-week position, but if you'd care to fill in
as a floor manager until something better develops, we'll be glad
to have you."

"I'll think it over," responded Blondy, appearing none too
eager. He discarded his pistol, bought a cutaway coat, and went
to work as a floorwalker with a carnation in his buttonhole.
Presently the hard-boiled ex-police reporter was promoted to—
of all positions—assistant buyer for the lingerie department. All
went well until a former Market Street madame, purchasing
silken panties, recognized him.

"You're the so-and-so who put that piece in the paper that

forced the cops to close my joint," she screamed at him, adding some choice Market Street invective. "I'll get your job if it's the last thing I ever do!"

Blondy bested her in a race for Sherman's office. Breathlessly he confessed all. Just and genial Sam Sherman chuckled.

"You've made good on the job. We'll be glad to have you stay with us."

He remained with the department store for some years, then established his own women's ready-to-wear store in another city, and prospered.

Development of the beet-sugar industry in Colorado brought an influx of Mexican beet-field labor and a new type of narcotic, marijuana. Known as "reefers," marijuana cigarettes sold for twenty-five cents each.

Following the arrest of a marijuana peddler, police confiscated a suitcase filled with the sage-green dried leaves and left it in the police reporters' room, precipitating an argument on the effects of the then little-known narcotic. Red-haired John Feeney, veteran police reporter, took no part in the discussion, for he was asleep in his chair, feet on his typewriter.

"One reefer gets the user pleasantly hopped up," explained a reporter who had come from El Paso, on the Mexican border. "Two will turn him into a bloodthirsty savage. The Mexican bandit, Pancho Villa, used to issue his men a ration of two marijuana cigarettes just before going into battle, and they'd fight like madmen. Enough marijuana will kill the user after making a raving maniac of him."

One of his hearers scoffed. He had never known of a death caused by marijuana. In fact, he was willing to back his position with cold, hard cash, for any amount up to one dollar. The former El Pasoan took the bet.

At hand were the requirements for a perfect demonstration— the sleeping Feeney and a whole suitcase filled with the deadly narcotic. The police reporters kindled a fire of old newspapers on the tile floor, poured the contents of the suitcase on the blaze, closed the doors and windows, and adjourned outside to watch the progress of their scientific experiment through the semi-basement windows. If Feeney were driven mad and died, the El Paso reporter stood to win a dollar.

White smoke from the burning weed slowly filled the room. The sleeping Feeney coughed, choked, awoke, stamped out the fire, opened the windows, and went back to sleep. The El Paso reporter never forgave him for ruining the demonstration.

The gloomy corridors of the police station basement were lined with lockers used by officers and the police reporters. During the Prohibition era police raided a North Denver bootleg establishment noted for the high quality of its "dago red" wine, and confiscated one hundred five-gallon kegs.

The kegs were trucked to the police station, where they were stored until needed for evidence. The newsmen generously offered to aid the crew to unload the truck, but strangely enough, five of the kegs wound up in the reporters' lockers.

Twenty-five gallons of wine should be sufficient to provide an evening's refreshment for all the newsmen in Denver. Word went out that the kegs were to be opened that night on the banks of Cherry Creek, two blocks from the police station. The response to the announcement was terrific.

The delicious wine from the first five-gallon keg lasted less than five minutes. But when the second was tapped, it was found to contain vinegar. So did the third, the fourth, and the fifth.

To mislead too-inquisitive officers of the law the proprietor of the bootleg establishment had hidden his real wine behind a tier of kegs containing vinegar. By chance the reporters who so thoughtfully had helped unload the police truck had obtained four kegs of vinegar and one of wine.

Gene Fowler, Denver newsman of the period, destined to achieve fame and riches as a novelist and Hollywood writer, relates in his *Solo in Tom-toms* that as a boy employed to deliver groceries for a Larimer Street store, he fell in love with a girl named Trixie, inmate of Mattie Silks's sporting house. In his innocence he sought to send her a valentine in an order of groceries, but was thwarted by his uncle, the store proprietor.

Police reporters were intimately associated with the underworld, but were not of it. They do not belong in a rogues' gallery of colorful Western characters, but rather in the category of chroniclers of their doings. Denver's Fourth Estate developed many other interesting personalities who had no connection whatever with the underworld. Among them was "Lord" Ogilvy.

He was an uncle of Mrs. Winston Churchill. In 1879, when but eighteen years old, he accompanied his father, David Graham Drummond Ogilvy, eighth earl of Airlie, on a tour of the Ogilvy ranching interests in Colorado with the earl of Dunraven.

Well over six feet in height and slightly stooped, he walked with a loose-jointed, gangling gait. Even as a young man, his chin was adorned with a square-cut stub beard. Customarily he wore a plaid waistcoat—the plaid of the Ogilvy clan.

Devil-may-care, spendthrift Ogilvy "made champagne pour around him like a river," says one chronicler. He staged a memorable tallyho party in a rented "drag" in Cheyenne, killing a horse in attempting to round a corner at a gallop with his six-horse hitch. The liveryman demanded $500 for the animal, which was worth at least one hundred dollars. Ogilvy gave him $1,000.

He was an early riser. At the Tedmon House, in Greeley, he took a rooster to bed with him to serve as an alarm clock.

Immersed in a Daudet novel while on a Denver-bound train from Cheyenne, he impatiently brushed aside the conductor's request for his ticket. The conductor stopped the train and gathered the rest of the crew to throw off the absent-minded passenger. Ogilvy threw the crew off the train, produced his ticket, and invited them all to be his dinner guests at the Windsor Hotel in Denver.

Young Ogilvy disapproved of the staid, dignified atmosphere of the Windsor. To liven things up he once loosed in the lobby a cage of rats and a pack of rat terriers.

For a time he lived with his sister, Lady Maude Josepha Whyte, on a ranch southeast of Greeley, where distinguished Britons were frequent visitors. One guest, while driving with Ogilvy in a buckboard, made a slighting remark about the speed of Western horses. To prove him wrong the young host threw the reins over the heads of the team, stood on the seat, and lashed them into a runaway that ended when the buckboard crashed into a telephone pole and the guest incurred a fractured arm. He never criticized Western horses again.

Ogilvy entertained another of his titled friends at the Windsor Hotel. The Britisher's hair was flaming red and he was immensely proud of his bushy red beard. Unaware of the perils of alcohol imbibed at high altitudes, he passed out shortly after midnight.

Ogilvy and his friends, inspired, shaved the distinguished guest's head and face clean, stripped him, laid him out in a bathtub, and placed long candles on the tub's corners.

When the visitor regained his senses in these strange surroundings, he thought he was dead. When he looked in a mirror and failed to recognize his clean-shaven reflection, he was sure of it. He departed Denver in a rage.

Ogilvy once sent Denver friends invitations to his own funeral. At the undertaker's parlors they found him laid out in a coffin banked with flowers.

As the service ended, the coffin was closed and carried out to the old-fashioned hearse with plate-glass sides. Behind a band playing the Saul Dead March, the procession started for Riverside cemetery.

Presently, the coffin became too stuffy for the corpse. Pushing back the lid, he sat up, flourishing a bottle. The mourners were terrified. So was the driver of the hearse. He leaped to the ground and the horses ran away, scattering the band as the laughing corpse leaped to the ground.

Reorganized, the procession proceeded to the cemetery, where they discovered in the new grave a keg of Scotch whisky. At the wake a wonderful time was had by all, especially the corpse.

In 1902 Ogilvy married and became a teetotaler. Lacking business ability, the reformed tosspot found his fortune dwindling away. In 1907 he moved to Denver and went to work as a switchman in the Union Pacific Railroad yards.

Here he was discovered by a former friend, Harry Tammen, who since had become one of the owners of the Denver *Post*. Tammen hired him as farm editor, a position he held for the rest of his life, except for intervals when he helped fight the world's wars.

In 1898 he enlisted in the United States Army and during the war with Spain became a member of Torrey's Rough Riders.

During the Boer War he joined the British Army, serving as a lieutenant of Scottish Horse and as a captain of Brabant's Horse. He was wounded in action and was awarded the British D.S.O. To his friends he was never known as "Lord" Ogilvy, but always as Captain Ogilvy.

He was fifty-three years old at the outbreak of World War I, but he served Britain again as purchasing agent for cavalry horses.

He was seventy-nine when World War II hostilities began. His hair and his stub beard were white. His stoop was no longer slight, and his step was faltering as he made his way to the United States Army recruiting station and once more offered his adopted country all he had left to give.

When, on April 5, 1947, gallant Captain Ogilvy, then eighty-five years old, died at Boulder, Colorado, the West lost one of its most colorful and beloved characters.

BOOK THREE

Denizens of the Overworld

(13)

Noblest Roamer of Them All

THE West's underworld possessed no monopoly on colorful characters. Book Three of this volume presents some of the interesting personalities developed, literally or figuratively, on "the right side of the tracks."

One of the earliest was the wealthy and eccentric Irish sportsman, Sir St. George Gore, whose name is borne by Colorado's Gore range of mountains, Gore Pass, and Gore Canyon.

Had he been less a sportsman he might have changed the history of the United States, for his discovery of gold easily could have led to the settlement of the West years earlier.

He made a formal offer to the United States government to recruit a "private army" to exterminate the Sioux tribe of Indians at his own expense. But his chief claim to a colorful page in the history of the West lies in his de luxe big-game-hunting expedition; the costliest, longest, and most astonishing hunting expedition ever staged in North America, and perhaps in the world.

It cost approximately $500,000, lasted three years, and covered at least 6,000 miles of trackless mountain and prairie. He bagged 2,500 buffalo, 1,600 elk and deer, 125 bears, and more antelope than he troubled to count, according to an official government report. He employed forty-one retainers, and is

129

said to have hired a tribe of 800 Indians to cut a road across a mountain range so he might enjoy a few days of hunting on the farther side.

Hollywood never dreamed up anything with the Arabian Nights atmosphere of Gore's luxurious adventuring in our wide open spaces, ending in a $50,000 bonfire when he destroyed all his equipment rather than be victimized by his American suppliers.

The Irish sportsman bore a remarkable resemblance to the cartoons of John Bull. He was a bachelor in his mid-forties, blond, ruddy, plump, and almost bald, with short, straw-colored Dundreary whiskers. He has been described as "mercurial, wrathful, effervescent and reckless," a man with a "kind heart."

Regarded as unsociable by all except his close friend, the rude and rugged frontiersman, Jim Bridger, he nevertheless was an animated conversationalist on subjects that interested him. He was short of temper, but "when addressed courteously, always gave a courteous reply." He drank sparingly and preferred wine to hard liquor.

His men respected but cherished no love for him. He generously rewarded extra duty, and none complained of injustice.

No one knows who or what inspired him to undertake the sumptuous expedition to western America, which for nearly three years cost him almost his entire annual income of $200,000 from rents in counties Sligo and Donegal. Possibly it was undertaken at the suggestion of his young friend, Sir William-Thomas-Spencer Wentworth-Fitzwilliam, K.G., D.C.L., who is known to have visited the Oregon country in 1853 during a leisurely round-the-world trip. The young man was Gore's guest for a few weeks at the beginning of the expedition.

First actual records of the Gore expedition are revealed by account books of the American Fur Company, which show he made huge purchases in May of 1854 while outfitting at St. Louis. His equipment was paid for with drafts on Baring Brothers, his London bankers.

The records show he bought twenty-one crimson two-horse *charettes*, of the type then used by French-Canadian *voyageurs* and American trappers and generally called Red River carts; four six-mule wagons; two three-yoke ox wagons and, for his personal use, a carriage. His purchases included one hundred twelve horses, eighteen oxen, and three milk cows. He also acquired thirty-six greyhounds to augment the pack of fourteen staghounds he had brought from Ireland.

His forty-one retainers were frontiersmen and *voyageurs*, mostly former trappers for the American Fur Company. His guide when he left St. Louis was Henry Chatillon, who was succeeded shortly by his brother Joe.

Noted *voyageurs* in the party included Louis Dapron and Jeremiah Proteau. The dress of the *voyageur* was unlike that of the American frontiersman. Customarily he wore a dark blue coat with hood, leggings fringed with scarlet-and-black beaded cloth, moccasins embroidered with stained porcupine quills, a crimson sash, and cross belts for beaded shot pouch and fringed and tasseled powder horn. The *voyageur* preferred a Rob Roy hunting pony with a beaded buckskin pad for a saddle. And how he could fiddle and sing and dance "French Fours"!

The party was soon joined by Wagon-boss Henry Bostwick, lean frontiersman in fringed buckskin, moccasins, and fur cap, who always rode with a long rifle in the crook of his elbow.

A search of existing files fails to reveal that St. Louis newspapers took note of the departure of the expedition. Unfortunately Gore employed no press agent. The only known contemporary newspaper description is contained in a dispatch in the Ohio State *Journal* from a correspondent writing of the departure of westbound immigrant trains from Westport, Kansas.

As the strange caravan passed through Fort Leavenworth, a small boy watched it in openmouthed wonder. Forty years later he mentioned it briefly in a magazine article. The boy was destined to become the last of the great scouts—Colonel William F. "Buffalo Bill" Cody.

With his temporary guest, who was known to the retinue as "Lord Fitzwilliam," Gore rode in state in the carriage at the head of the long string of wagons. Fitzwilliam, an amateur astronomer, carried with him a telescope with a six-inch lens. He went along just for the ride and after a few weeks returned to St. Louis to resume his round-the-world journey.

Gore carried with him a brass bed, an iron washstand, and an iron table, and slept in a ten-by-eighteen-foot green and white striped linen tent. The bed was carried in a strange wagon, constructed with cranks at all four corners. When rain threatened, four henchmen would spring to the cranks, whereupon, according to a historical account, a canvas top "lifted into view out of the bed," converting the vehicle into a covered-wagon bedroom.

Gore's personal fishing tackle filled two wagons in charge of a specialist, an expert at tying trout flies. Another wagon contained only the wealthy sportsman's personal weapons—seventy-five muzzle-loading rifles of such famous makes as Joe Manton, Purdy, Hawken, and Westley Richards, one Sharp's rifle of the then new breech-loading type, fifteen shotguns, and so many pistols that no one ever recorded the number.

An arsenal was essential for his style of shooting. He never hunted alone and usually was accompanied by as many as seven heavily laden gunbearers. In hunting buffalo he hid himself and his gun caddies in a blind and waited for his master of hounds to flush the quarry.

As the herd thundered past, Gore, resting his rifle on a forked stick, would blaze away and then snatch another weapon from the hands of a gunbearer, banging away until the supply of guns or animals was exhausted. He never deigned to load his own gun.

His marksmanship was excellent when firing from a rest, but he was an indifferent shot when it came to offhand snap shooting. By frontier standards he was an unskilled horseman, preferring his carriage to the saddle, but not because of laziness. He could outwalk any member of his party. His favorite mount was a tall, gray Kentucky thoroughbred named Steel Trap.

Except for the scout, Jim Bridger, no American ever succeeded in penetrating his wall of reserve. He just wasn't the kind to encourage a palsy-walsy attitude on the part of the hired help.

However, his liberality made it a pleasure to work for him. On one occasion he paid Joe Merrival $150 for a horse. After riding the animal all afternoon, he paid the horse trader an additional one hundred dollars, insisting that Joe had cheated himself. It was an error that was to lead two years later to the spite burning of his own equipment, for from that time on the natives overcharged him outrageously.

By the end of June, 1854, the party reached the junction of the Platte and Laramie rivers. Here stood old Fort Laramie—not to be confused with the Laramie, Wyoming, of today. Under the guidance of Joe Chatillon, he struck out to the southwest into Kansas Territory, hunting in the wide mountain valleys of what today is northern Colorado. The French-Canadian trappers called such a valley a *parc*, or hunting preserve. Today Westerners call them "parks." Gore penetrated North Park and Middle Park and probably reached Lost Park and Middle Park.

While camped in Middle Park he learned that elk were numerous on the far side of a towering mountain range—the mighty ridge that today bears the name of the Gore Range. Legend has it that he employed a tribe of 800 Indians to cut a road through the timber so his wagon train could cross the range and then remained only four days on the far side. It is more likely that he left his wagons behind and packed across on horseback. In whatever manner the crossover was made, it must have followed the approximate route of today's paved highway which reaches the crest of the range at 9,000-foot Gore Pass.

A few miles to the south the range is gashed by the red depths of mighty Gore Canyon. Gore found it impassable, but today streamlined trains of the Denver & Rio Grande Western Railroad speed through its rugged depths.

Forty years after the crossing that won the Gore Range its name, Henry Chatillon, son of the wealthy sportsman's guide, in a letter now in the files of the Colorado State Historical Society, wrote that his father, Joe Chatillon, told him the party continued through Middle Park, crossing the continental divide, and "camped on all four sides of Pikes Peak" before returning to Fort Laramie for the winter.

If this be true, and Gore built his own roads for his wagon train through some of the most rugged mountain terrain in the United States, he performed a feat unequaled in the history of Western exploration. In view of the short summer season at high elevations and the time required for such a road-building feat, it is more probable that Gore left his wagons behind and made this loop on horseback. However, gold-seekers who swarmed through the region a few years later reported the discovery of log bridges over mountain streams where no wheeled vehicles had been known to have penetrated. Gore might have fathered an earlier Pikes Peak gold rush, for he covered most of the region where gold was discovered only a few years later.

Meanwhile, the famous scout and frontiersman, Jim Bridger, had been expelled by the Mormons from his trading post at Fort Bridger, in what today is southwestern Wyoming, and was returning from Westport after visiting his third Indian wife. Gore encountered him at Fort Laramie and promptly hired him as head guide and storyteller.

Although the illiterate, rawhide-tough scout and his cultured but eccentric employer seemed to possess nothing in common, they speedily became fast friends. Sir St. George was accustomed to read until late at night and then remain in his brass bed until ten or eleven o'clock in the morning, when he arose, bathed, downed a glass of wine, and girded himself for the day's hunt. But Jim, child of nature, slept whenever he became sleepy, and ate, not by the clock, but strictly from hunger. Historians note that for seventeen years he ate no bread.

As often as not, in mid-afternoon Jim would be seized with a desire to sleep. Awakening, refreshed, shortly after midnight, he chose to entertain himself until daylight squatting by the fire eating venison and "singing Injun" to the accompaniment of a tin-pan and spoon tom-tom.

He scorned to address his employer by his title and always called him merely "Mister Gore." The Journal of Captain R. B. Marcy, who talked with Gore at the conclusion of the expedition, relates that the titled Irishman was accustomed to invite the scout to dine in his striped linen tent and after a few glasses of wine to spend the evening reading aloud to him and listening to his comments.

As to Shakespeare's Falstaff, Jim "rather calculated that thar big Dutchman, Mister Full-stuff, was a little too fond of lager beer."

Since Jim already had achieved the reputation of being America's champion teller of tall tales, Gore like to read to him from the adventures of Baron Munchausen. Skeptical Jim insisted cagily, "I didn't swaller everything he said. I reckon he was a durned liar."

Although Jim was making history, history as such left him cold. He politely conceded that the account of the battle of Waterloo, as read to him by Gore, described "considerable of a scrimmage," but his sense of patriotism led him to add, "The Britishers must have fought better'n they did at New Orleans, when Old Hickory gave 'em forked chain lightnin'."

The following summer the hunting party followed the Big Horn River north through the heart of the buffalo country to the Yellowstone. Gore established quarters for the ensuing winter on the Tongue River, a few miles above the site of the present Miles City, Montana.

He built a log fort, including stables, storehouses, and barracks, all surrounded by a stockade. But Henry Bostwick knocked the ashes from his pipe in the wrong place, causing a prairie fire that destroyed most of the forage for miles around. Through the winter of 1855-56 the horses existed largely on the bark of cottonwood trees, of which each man was required to gather 125 pounds daily.

Meanwhile, Gore had ordered a cabin built at the mouth of the Tongue for himself and his horse. While the other animals fed on cottonwood bark, Steel Trap ate corn meal from the hands of Sir St. George.

Virtually the only appurtenance of civilization the party did not possess was a coffin, which was needed when a wagoner named Uno died. Gore was shocked at the assumption of his men that Uno would rest just as well buried in "nothing but his clothes."

He ordered a coffin built from a precious wagon bed, and caused it to be lined with woolen cloth from his dwindling stores. Above the grave he built a log mausoleum. He wrote to the wagoner's kinfolk, offering to bring back the body for burial in "the states." The kinfolk reckoned Uno would rest right comfortable where he was.

Generous Gore showered the Indians with gifts of beads and tobacco. He flew into a rage when a white profiteer demanded blackmarket prices for six beefs. From another cattleman he bought an entire herd of fifty head and gave the forty-four unneeded animals to the redskins.

The Indians showed their gratitude by raiding his Tongue River camp and stealing twenty-one horses. His men pursued the horse thieves sixty miles until a snowstorm blotted out the trail. But Gore gave them a hot reception when they made a second raid.

According to the Lieutenant James H. Bradley manuscript in the files of the Historical Society of Montana, in the ensuing melee Gore's cook wounded one of the raiders, Big Plume, who turned out to be the Indian brother-in-law of "Major" Alexander Culbertson, the American Fur Company trader at Fort Union. Culbertson was one of the most influential white men west of the Mississippi, and he took a dim view of the wounding of his Indian wife's brother.

Presently, accompanied by Colonel A. J. Vaughan, Indian agent at Fort Union, he visited Gore's camp, demanding to know by what right a British citizen had built a fort on United States soil. The sportsman showed him the passport he had obtained from the superintendent of Indian Affairs at St. Louis. When the officials refused to recognize the passport as authority to build a fort, Gore lost his temper and in cultured Irish accents told them exactly where they could go. It wasn't the best judgment.

Vaughan filed a complaint with his superiors, charging that Gore was causing unrest among the Indians by killing so much game. Culbertson bided his time.

In the spring the party ascended the Tongue River and crossed to the Rosebud to buy fresh horses from the Crow tribe. While some of his men floated his trophies down the Yellowstone in flatboats, Gore traveled overland and joined them at Fort Union, where the Yellowstone joins the Missouri.

He was paying out a huge amount to maintain his small army of retainers, but oddly enough, in a wilderness where he was spending nearly three years without visiting a town, his banking problems were the least of his troubles. Any trading post of the American Fur Company would honor his drafts on Baring Brothers.

His party swung south from Fort Union, ascending the Little Missouri to the Black Hills. No sooner had they reached the marvelous troutwaters of the Belle Fourche than catastrophe befell them.

They discovered gold!

Historian Robert E. Strahorn, quoting *voyageur* Jerry Proteau, describes the discovery as follows:

"One Sunday I went out to the falls of Swift or Rapid Creek with Lamourie. As we were standing by the falls I noticed some yellow-looking stuff in the water, and I said to Lamourie, 'By George, there's gold!'

"I took off my shirt and scooped up three double handfuls of the yellow stuff and put it in my shirt. Then we went back to camp. Sir George noticed me and asked me what I had in my shirt. I said 'Gold!' He looked at it a little while, then he said, 'Oh, no, Jerry, that's not gold. That's mica.'

"I was not very well posted about gold and thought Sir George was. He took it and put it in two black bottles and placed them in his chest. The next day we marched out of the Black Hills and two or three days after, Bridger told me that Sir George told him it *was* gold. Sir George also told Lamourie that if he would prospect on the head of Swift Creek he would find rich gold there."

For fear his men would desert him to pan the sandbars, Gore departed precipitately from the Black Hills. Although he might have made millions from the discovery, he was interested only in sport, not in additional riches.

Twenty years were to elapse before gold was rediscovered in the Black Hills. Had Gore proclaimed his discovery, the Deadwood country would have been settled two decades earlier and warfare with the Indians might have assumed vast proportions.

As he headed back down the Little Missouri, the Sioux raided his camp and stole almost all his horses. It was then, according to Buffalo Bill Cody's account, that he sent the government a formal offer to raise a private army to exterminate the tribe. At the time it seemed a good idea to everyone except Uncle Sam.

In the autumn, back again at Fort Union, Gore lost Jim Bridger to the army which requisitioned him to serve as a guide for the expedition against the Mormons. Sir St. George decided to call it a day.

He offered to sell all his wagons and equipment to the American Fur Company and asked the none-too-friendly Culbertson to build him two sixty-foot mackinaw boats in which to float his trophies the 2,200 miles down the Missouri to St. Louis.

Perhaps Culbertson felt that now he had the Irishman over

a barrel. His price for building the boats was so high and his offer for the equipment so low that he merely succeeded in killing the goose that laid the golden eggs.

To spite him, Gore heaped all his wagon, harness, and other equipment on the bluff across the Missouri from the trading post, touched a match to them, and enjoyed his $50,000 bonfire. To make sure the trader could recover nothing of value, he even combed the ashes the next day for wagon tires and other metal, and dumped them into the river's deepest channel.

He disbanded his party, presenting Bostwick with $1,000 worth of firearms. When the wagon boss insisted on paying for them, he charged him only twelve dollars. He gave away all his horses and his dogs. An odd item in the South Dakota Historical Collections notes that many years later Fort Kearney was overrun with dogs descended from Gore's Irish staghounds.

Gore spent the winter of 1856-57 at Fort Berthold, living in an earthen hut as the lavishly paying guest of the Minatare tribal chief, Crow's Breast. When the ice broke up in the spring he boarded the first steamboat for St. Louis and returned to Ireland, where he died in 1878.

Between 1834 and 1843 Sir William Drummond Stewart of Murthley, Scotland, made six summer trips from New Orleans to the Green River fur traders' rendezvous in the Rockies.

Sir John Watts Garland, who had hunted big game in India and Africa, staged a notable buffalo hunt in 1869.

In the same year Lord Adair, later earl of Dunraven, spent four weeks hunting buffalo with the aid of a military escort. Later he bought, as a private hunting preserve, the land now approximately included within the boundaries of the Rocky Mountain National Park.

James Gordon Bennett and a party of New York millionaires were guests of General Phil Sheridan on a buffalo hunt centering at Fort McPherson in 1871.

During the winter of 1873 the Grand Duke Alexis, with a

military escort, hunted buffalo in the vicinity of North Platte, guided by Buffalo Bill Cody.

But for costliness, elapsed time, territory covered, and amount of game killed, none of these hunting parties could hold a candle to the fabulous expedition designed to provide sport for but one man, the eccentric eighth baronet of Manor Gore.

(14)

Queen Victoria's Colorado Cousin

THE West's vast cattle ranches, its mines, and to an extent its railroads were financed largely by European capital, chiefly from Great Britain. Titled Europeans were not uncommon in Denver and other Western cities, nor were remittance men and fortune-seekers of the shabby genteel.

Many titled Britishers who invested in the cattle business made their homes, at least temporarily, on their ranches. Colorado Springs became the headquarters of wealthy English investors in mines, and for that reason was frequently called "Little Lunnon." In the seventies Julius Stockdorf's City House, on Blake between F and G streets, was the center of Denver's foreign colony. Most of his guests were German or French. Many were cultured and affluent, and some remained to found fortunes and families in the frontier Western city.

Among those who met at the City House for rye bread and beer were the Gotteslebens and the Steinhaurs and the O. P. Baurs—names that within a generation were to become widely known in Denver's business circles.

The rye bread was baked by Stockdorf's eccentric cook, fat and frivolous Charles Gleichmann, formerly chef for the king of Denmark. His cooking pleased the palates of Stockdorf's

141

European guests. Most of them paid well for their accommodations, but there were some who were welcome though they could not pay at all—some in velvet gowns.

During the summer of 1872 Denver newspapers published an announcement of a concert at Occidental Hall by Stephanie, baroness di Gallotti, recently of the Pareda-Rosa Grand Opera Company, direct from the Academy of Music and Niblo's Garden, New York, where she had sung in *Il Carnevale di Venezia* and *Medea*.

Frontier Denver was not noted for its interest in the arts. In the realm of music its needs were amply satisfied by the singers in the honky-tonks. But Denver had never seen or heard anything quite like the baroness and her aristocratic husband, Don Carlos.

Even the girls of Holladay Street never wore anything to approach the stunning silk-and-lace garb of Stephanie. Denver housewives, accustomed to a wardrobe consisting of a "Sunday dress" and the "other dress," gasped as her four trunks of costumes were delivered at the City House.

They were deeply impressed by the aristocratic air of the lovely young baroness as the baron handed her into the rented carriage for the short trip to the concert hall.

She appeared to be in her late twenties, although she was thirty-two years old at the time. She was about five feet eight inches tall, with black hair worn in a fashionable and fetching chignon. Her eyes were brown and flashing, her complexion olive, and her nose was rather prominent. In public her manner was distinguished by a marked reserve, but with the Europeans of the colony at the City House she unbent with a ready and hearty laugh and irrepressible good humor. Her energy was tireless. Her hands, shrug, and glance were of the most eloquent. Denver had seen nothing to equal the exotic silks she wore. No woman outside Holladay Street possessed so many diamond rings, earrings, and diamond-studded bracelets.

At first Denver was slightly awed by Don Carlos, her dignified and unsmiling husband, thirty-five years older than Stephanie, but who lacked half an inch of equaling her in height. Although his hair was graying at the temples, his bushy mustache remained glossy black. His complexion was sallow and his cheeks were thin, but he walked with an erect, military bearing.

The baron wore a stovepipe hat and carried an enormous, fat gold watch bearing a strange, foreign, jewel-studded coat of arms. He decidedly lacked his young wife's personal magnetism. At the concert he provided her piano accompaniment.

Although her rich, golden contralto almost lifted the rafters of Denver's second-floor Occidental Hall in her selections from *Tannhäuser*, the hall was but half-filled and the engagement fell short of being a financial success.

Nevertheless, the baroness announced plans to abandon her concert tour and to remain in Denver at least for the remainder of the summer. The dry, mile-high climate was just what the baron needed for his "lung trouble." The di Gallottis engaged the most elaborate suite in the City House by the month. On their oaken washstand, alongside the china washbowl, stood a framed picture of Queen Victoria.

The baroness let it be known that she was not averse to picking up a few dollars for a concert now and then. Julius Stockdorf arranged for her to sing at the Turnverein meetings, in Turner Hall upstairs across the street from the old Elephant Corral, where the immigrants put up their wagon teams. Although the railroad had reached Denver two years earlier, many families still crossed the plains by the less expensive ox team.

The golden contralto of the baroness at first was in much demand at banquets, where she made the rafters ring with her rendition of the Marseillaise. Autumn came, and winter, and the di Gallottis remained in Denver.

Stephanie loved children, especially twelve-year-old Bertha Stockdorf and her little sister, Mathilda, who used to play in her room. These gay hours have not been forgotten by Bertha, who celebrated her ninetieth birthday in 1950. The baroness and her husband, Don Carlos, talked incessantly of Europe—of Paris, of London, of Salzburg, but most of all, of Italy.

"When the pardon comes, we can leave this crude country and return home, my darling," the baron would assure his young wife confidently, Bertha Stockdorf recalls. "It can't be much longer, now. It can't!"

"And then," Stephanie would ask, eyes gleaming with anticipation, "we can go back to the palace?"

Don Carlos would shrug. To the listening child, who had never seen a palace, this was too much to expect.

"What is a really-truly palace like, *Tante* Stephanie?" she asked when Don Carlos had departed. "I have seen pictures in the picture books, but I thought they were make-believe like the fairy stories, 'cause they were grander than the City House, and it is hard to believe anything could be grander than that."

"I lived in two palaces, but my favorite was in Naples," explained the baroness. "That was where I went as a bride, when I was only fourteen years old and fresh from the convent."

She described the palace in detail, and the gay years she spent there, but in the ensuing eight decades the description has merged in Bertha's memories with the impressions she gained from her picture books, and all she can say with certainty is that it was grand and most impressive to the mind of a twelve-year-old.

The di Gallottis spoke five languages fluently, and received mail from Europe. One of the envelopes bore a strange seal, which Stephanie showed to Bertha, explaining that it was the royal seal of King Vittorio Emmanuele, of Italy.

During the long winter, between infrequent concert engagements, the baroness found plenty of time on her hands. She made dolls for the Stockdorf sisters, using the finest silks and laces from her four wardrobe trunks.

Upon one occasion the sisters, playing "house," dressed themselves in their mother's garments and paraded into the di Gallottis' rooms to show off.

"Come, I shall do better than that for you," the baroness told blond, pig-tailed Bertha. "I shall dress you like my cousin, when she came to visit us at Laugensberg. I shall teach you how to curtsy; how to deport yourself in the presence of royalty."

From the garments in her trunks she garbed Bertha in dazzling finery. As the child strutted through the door, drawing a long train behind her, Stephanie, baroness di Gallotti, executed a deep curtsy and addressed her as "Your Majesty."

"Who is your cousin?" asked the curious child.

The baroness handed her the framed picture of Queen Victoria.

"Victoria," she explained, "is the daughter of Edward, duke of Kent, and of Victoria Mary Louisa, the duchess of Kent and fourth daughter of Francis, duke of Saxe-Coburg-Saalfield.

"My grandmother was the duchess of Luxembourg, sister of the duchess of Kent. She married General Dalaruche, one of Napoleon's famous officers. His daughter married my father, Ghillardi, a wealthy silk merchant of Milan. That is how I come to know so much about fine silks. In Italy it is the duty of the women and girls to attend to the silk worms.

"I was born in 1840, one of twelve children. When I was eight years old I was sent to Salzburg, Austria, to a convent which educated only the children of the aristocracy. I was visiting at the summer home of my grandmother, the duchess of Luxembourg, at Laugensberg, Bavaria, when Queen Victoria came to visit her aunt.

"Victoria was quite young at the time, in her twenties, and she held out her hand to me to kiss. I refused to kiss it, not from shyness, but from haughtiness. I had been taught that members of my family bowed to no one. Her majesty seemed amused rather than annoyed, and bent over and kissed me."

The Princess Clothilde, daughter of King Vittorio Emmanuele, was only fifteen when she was married to Prince Napoleon Jerome, son of Napoleon III. Stephanie was considered of marriageable age at fourteen when she left the convent and returned to the home of her parents at Milan. She was married almost immediately to Don Carlos, then forty-nine years old. He was an uncle of Salvatore Gallotti, who became a distinguished composer of sacred music and director of the choir at the Milan cathedral.

The next few years, when Stephanie, still in her teens, was mistress of a magnificent palace in Naples, were the happiest of her life. Italy had not yet been united into a single kingdom. The entire peninsula was seething with political strife, plots, and counterplots, schemes for revolt and revolution. Garibaldi came to Italy in 1854, but several years were to elapse before he took part in the war of Sardinia and France against Austria and succeeded in establishing a united Italy under a single king.

Don Carlos, along with seventeen other noblemen, was arrested, charged with plotting against the king of Sardinia. All were sentenced to be shot. But Don Carlos' brother, Frederego, chanced to be Sardinia's secretary of war. Using passports provided by his brother, Don Carlos escaped and succeeded in fleeing to France with Stephanie.

At that time Napoleon III was blowing hot and cold toward Vittorio Emmanuele, and during the periods when they were on good terms France was not the safest place for an Italian political refugee who had plotted to overthrow the king. The baron and his child-wife fled to Switzerland, hoping they would be readmitted to Italy within a matter of months. But when, by 1858, Vittorio refused to forgive his expatriate enemy, the baron and his wife went to London and presently sailed for New York.

They were almost penniless, but Stephanie had gained a splendid musical education at the Salzburg convent. She found employment with an Italian grand opera company, and for the next decade the di Gallottis toured the United States with the company. When it gave up the ghost in an Iowa town, they organized their own concert tour. It was none too successful, and this, as well as the baron's health, probably motivated them to remain in Denver.

Stephanie was just beginning to take on a touch of plumpness that was to develop, as the years passed, into a massive prima-donna figure.

Her paid concerts in Denver realized far too little to support the couple. Denverites wondered why the baron didn't get a job. Plainly he was living on his wife's concert earnings, and Denver had scant respect for men of this type, who were classed with the scorned males who lived on the earnings of the girls of Holladay Street.

Don Carlos was not too ill to work, but he had been educated to scorn manual labor, and in frontier Denver no jobs existed suited to his educational training. He was devoted to his beau-tiful young wife. Bertha Stockdorf says he waited on her as if she were a child. They wrote frequent letters to their influen-tial friends in Europe, always hoping the next mail would bring the baron's pardon.

One by one Stephanie's jewels began to disappear in the pawnshops of Larimer Street. So, too, did the baron's fat watch with the jeweled crest. For a year or two Stephanie would accept only concert engagements. Then, as their resources con-tinued to shrink, she was found singing in Denver's variety halls, and finally in its saloons and gambling joints.

In an attempt to recoup his fortunes, the baron began to spend much of his time at Ed Chase's Cricket Club gambling hall, only a few doors from the City House. But luck and the law of prob-abilities were against him.

Meanwhile, the panic of '73 had gripped the nation. Money was fearfully tight. Mines began to close down. Boom-town Denver was beginning to lose population.

But Don Carlos and his wife felt that ill fortune could not last forever. Every day he would go to the post office, seeking the envelope containing the expected pardon permitting his return to Italy.

Stephanie was filling a matinee singing engagement at a honky-tonk on an afternoon in the summer of '74 when the baron stalked to the post office and found a letter bearing the royal seal of King Vittorio. He hurried back to the City House—to the single back room into which they had moved from their original suite. His heart was pounding as he opened the envelope with trembling fingers.

Late in the afternoon Stephanie, gaily humming a lighthearted Italian folk song, returned to the City House from her engagement at the honky-tonk. She found her husband on the floor, dead, the king's pardon gripped in his fingers. The shock had been too much for his heart.

After the death of Don Carlos Stephanie made a concert tour of Colorado mining camps. She disappeared from Denver for a year and on her return said she had been on a concert tour of Eastern states.

Meanwhile she had become acquainted with Charles H. Tanner, a man much older than she, described both as an attorney and as a musician. The Denver city directory for those years, however, lists him as a bartender, living at 270 Curtis Street.

Charley and Stephanie were married in 1878. The effects of the panic of '73 were wearing off. Business was picking up. Silver and lead had been discovered at Leadville. A new boom was in the making.

In '79 Stephanie and her second husband went to booming Leadville. Gus Voges, operator of Carbonate Hall, offered her a job singing to the miners and put her bartender-husband on the payroll, too.

She no longer used the name, Baroness di Gallotti. Now she was just Charley Tanner's wife. She was putting on flesh. Her stature, if not her voice, reached prima-donna proportions. Although her hair was black and her skin was touched with olive, her nose and profile bore a remarkable resemblance to those of Victoria in the queen's later years.

When the Tanners moved to Leadville, Stephanie packed all the mementos of her first marriage and of her life in Europe in the four trunks containing her opera costumes, and hired a freighter to haul them to the new mining camp. The freighter vanished, and so did the trunks.

With the passage of the years, Stephanie became too fat to please the customers of Carbonate Hall. Julius Stockdorf, who had gone bankrupt during the panic, had quit the hotel business and had moved from Denver to Leadville, where he conducted a prosperous florist's shop.

Julius had always liked Stephanie and her aristocratic first husband. Now, although the di Gallottis' Denver hotel bill remained unpaid, he tried to help her by arranging a concert at the Grand Central Theater. It failed to start her on the comeback road, proving only that her voice was beginning to crack and that she was washed up as a singer, even as a honky-tonk singer. Leadville forgot about old Charley Tanner, the barkeep, and his fat wife, who lived in a tiny log cabin at 510 East Tenth Street.

Queen Victoria died in 1901. The editor of the Leadville *Herald-Democrat* remembered that someone had told him, back in the eighties, that Charley Tanner's old woman had some crackpot yarn about being kin to the queen. He sent a reporter to interview her. This was on January 23, 1901.

The reporter found her bedridden, kissing the framed picture of her cousin, Victoria, and sobbing, "My poor darling!" He noted her remarkable resemblance to the picture of the queen.

He noted, but did not report, that Charley was too old to tend bar any more. The two were virtually destitute, although the old man occasionally picked up a few dollars doing odd jobs.

Stephanie, third cousin of a queen, second cousin of Edward VII, born to riches, once mistress of a palace, wife of a baron, had completely dominated the lives of two men. She virtually had supported Don Carlos during the years he was too proud to work. She had done the same for Charley Tanner, the amiable but shiftless barkeep.

Now she was bedridden, but not without hope. Eagerly she saw in the reporter's newspaper article an opportunity to retrieve her shattered fortunes, to stage a comeback. Her spirit was indomitable. Fired with enthusiasm, she told him of her plans. She was only sixty-one, and believed she might pass for fifty behind the footlights. True, her voice was a trifle unsteady, but that was due merely to her temporary illness! Newspapers throughout the world published the story of Queen Victoria's Colorado cousin.

The next item about Stephanie in the *Herald-Democrat* did not tell of a comeback concert. It told of her death, April 21, 1904, and it called her husband not a bartender but a lawyer. Besides old Charley only three persons attended the funeral, at the Church of the Annunciation, of this kinswoman of royalty.

No one knows whatever became of Charley. No one ever took the trouble to find out.

(15)

Barren Gain and Bitter Loss

MUCH—but not all—of the amazing story of the Tabors has been chronicled in book form in recent years and in one highly inaccurate motion picture. Without repeating more than enough of the oft-told Tabor biography to provide an intelligible background, this account, taken largely from court records, will present only that part of the Tabor story that has not appeared in published biographies.

H. A. W. Tabor, the Maine stonecutter who was to become Colorado's bonanza king, was an unlearned but friendly, honest, and generous man before he "struck it rich." After he grubstaked prospectors August Rische and George T. Hook at Leadville and the riches of the Little Pittsburgh mine began pouring into his hands faster than he could spend it, certain changes became apparent in his none-too-rugged character. In some respects he was totally unprepared to "stand prosperity."

His first wife, Augusta, was a handsome woman when he married her at Augusta, Maine, January 31, 1857. She endured the hardships of pioneer life uncomplainingly for many years, operating a bakery and a store serving customers and keeping his books as well as attending to her household duties and rearing their son, Maxcy. She was bewildered by the wealth that sud-

denly poured in upon them. As for Tabor, with the coming of
wealth he began to drink heavily, to gamble for high stakes, and
to seek the companionship of other women. Little wonder that
as middle-aged Tabor began to tire of his middle-aged wife,
this wife who had aided him so faithfully for so many years became sharp of manner and acid of tongue!

The most imposing building in Leadville was the Tabor Opera
House, adjoining the Clarendon Hotel on Harrison Avenue. At
the time it was built it was the finest theater west of the Mississippi. It contained stores on the first floor and the theater auditorium seating 500 persons on the second. Gaslights illuminated
the theater. The building also contained apartments occupied
by Tabor and his business manager, Billy Bush.

Before he built his own theater at Leadville, Tabor liked to
attend the variety shows at the Grand Central where he occupied a private box. Actress Erba Robeson, who did a turn on
the stage and sold drinks to the boxholders on the side, served
many a drink to the bonanza king who, she said, was usually
drunk.

"He gave me a dollar for each service," Erba told William
B. Thom in an interview published in the Leadville *Herald-
Democrat*, January 1, 1936, "and as often as not, when I
brought him a bottle of wine, he'd pour it into the cuspidor.
When he was very drunk he'd ask me to look after him, and
once I cared for his watch and money overnight. He was exceedingly vulgar, and cleanliness wasn't next to his cuticle.

"Prior to his marriage to Baby Doe he had a flame in Alice
Morgan, a club swinger at the Grand Central. She told me the
only way she could stand him was to get drunk."

Once-attractive Augusta, at middle age, was thin, toil-worn,
angular. She was nearsighted and wore blue tinted glasses. Her
voice was soft. Since her education was limited, her English was
none of the best, although she wrote a fine Spencerian hand. She
loved Tabor devotedly, even after she became aware of his affairs with other women.

Augusta kept a scrapbook in which she pasted newspaper clippings, pictures, programs. As her husband broke into print more and more frequently, she added two more scrapbooks. One of the earliest of the clippings in these Books of Memories —of memories that bless and burn—is an undated cutting from the St. Louis *Post Dispatch*.

The newspaper article reports an interview with Willie Deville, a prostitute, who said she met Tabor while she was an inmate of Lizzie Allen's parlor house at Chicago, while the bonanza king was in that city on a business trip.

Willie related that she became Tabor's companion and traveled with him in the West for more than a year. They attempted to keep their affair secret, but after Augusta discovered her, the two pretended to sever their relations but continued to meet secretly. Willie said she accompanied him on a trip to New York, where a woman of that city learned of their relations and used her knowledge to blackmail Tabor. He then told Willie she had talked too much and thoughtlessly had caused him a great deal of trouble. He gave her $4,000, she said, and informed her that their relations must end.

No Denver newspaper published this story about the powerful multimillionaire, many of whose business enterprises were purchasers of advertising space. But Augusta knew about Alice Morgan, the Indian-club swinger, about Willie Deville and his other affairs. She also knew about her rival, Baby Doe, although at that time had never laid eyes on the lovely young wife of Harvey Doe. Her scrapbook of burning memories contains a newspaper clipping in which Tabor's name is mentioned in connection with that of a "Mrs. Doe."

Elizabeth B. McCourt was only seventeen years old when she married William Harvey Doe, Jr., at St. Peter's Catholic Church at Oshkosh, Wisconsin, on June 27, 1877. The two left for Colorado on their wedding night. Known to her family and friends by the pet name, Baby, from the time of her marriage to Doe, during her marriage to Tabor and until the time of her death she was known as Baby Doe.

Baby Doe was a doll-like creature with honey-gold hair, a peaches-and-cream complexion, and intense, expressive blue eyes. Her sparkling Irish wit, her complete self-possession in any company, her rich, golden contralto, all contributed to a magnetic personality that charmed most men and even a few women.

The young couple came to Central City, whose mining boom was fast subsiding. Harvey worked as a mucker in the mines—when he worked. At times his bride helped support him by taking in washing. As the wife of Harvey Doe, Baby Doe gave birth to the first of her four children, a stillborn child.

Just where and when Tabor and Baby Doe met is uncertain. One account has it that they met in a restaurant at Leadville, where she had gone with the deliberate intention of making his acquaintance.

Another account, unverified, has it that Tabor was seated in the lobby of Denver's Windsor Hotel, chatting with William A. "Bill" Hamill, superintendent of the celebrated Terrible mine at Silver Plume and at that time political boss of Clear Creek County, which included the mining towns of Central City, Blackhawk, and Georgetown.

When Harvey Doe and his lovely young wife crossed the lobby, Hamill remarked, "There goes the most beautiful woman in Colorado."

"I know it," said Tabor, "I have just promised Harvey Doe a thousand dollars for an introduction."

The Windsor Hotel, at Eighteenth and Larimer streets, was slightly more than two blocks from Lizzie Preston's Holladay Street sporting house. At ten o'clock on the night of March 2, 1880, less than three years after her marriage to Harvey Doe, she led the police raid on Lizzie's place to gain evidence for a divorce action. Two days later she filed her divorce suit in the

Arapahoe County court, charging her husband with adultery and nonsupport.

The case was heard March 19 before Judge Amos Steck. Her attorney was C. W. Wright. She signed the complaint, "Elizabeth B. Doe, Jr."

"I saw the defendant enter Lizzie Preston's house," her testimony in the court record reads. "I went to the door of the house and told the woman I had seen my husband go in, and wanted to follow him. The woman said that if I came in, I would be in a house of ill-fame, too. I then pushed past the woman and saw my husband in one of the rooms. I came right out. Policeman Edward Newman accompanied me. I never thought my husband would go to such a place because he told me he wouldn't. I had been compelled to sell my jewelry and furniture and clothes to support us." She said she and her husband had been residents of Colorado since July 3, 1877.

Officer Newman corroborated her story, telling the court that he had accompanied Baby Doe on the raid and had seen Harvey Doe seated on a lounge in Lizzie's establishment.

Judge Steck granted her a divorce decree. The judge was soon to be retained by Augusta Tabor to represent her in her suits against Tabor. Strangely, too, the record of the Doe divorce hearing disappeared completely from the court records —which may have been the reason not a line about the case was published in Denver newspapers. Its disappearance was destined to lead to serious complications.

On the other hand, since the filing of the case was a matter of public record, it is entirely possible that, because the name of the lovely Baby Doe had not yet been linked publicly with that of Colorado's bonanza king, it meant nothing newsworthy to the newspaper reporters.

There is no shred of evidence to indicate that Tabor paid for Baby Doe's divorce, nor that he paid Harvey Doe $5,000 to give up his wife. Since the record of the hearing vanished completely for some years, there could be no basis for the belief

that the evidence indicated collusion on the part of the parties
to the divorce, as in many states where it is fairly common practice for a husband to provide grounds for divorce by permitting
himself to be found by witnesses in a compromising situation.

Now Baby Doe was free to remarry, but Tabor was not. As
disclosed in subsequent court proceedings, he had sought un-
successfully to induce Augusta to sue him for divorce. Presently he persuaded W. H. "Billy" Bush, his business agent,
opera house manager, and general "fixer," to attempt to arrange for Augusta to divorce him. "Fixer" Bush later testified
in court that Tabor promised him $10,000 for arranging the
affair. This was in 1881, when Bush was the manager of the
Tabor Grand Opera House in Denver and of the Windsor
Hotel.

But they failed to take into account the stubbornness of
Augusta. Immeasurably shocked, she informed Bush flatly that
she would never ask for a divorce. Two reasons are given to
account for her refusal to agree to his proposition: first, she
was opposed to divorce on religious grounds; second, hers was
the natural reaction of a middle-aged wife who knows she is
being cast aside for a younger and more comely woman—that
she still loved Tabor and desperately wanted to prevent Baby
Doe from taking him from her.

By this time the Tabors were living apart—he at Denver's
Windsor Hotel and at Leadville's Clarendon, and Augusta at
the Tabor mansion between Broadway and Lincoln Street,
and Seventeenth and Eighteenth avenues. The destitute Baby
Doe was dividing her time between the West's two most expensive hotels—the Windsor at Denver and the Clarendon at
Leadville.

Failing to win Augusta's consent to a divorce, Bush arranged
through a firm of Chicago attorneys for Tabor to file suit himself, in secret. The suit was filed at Durango, in southwestern
Colorado, and the hearing was held in secret and a decree was
granted Tabor on March 24, 1882, on the ground of desertion.

Augusta was wholly unaware of her husband's divorce. Bush swore to Tabor's lawyer, L. C. Rockwell, that he had seen the process server hand her notification of the divorce action. Later he testified on the witness stand that he had lied. "I confess it with shame," he told the court.

Presumably the secret Durango divorce left Tabor free to marry Baby Doe. Actually it proved to be only a preliminary skirmish in his court battle to discard his first wife.

Having rejected Fixer Billy Bush's offer on Tabor's behalf, Augusta retained as her lawyer Judge Amos Steck, who had granted Baby Doe's divorce, and began to prepare for a separate maintenance action, which was filed in the district court in Denver on March 15, 1882, just eleven days after Tabor's secret Durango divorce decree had been granted.

Although the lengthy complaint, written in longhand, gave an extended history of the Tabor marital difficulties and presented some startling facts concerning the size of his fortune, one Denver newspaper ignored it altogether, two dismissed it with a single paragraph, and one printed an article of several paragraphs under a one-column head. No newspaper printed any of the charges Augusta made against her husband.

She charged that Tabor repeatedly had asked her to divorce him, offering her a substantial part of his huge fortune if she would agree to a divorce. She set forth that she had refused, and still continued to refuse to ask for a divorce, and pointed out specifically that she was seeking only separate maintenance.

She charged that he had threatened to sell the $100,000 Tabor mansion on Broadway, and claimed he had deserted her and had refused to pay her bills. Augusta said she had been compelled to rent rooms to support herself. She petitioned the court to direct that the Tabor mansion be placed in her name and that he be directed to pay her $50,000 a year support money.

Although biographers have estimated Tabor's fortune at everywhere from ten million to one hundred million dollars, the itemized inventory listed by Augusta in her complaint shows he had assets of at least $9,076,100 at that time. Since she had served as his bookkeeper for many years, she should have been in a position to know of his holdings. His fortune may have been greater than the total shown in Augusta's complaint, for she charged that he possessed "other property of great value, unknown to the plaintiff."

Following is the inventory of Tabor's assets, as listed in the complaint:

Tabor Grand Opera House, Denver . . . .$ 800,000
Tabor Office Building, Denver 250,000
    (Now the Nassau Building)
Tabor residence 100,000
Two dwellings on Welton Street 20,000
Eight blocks of unimproved East Denver real estate 100,000
Four lots, Block 107, East Denver 50,000
Ninety-seven shares, First National Bank, Denver 500,000
Bank of Leadville stock 100,000
Coliseum Theater, Leadville 20,000
Chestnut Street Building, Leadville 20,000
Interest in Leadville Post Office Building 100,000
Five houses in Lake County 10,000
Loan to gas company and stock, Leadville 100,000
Houses at Malta 1,000
Hotel at Gunnison 20,000
Gunnison Bank stock 50,000
Telephone Company stock 15,000
Tabor mill, near Leadville 60,000
Matchless Mine, Leadville 1,000,000
Henrietta, Maid of Erin, Waterloo mines 1,000,000
Chrysolite Mine 50,000
Breese Iron Mine 300,000
Hibernia Mine 100,000
Glen Pendry Mine 100,000
Oolite and group of mines 100,000
Interest in Bull Domingo and Robinson 1,000,000
Smuggler, Lead Chief, and Denver City Mines 500,000

Mines in Summit County	200,000
Mines in San Juan County	200,000
Torrance and other mines, New Mexico	50,000
Interest in manufacturing company, Mexico	50,000
275 acres, new stockyards	50,000
Lands and mortgage bonds, near Chicago	500,000
320 acres in Kansas	15,000
Lots in Manhattan, Kansas	100
Coal lands in South Park, Colorado	30,000
Railroad stocks	50,000
Steam-heating plant shares, Denver	10,000
Livery and stage line, Durango, Colorado	15,000
Government bonds	200,000
23/48 shares Tam O'Shanter Mines	1,000,000
Cash in bank, notes, miscellaneous securities	200,000
Interest, Denver, Utah & Pacific Construction Company..	10,000
Diamonds and other jewels not worn by defendant	100,000

Prior to the date of this inventory, Tabor had sold his interest in the Little Pittsburgh Mine to Chaffee and Moffat for $1,000,000. Since other of his known holdings are not listed, presumably they were acquired at a later date. These included 175,000 acres of copper land in Texas; copper-mining properties in Arizona, and alternate sections of mahogany and ebony timber lands for 400 miles bordering the Patook River in the Republic of Honduras.

His income, as set forth by Augusta in her complaint, was $100,000 a month.

Although Tabor already had been granted his secret divorce at Durango, nevertheless he promptly filed a demurrer to Augusta's separate maintenance complaint. He alleged that in 1879 he had given her $100,000 in government bonds as pin money but that she had spent most of it and had lost the rest through unwise investments. He claimed that she owned a one-third interest in the Windsor Hotel which yielded her $14,000 a year.

The court overruled his demurrer. In April Augusta sold her interest in the Windsor for $38,350.

On September 30, 1882, six months and twenty-six days after the secret divorce proceedings at Durango, Tabor and Baby Doe were married secretly at the Southern Hotel, St. Louis. Augusta was blissfully unaware of his secret Durango divorce and of his secret marriage to Baby Doe and, never doubting she was still his wife, was confidently awaiting the outcome of her separate maintenance action.

Meanwhile, a new set of town officials had been elected at Durango. A new deputy in the office of the district clerk chanced to be thumbing through the docket book when he discovered two pages pasted together. His curiosity aroused, he slit the glued pages and discovered the record of the Tabor divorce. It was not recorded in the handwriting of the former clerk of court, as were all other cases, but was in the handwriting of the judge.

The clerk realized that his discovery was of immense importance. The newspapers were filled with stories of Tabor's campaign to win a seat in the United States Senate. At the time he was nearing the end of his second term as lieutenant governor of Colorado and was state chairman of the Republican party. The legislature which was to meet in January was to elect two United States senators—one for a full six-year term and one to fill a thirty-day vacancy caused by the appointment of Senator Teller to a cabinet post. Money was being spent like water. Tabor was determined to win the six-year term.

The clerk realized he had discovered a political bombshell. Although he knew nothing of the secret St. Louis marriage to Baby Doe, he knew that if Tabor's opponents learned of the bonanza king's secret divorce from his highly respected wife, it might cost him the election.

He made a copy of the secret proceedings and mailed it to Augusta in Denver. Needless to say, she was profoundly shocked by the discovery that Tabor had divorced her. Her attorney,

Judge Steck, advised her that since she had not been served with notice of the divorce action the decree was completely invalid. He immediately got in touch with Tabor's attorneys and, fully aware that he was in possession of facts that were political dynamite, urged them to permit Augusta to gain her separate maintenance decree without opposition.

He did not, of course, know of Tabor's secret marriage to Baby Doe. Of course, if the secret Durango divorce was invalid, the marriage to Baby Doe was bigamous.

Although Augusta and her lawyer were not aware of this situation, Tabor and his lawyers decidedly were. He was facing a scandal that could well ruin him. He could not agree to let Augusta have her separate maintenance decree, for that meant he could never marry Baby Doe and that their secret St. Louis marriage would be branded as bigamous and her reputation would be blasted.

Fixer Billy Bush's testimony during subsequent litigation with Tabor indicates that at first, when questioned by the latter's lawyers, he stuck to his story that he had seen Augusta served with the papers in the divorce case, but that he later admitted he lied. Bush's admission left Tabor and his lawyers panicky, for the senatorial election was fast approaching. Something must be done, and speedily, if Tabor was to avoid disgrace and political ruin.

He discharged his Chicago lawyers and retained Attorney L. G. Rockwell of Denver, who advised him that the Durango divorce was not worth the paper it was written on.

The bonanza king fired Billy Bush promptly for his blundering attempt to "fix" the secret Durango divorce, and refused to pay him the promised fee. Bush later brought suit to recover the fee for arranging the Durango divorce and for other sums he claimed Tabor owed him, and the testimony at the hearing of his suit and Tabor's countersuit aired much of the bonanza king's dirty linen.

Bush's claim that his duties included the shielding of Tabor's amorous dalliances from publicity was ruled by the court to be scandalous, and when his attorney insisted it was true and refused to withdraw it, he was fined $500 for contempt and the charge was ordered expunged from the record.

Through his attorney Tabor made another and much more generous offer of a quarter-million-dollar cash settlement if Augusta would drop her separate maintenance suit and sue him for divorce, which they assured her would be uncontested.

Augusta, still unaware of his secret and probably bigamous St. Louis marriage to Baby Doe, steadfastly refused all advances. She was opposed to divorce on religious grounds and, beyond support money, was completely uninterested in a financial settlement.

Such was the situation a week before the legislature was to meet to elect two Colorado senators. Tabor was desperate. His lawyer had one more card to play. He was convinced Augusta was still devotedly in love with her unworthy, philandering multimillionaire husband. If money could not sway her, perhaps sentiment could.

As she stated later in a newspaper interview, it was the argument of her own lawyer, Judge Steck, who had granted Baby Doe her divorce from Harvey Doe, that finally persuaded her to forget her religious scruples, drop her separate maintenance suit, and sue Tabor for divorce. He brought pressure on her by telling her it was hopeless to try to wage a court fight against a man worth so many millions, that a man of Tabor's character would blast her reputation through purchased testimony, sue for and win the divorce himself, and she would get nothing.

Augusta still loved Tabor. She wanted desperately to hold him, to keep him from the arms of the beautiful siren who was breaking up her home. But she knew his greatest ambition was to serve in the United States Senate, knew that a scandal would thwart this ambition. It is interesting to speculate as to whether she would have agreed to divorce him had she been aware of Tabor's secret St. Louis marriage to Baby Doe.

On January 2, 1883, shortly before the legislature was to choose Colorado's senators, Augusta filed suit for divorce in the county court and two days later dismissed her separate maintenance suit in the district court. Her complaint—an original copy is preserved in her Book of Memories—was brief and conventional, charging desertion.

The divorce hearing was not held in open court but in the chambers of Judge Benjamin F. Harrington. Asked if she were aware of her husband's Durango divorce, she replied that she was and that she knew it to be fraudulent.

The court asked her the customary routine questions as to whether there had been collusion between her husband and herself in arranging the divorce. She astonished court and lawyers by replying, "Yes."

Instantly her attorney, Amos Steck, leaped to his feet. "She does not mean that, your honor," he put in hastily. "She does not understand the question. What she means is simply that there was an agreement reached as to a property settlement. She is to receive the Tabor home and the La Veta apartments." The apartment building stood on the site now occupied by the Denver Public Library.

The testimony was brief, relating only to Tabor's desertion, which he admitted. Before she stepped down from the witness stand, Augusta again startled the court by stating, "I wish the record to show that this divorce was not willingly asked for."

She had maintained her composure up to this point, but now she burst into hysterical sobbing, crying, "Oh, God! Not willingly! Not willingly!"

In spite of her testimony as to collusion, in spite of her declaration that she was not a willing party to the action, the court granted the decree. When lawyer Steck handed her the papers to sign, she cried hysterically, "What is my name? Am I still Mrs. Tabor?"

After the hearing her attorney told newspaper reporters, "She loves him. She has always loved him, and she always will love him. Some day this creature, Tabor, will lose his fortune and will come whining to Augusta to help him, and she will help him."

Interviewed that evening in the lobby of the Windsor Hotel, Tabor denied to a reporter for the Denver *Republican* that he was planning to marry Baby Doe. "But," he added with a knowing grimace, "that isn't saying I wouldn't like to."

This was less than four months after his secret St. Louis marriage to the lovely divorcee, and less than two months before his second and public marriage to the celebrated beauty.

Augusta, with a comparatively small settlement and her books of burning memories, departed immediately for California. An undated, unidentified newspaper clipping in one of her scrapbooks reads in part:

> A bonanza king can purchase anything that he wishes, even a divorce in four hours. Tabor's friends are probably as glad as Tabor to have an affair speedily and quietly concluded, which if sifted thoroughly by daylight, might prove dangerous to the lofty senatorial aspirations of the governor. [Lieutenant governor Tabor.]
>
> Mrs. Tabor possibly has it in her power to tell some very ugly truths about her ex-spouse, but as Judge Steck [her attorney] says, "If the truth were known, it would be enough to ruin him forever. She loves him and that settles it. She will not say a word.". . . In the courtroom she prays the judge to enter upon the record that the divorce was "not willingly asked for." . . . She seems a woman mortally wounded through the shield of her affection.

Another undated scrapbook clipping is a poem identified only by the name of its author, Carlotta Perry. Three verses read:

Though I loose my hand from yours and go
Away from you bitter-hearted
And we say it is best, do you think that so
We two shall be truly parted?

Still forever the bond endures
With resolute [*sic*] and persistence,
And never a word of mine or yours
Can will it out of existence.

Though I loose my hand and say good-bye,
In vain is our weak decreeing.
There is no power that can break a tie
That is one with our very being.

(16)

Memories that Bless and Burn

TABOR failed to win the six-year senatorial term, but on January 27 was elected to fill the thirty-day vacancy and left at once for Washington. When he took his seat in the United States Senate the impression the bonanza king made on his colleagues was far from favorable. Senator John J. Ingalls wrote to Mrs. Ingalls:

> The Colorado millionaire, Tabor, took his seat last week. A fouler beast was never depicted. He is of the Harvey type, but indescribably lower and coarser. Such a vulgar, ruffianly boor you never beheld; uncouth, awkward, shambling, dirty hands and big feet turned inward; a huge solitaire diamond on a sooty, bony, blacksmith hand; piratical features, unkempt, frowsy and unclean, blotched with disease, he looks the brute he is. He was stared at with curious but undisguised abhorrence.

Now legally divorced, Tabor was free to contract a legal marriage with Baby Doe. Originally scheduled to be held at the White House, the ceremony was transferred to the Willard Hotel when President Chester A. Arthur learned that the wives of the other members of the Colorado Congressional delegation had flatly refused to attend the wedding. So, on March 1, 1883, one day less than three years after she had led the police raid on Lizzie Preston's sporting house, Baby Doe was married publicly and legally to the multimillionaire Colorado senator at one of the nation's most costly and magnificent weddings, in the presence of a president of the United States.

By chance Tabor and his new wife returned to Denver on the same day Augusta returned from California. While Baby Doe sat alone in her chamber at the Windsor Hotel, thoroughly snubbed by Denver's social leaders, thirty-two of the city's most prominent women called upon Augusta to pay their respects.

Tabor had every reason to believe that he was legally married at last and that the legal books were closed on his marital difficulties. However, a clerk in County Judge Harrington's court, during a routine clearing of the docket during the 1884 March term of court, discovered that the records showed Baby Doe had filed suit for divorce against Harvey Doe in 1880 but that there was no record of the disposition of the case. The divorce decree issued by former Judge Steck was missing from the files. So far as the court record showed, no action had ever been taken in Baby Doe's divorce suit.

On his own motion, on March 4, 1884, Judge Harrington issued an order directing Baby Doe Tabor to appear in court and show cause why her divorce complaint should not be dismissed because of failure to prosecute her suit. For some reason the order was not served until nearly a year later. On January 20, 1885, it was served on Hugh Butler, at that time one of Baby Doe's lawyers. It directed her to appear in court in ten days and show cause why her complaint should not be dismissed.

The consternation that this new development caused in the Tabor household may only be imagined. If Baby Doe's divorce from Harvey Doe could not be established, then the public marriage in Washington was invalid and the second marriage was bigamous. And to add to the distressing situation Baby Doe on July 13, 1884, had given birth to a daughter, Elizabeth Bonduel Lillie Tabor, her second child and her first by her second husband. Unless the legality of Baby Doe's divorce could be established, this child might bear the stigma of having been born out of wedlock.

Another year, and more, dragged along before C. W. Wright, Baby Doe's lawyer in her divorce suit against her first husband, filed a motion on April 24, 1886, pointing out that Judge Steck's decree, although issued, had never been entered in the court records, and asking Judge Harrington to decree that the 1880 divorce had been granted. In the motion her name appeared as Elizabeth B. Tabor. It set forth that she had always believed the decree had been properly recorded until recently advised otherwise, that she later had married H. A. W. Tabor and had borne him one child.

The court records fail to show that Judge Harrington ever took formal action on attorney Wright's motion. However, the jacket containing the documents in the case now includes the Doe divorce decree, written in longhand, as originally issued by Judge Amos Steck.

Lawyers today express the opinion that Judge Steck's decree originally had been withheld from the court files to suppress the case from the newspapers, and that it was restored six years later after Judge Harrington's order revealed it to be missing. The name of the person who abstracted it from the files, only to replace it years later, remains a matter of conjecture.

At the time of this latest threat against his marital status, Tabor was at the height of his wealth and investment activities. No Denver newspaper carried an account of the court order which threatened the legitimacy of his public marriage to Baby Doe.

One biographer coined for Tabor the nickname, "Haw," and the error has been perpetuated by other writers. According to

Tabor's friends, he never, never was known as Haw, and there is no documentary evidence whatever that he was ever called by this nickname. In his early storekeeper days he was frequently called Hod, a nickname for Horace, and some of his letters are so signed. It is entirely possible that he may have been addressed by his initials, H. A. W. His first wife, Augusta, called him merely "Tabor." After the birth of their first child, Baby Doe's pet name for her husband was "Papa" or "Pappy."

From her girlhood on, she was always called Baby, by members of her own family, by Harvey Doe, by Tabor, and by her friends. She used this diminutive in signing letters. It appears under a poem in her handwriting found in a scrapbook now in the possession of the Colorado State Historical Society.

Baby Doe's third child (her second by Tabor), a boy named Horace Joseph Tabor, was born October 17, 1888, and died the same day. Her fourth and last child, the widely publicized Silver Dollar Tabor, was born December 17, 1889, and was baptized July 30, 1890. According to some accounts, her name was suggested to Tabor by William Jennings Bryan. When she was in her twenties, Silver Dollar gave the author the following version of how she came by her name.

"Before I was born papa was expecting a boy. He decided to name him Silver Dollar because the silver dollar symbolized the fortune he had made in silver. When I turned out to be a girl, he still wanted to name me Silver Dollar. Mama insisted I be named Echo. She thought Silver Dollar a terrible name to wish on a girl. They compromised by giving me both names.

"However, neither papa nor mama ever called me either Silver Dollar or Echo. They had their own pet name for me—Honeymoon. So my real name is Silver Dollar Echo Honeymoon Tabor."

The records show she was christened Rose Mary Echo Silver Dollar Tabor.

The author never heard her called "Silver"; it was always Silver Dollar. At that time she was haunting Denver newspaper offices, promoting a publicity campaign to induce the federal government to deed to her then destitute mother the site of the old post office building, which her father had donated to Uncle Sam. It was across the alley from the Tabor Opera House and was valued at $62,000 at the time Tabor conveyed it to the government. Denver's present post office building was under construction at another site. In the heart of the business district, the old post office site with its building (still standing) would have been sufficient in value to have provided amply for Baby Doe and Silver Dollar.

Like her mother, Silver Dollar was strikingly beautiful, but her hair was almost black while Baby Doe's was light. She was afflicted with a speech defect that caused her to speak with a decided lisp. She was a lighthearted girl, blessed with a gay disposition, and at the slightest excuse would throw back her head and laugh merrily. The best likeness of Silver Dollar is the mural by artist Herndon Davis, on a wall of the Windsor Hotel.

While promoting her publicity campaign Silver Dollar picked up a few dollars by writing verse for the newspapers. It was terrible and was generally turned over to a reporter to rewrite. The newspapers used it only because it carried the Tabor by-line.

Silver Dollar cherished an ambition to become a writer, and had written an atrocious book entitled *Star of Blood*. A conglomeration of fact and fiction, the privately printed volume dealt with the life story of a Western bandit.

Her campaign to regain the post office site ended in flat failure, for Uncle Sam believes it is more blessed to receive than to give. Silver Dollar left Denver and, in her mid-thirties, was scalded to death in September, 1925, in Chicago.

Various biographers of Tabor have told, quite adequately, the story of the bonanza king's magnificent opera house in Denver (now a motion picture theater). However, the history of the famous drop curtain, almost as widely known as the theater itself, has never been told in its entirety. Frequently quoted—perhaps because they apply so aptly to the Tabor story, are the lines on the curtain:

> So fleet the works of men, back to the earth again;
> Ancient and holy things fade like a dream.

One biographer erroneously adds a third line:

> And the hand of the master is dust.

The painting depicts an ancient, ruined, deserted temple. The same biographer erroneously attributes it to artist Edward Daingerfield, although the curtain plainly bears the signature, "Hopkin."

Actually the quotation is from a parable, "Old and New," by Charles Kingsley, written at Eversley, May 13, 1848. The reason early researchers were unable to trace it to its source probably is due to the fact that it originally was printed anonymously in an English newspaper and was not included in Kingsley's collected works until some years later. It follows:

OLD AND NEW
A PARABLE
By Charles Kingsley

> See how the autumn leaves float by decaying,
> Down the wild swirls of the rain-swollen stream.
> So fleet the works of men, back to their earth again;
> Ancient and holy things fade like a dream.
>
> Nay! see the spring-blossoms steal forth a-maying,
> Clothing with tender hues orchard and glen;
> So, though old forms pass by, ne'er shall their spirits die,
> Look! England's bare boughs show green leaf again.

Eversley, 1848

Canon Kingsley, author of the immortal *Westward Ho*, came
to Colorado with his son, Maurice, and daughter, Rose, in 1874
and for a short time occupied the pulpit of Grace Episcopal
Church at Colorado Springs. Kingsley lectured at Guards' Hall,
Denver, on July 17, 1874.

The condensed story of the origin of the curtain substantially
as told by Tabor to Joseph Emerson Smith, Denver newspaperman, follows.

When Tabor was operating a store at Oro City he passed
through Colorado Springs on his way to Denver, attended services at Grace Church, and was greatly impressed by Kingsley's
sermon. After the services he introduced himself, and Kingsley
presented him with a thin volume of his verses. Years later, when
he was making plans for the opera house, Tabor told the architect, "I want these lines by Kingsley on the curtain."

The Sullivan Scenic & Decorative Co., of Chicago, was com-
missioned to provide the curtain at a cost of $1,500. This firm
employed Robert Hopkin, Detroit artist, to paint the drop curtain. Hopkin previously had painted curtains for theaters in
Chicago and elsewhere. His most noted works were the murals
painted for the Rice Exchange at New Orleans.

When Hopkin read the instructions he said, "There was a
queen and she came from cool, green mountains to become the
bride of Nebuchadnezzar. She came down into the Mesopota-
mian plains into the furnace heat. Slaves fanned her but she
paled, and her heart longed for the green coolness of the mountains.

"And so it was that the love of a king builded one of the won-
ders of the world—the Hanging Gardens of Babylon. There
water was forced up from the Euphrates and on the truncations
making the hanging garden. Earth was planted. Trees were
planted, and gardens, and there were brooks and waterfalls and
the birds came and it was a garden cool and beautiful between
heaven and earth and the queen was happy. . . .

"And so the curtain was born. A great palace, the pillars totter-

ing, parasites pulling the mortar out of the wall, a rotting gon-
dola upon a stagnant pool. A thing of horror that had once been
a thing of beauty."

It is possible that one of the paintings of the Italian artists, the
Ricci brothers, who specialized in ancient ruins, may have inspired scenic artist Hopkin. Quite similar in general to the Tabor
curtain is a Ricci painting now hanging in the National Gallery
of Art, Washington. It certainly does not depict the ruins of the
Hanging Gardens of Babylon, for the ruins bear a carved in-
scription including the name of the Roman official, Publius
Cornelius Dolabella.

Tabor's fortune melted away rapidly in the late eighties and
early nineties. The collapse in the value of his mining properties
following the demonetization of silver found him loaded with
real estate and other investments he was unable to retain, and his
fortune melted away as swiftly as it had been gained. Strangely
enough, bumbling Billy Bush, who had failed to fix the Durango
divorce, became associated with Augusta Tabor after his dismiss-
al by the bonanza king. She acquired an interest in the Brown
Palace Hotel, and named him manager. She died at Pasadena,
California, in 1895, still devoted to the man who had proven
himself so unworthy of her love. Had she lived a few years
longer, it is entirely possible that the prophecy of her lawyer,
Judge Steck, might have been fulfilled—"Some day this creature,
Tabor, will lose his fortune and will come whining to Augusta to
help him, and she will help him."

In 1898 Tabor, his huge fortune gone, was appointed post-
master of Denver to save him from starvation. He died the following year—not on the stage of the Tabor Opera House, as
depicted on the motion-picture screen—but in his bed at home.

Baby Doe quarreled violently with her older daughter over
Lillie's marriage to her first cousin, which was not condoned by
her church. Baby Doe was of a deeply religious nature, and even
though she was herself divorced and had married a divorced man
(twice divorced, if the Durango divorce be included) in opposi-

tion to the teachings of her faith, she never saw Lillie but once thereafter.

Baby Doe was nearly forty years old when Tabor died. Her beauty was fading. She was virtually destitute, and with two teen-age daughters her matrimonial prospects were anything but promising. After a few years spent in Denver she went to Leadville, where she lived as a squatter, in poverty and rags, at the once-rich but now played-out Matchless mine. Here, in March, 1935, ten years after the death of Silver Dollar, she was found frozen to death.

(17)

The Happy Dutchman

THE day after district attorney Philip Van Cise's raid on Lou Blonger's million-dollar bunco ring, the Denver *Post* failed to list the name of the leader of the gang of confidence men in its account of the wholesale arrests, but thereafter Blonger's name appeared regularly in the *Post's* stories of the raid and subsequent lengthy trial.

The reason his name was first suppressed and later used was explained a few days later to the reporter who had covered the raids; explained by the genial and pixy-like little Dutchman, Harry H. Tammen, who with Fred G. Bonfils, starting on a shoestring, had built the *Post* into one of the most prosperous newspaper properties in the United States. Tammen was a plain man who didn't mind mingling with the hired help, and on this occasion was lounging on the reporter's typewriter desk.

"You know, son, I'm sure sorry we had to print old Lou's name," he remarked thoughtfully, "but the story got so damn big we simply couldn't hold it out any longer." He paused a moment, finally adding loyally, "My conscience troubles me, because I owe a lot to Lou Blonger. He taught me the most valuable thing I ever learned."

Naturally the reporter asked, "What was that, Mr. Tammen?"

"He taught me how to catch a sucker." The publisher smiled puckishly. "I caught one—and I've still got him." He jerked a thumb toward the office of his partner, Bonfils.

Almost since his birth at Baltimore in 1856 the little Dutchman had been obsessed with a burning ambition to make something of himself. His father was Heye Heinrich Tammen, born in Hanover, Germany, a minor employee of the German consulate at Baltimore. The son was christened Heye Heinrich after his father, but Harry was the nearest his American schoolmates could come to pronouncing his first name, so Harry he became for the rest of his life.

His father died when Harry was only thirteen years old, and the ambitious boy was thrown on his own resources. When he was twenty he married Elizabeth Evans of Baltimore. Two years later the Baltimore city directory listed a Harry H. Tammen as proprietor of a saloon at 352 West Baltimore Street. Another two years and the Tammens were in Chicago, where the Chicago directory listed him as a bartender at the Gardner House.

This was the year the Windsor Hotel had been completed in Denver by the Denver Mansions Co., a corporation owned by English capitalists. The pretentious hostelry was operated under the management of W. H. Billy Bush by a company controlled by Tabor and his son, N. Maxcy Tabor.

Its huge, glittering diamond-dust mirrors were to reflect the images of the West's greatest personages, and some of the nation's greatest. Every guest room boasted its own fireplace, no two alike. The lobby was roofed with stained glass. To foil robbers the safe was built into the wall behind the clerk's desk ten feet from the floor, reached only by means of a ladder. The Windsor still stands, and each year thousands of tourists gaze into the diamond-dust mirrors and admire the luxurious suite once occupied by Senator Tabor and his lovely young second wife, Baby Doe.

All the employees of the new hotel were brought from Chicago in a group. They included Tammen and his wife, who died

in 1890. The 1883 Denver city directory listed the bartender as
Heye H. Tammen, but thereafter he was listed as Harry H.
Tammen.

He served drinks to most of the West's notables, one of whom
confided to him in a befuddled moment that he had just been
thrown out of Mattie Silks's sporting house on Holladay Street.
"But I'm going back," he muttered. "Don't want to be tossed
out again. I'm all bruised up from landing on that stone sidewalk.
I'll give ten dollars to anyone who can guarantee I won't get
any more bruises."

Tammen took the ten dollars, and after the customer had
departed for a second visit to Madame Silks's place, used the
money to buy a rack of hay from a farmer. He overturned the
vehicle so the hay spilled on the sidewalk in front of the Silks
establishment, and drove away satisfied he had saved his friend
from further bruises when Mattie threw him out again.

Ambitious young Tammen had no intention of remaining a
bartender all his life. He was constantly devising schemes to go
into business for himself, but all required capital, which he
lacked. So he set about finding an "angel" to finance him—"catching a sucker," he called it.

C. A. Stuart provided the capital for a partnership in the manu-
facture of mineral inkstands for sale to tourists. They rented a
storeroom adjoining the Windsor Hotel entrance and gradu-
ally developed a prosperous curio business. A few years later
the Tabors and Bush padlocked the door leading from the hotel
lobby into the curio store. Tammen brought suit and gained a
court order requiring them to unlock the door. Today the H. H.
Tammen Curio Company sells its wares throughout the entire
United States and in many countries abroad.

Presently he found a partner for another venture and with
Stanley Wood began publication of a weekly known as *The
Great Divide*. The publishing venture was not successful. In
1889 Wood and Tammen aided in the publication of a book,

Young Konkaput, the King of the Utes, by Thomas Nelson Haskell, a contributor to their weekly.

Meanwhile, Tammen learned that the Denver *Post,* a struggling daily, was about to give up the ghost. Once more he set out to find an angel to finance the purchase of the publication.

He learned that Bonfils, a young ex-West Pointer, had just cleaned up a small fortune operating the Panhandle Townsite Co. at 802 Delaware Street, Kansas City. He sold Bonfils on the possibilities of the publication, and they formed a partnership that lasted a lifetime. With Tammen's sense of showmanship and innate knowledge of mass psychology and Bonfils' drive and business ability, each provided qualities the other lacked.

Tammen liked to belittle his own contribution to one of the nation's most successful newspaper enterprises. He once told the author, "This sheet earned half a million dollars last year, due entirely to Fred's efforts. He made a deal with our paper mills that saved us exactly that amount. Except for Fred's business shrewdness, we wouldn't have made a cent."

Tammen, with his impish sense of humor, loved to torment his humorless partner.

"Fred's the tightest man in the world," he told the author. "Last year I needed some money, and borrowed a thousand dollars from him. He made a note of the loan in a little black loose-leaf notebook he keeps in his desk.

"About a month later, when I thought he'd forgotten about it, I sneaked into his office while he was gone and tore out the leaf containing the record of my loan. Nothing happened, and I thought I'd got away with it. A few days later I looked in the notebook to make sure.

"I found he'd replaced the notation. Hadn't said a word to me, mind you. Well, I tore out the page again. After another month I looked in his notebook and found he'd replaced the page again. Well, I gave up; told him I was licked, and paid him the thousand dollars. Told him I should have known he'd never forget anything involving money, but he couldn't see the joke."

After Tammen and Bonfils bought the Kansas City *Post*, it was customary for each to operate one of the two newspapers for thirty days, and then switch assignments. "Baron" Nelson, owner of the rival Kansas City *Star*, sued them for libel, and a special examiner was sent to Denver to take a deposition from Tammen.

Nelson's attorneys hoped to establish two facts for the court record: First, that although neither Tammen nor Bonfils had actually written the editorial upon which the suit was based, they had directed that it be written and hence were responsible; and second, in the belief that a jury will always "soak" a rich man, they hoped to establish the fact that the defendants were wealthy.

"You and Mr. Bonfils are wealthy men, aren't you?" the Kansas City lawyer asked Tammen.

"I can't speak for Fred," answered the witness amiably, "but I'd say I'm pretty well fixed."

"How well fixed? Please tell the examiner just how wealthy you are."

"Well, that's pretty hard to say."

"But you must have some basis for your assertion, Mr. Tammen. Please tell the examiner what that basis is."

"Sure, sure," agreed the little Dutchman pleasantly. "When I was running my little curio shop I learned to pay my bills on the first of the month and keep out of debt. Anyone who pays his bills on the first of the month and doesn't owe anyone a damned cent is a rich man."

In attempting to establish the responsibility of the two publishers for the editorial on which the suit was based, the lawyer asked:

"Now, Mr. Tammen, when one of you is in Denver and the other in Kansas City it is your practice, isn't it, to exchange lengthy telegrams every day discussing matters of newspaper policy?"

"That's just half true," Tammen replied.

"Half true?" repeated the puzzled lawyer. "Will you kindly explain for the record just what you mean by 'half true'?"

"Well, sir, it's like this. I send those long, long telegrams to Fred, but he never sends any to me."

"And the reason you send them is to discuss matters of policy, is it not?"

"The reason I send 'em," said Tammen, "is because Fred is so damned tight, and I send 'em 'collect' because I get a kick out of thinking how he'll squeal when he has to pay for 'em."

Tammen knew how to play a prank and make the victim like it. He once pulled a fast one on the people of Denver that left them laughing at themselves for years.

Denver had just completed a splendid new municipal auditorium to house the 1908 Democratic national convention. It was the city's pride and joy. A few days before the opening of the convention the *Post* published a story under an eight-column screamer head, telling of the destruction of the auditorium by fire. An eight-column cut showed firemen pouring streams of water on the burning building, from which poured huge columns of black smoke.

The entire page was devoted to a detailed description of the fire. In small body type the last sentence read, "After a thorough investigation, the *Post* has discovered that every word of this story is untrue."

Few readers ever reached the qualifying last sentence. For hours the city was in an uproar. The *Post's* street sales soared. Those who read the pay-off sentence carefully concealed it from their friends. Tammen was shrewdly counting on the quirk of human nature that leads a person who is taken for a sucker to lead his friends to fall for the same gag.

When Bonfils hated anyone, he hated his wife, his children, his aunts, and uncles and cousins and friends. Tammen was somewhat more tolerant. During World War I, when Tammen was in Kansas City, the son of one of the *Post's* most bitter enemies won a commission in the army. It was customary to publish such stories, with photographs, but in this instance the then managing editor, William C. Shepherd, submitted the story and picture to Bonfils for clearance.

"Kill the story," snapped the publisher. "His old man's a so-and-so."

The following day he departed to take over direction of the Kansas City *Post,* and Tammen returned to Denver. Noting the young man's photograph on Shepherd's desk he took it up, studied it, and commented, "A fine-looking, clean-cut young American. Who is he, Shep?"

Shepherd explained that Bonfils had killed the story because the youth was the son of an enemy of the *Post.*

"Sure, the old man's a so-and-so," agreed Tammen. "But why hold that against this grand kid?"

Caught between two bosses, Shepherd could only shrug and repeat, "F. G. killed the story."

"Listen, Shep," said the little Dutchman, "you know how this paper is owned, don't you? Fred owns half and I own half. Well, you run that story in my half!"

The story was published.

One of the *Post's* favorite enemies was William E. Sweet, wealthy investment banker who later became governor. He incurred the enmity of Bonfils by besting him in a bond deal.

At the time Bonfils had just acquired an imposing mansion on Humboldt Street, adjoining Cheesman Park. Tammen wished to build a home in the same neighborhood. The only available site was owned by Sweet and adjoined his mansion across the street from the Bonfils home.

Later, when campaigning for governor, Sweet professed to be a friend of the common man, but at this time he was acutely conscious of class distinctions and his own social eminence. When Tammen phoned him and offered to buy the site, Sweet replied:

"Mr. Tammen, I'll have you understand that this is Denver's finest residential district, and only the best people live here. I don't propose to have an ex-bartender living next to me. The property is not for sale to you at any price."

Tammen liked to boast that he had risen from a humble beginning. In fact, he loved to confound critics of the *Post's* policies by saying, "Well, what can you expect of a so-and-so like me? I'm nothing but an ex-bartender." Actually, he was a soft touch for any worthy cause, and today much of the income from his huge estate goes to Denver's Children's Hospital, which was always close to the heart of the childless and sentimental little Dutchman.

Despite his pride in his rise from the status of bartender, he didn't care to have others rub it in. Sweet's scorn hurt him, but he bided his time and after some months succeeded in buying the property through an intermediary. Knowing Sweet to be utterly lacking in humor, he loved to puncture his dignity by calling him "Willie." So he phoned him again.

"Hiya, Willie. This is Harry Tammen. Thought you'd like to know we're soon to be neighbors. Just by chance I learned you'd sold those lots next to your place, so I bought 'em."

Sweet sighed. "Well, I suppose there's nothing I can do about it, now. But I want you to understand, Mr. Tammen, that only the best people live in this neighborhood, which is subject to the most rigid building restrictions. No one can build anything but the very finest residences here."

"That's the very reason I called you, Willie," said Tammen. "You know Fred and I own the Sells-Floto circus. Being in the circus business, I've got some ideas for a home that will simply knock your eye out!

"Remember our baby elephant that died? I loved that little elephant like a brother, Willie, and I aim to have it reproduced in bronze on a pedestal right in front of your sun-porch windows. The pillars of my veranda are to be of Carrara marble, with carved boa constrictors coiling round 'em.

"And remember that lovely baby gorilla that died? I'm having it cast in bronze with an outstretched paw, for a hitching post. You'll love it, Willie. You'll simply love it!"

Humorless Sweet was almost frantic. "You can't do it," he screamed. "I'll get an injunction against you!"

Actually, Tammen built a tasteful and magnificent home, notable for its exquisite inlaid woodwork installed by a special crew of skilled craftsmen from the Pullman Company.

When Sweet became a candidate for governor, it was only natural that the *Post* opposed him. Wholly inexperienced in politics, he was what is known in political circles as a "fat cat"— a wealthy man willing to spend liberally to further his political ambitions. He was elected in spite of—or perhaps because of— the *Post's* opposition.

It was said of the *Post* that everybody cussed it but everybody read it. In those days it was almost wholly lacking in political influence, and when it won an election it was often a surprise and usually a disappointment to its owners.

Few persons in Denver realized that, as a deliberate circulation-building policy, the *Post* did not want to win elections. It preferred to be against the administration. Its owners theorized that no one buys a newspaper to read paeans in praise of public officials, while thousands will buy it to read of crusades against the politicians. They held that the newspaper that is always raising hell and calling names builds circulation and consequently advertising revenue, while the sheet that is filled with praise of officeholders ultimately dies of dry rot. When the *Post* surprised itself by occasionally winning an election, within a few months it usually turned against its own candidate.

When Sweet took office in 1923, *Post* reporters covering the statehouse were instructed to handle all political matters as "straight news," strictly without bias, so the new governor might have an opportunity to prove himself.

Shortly thereafter Sweet summoned one of the *Post* statehouse reporters to his office for a dressing down.

"That story of yours in yesterday's paper was nothing but a

pack of lies," he charged angrily. "The next time it happens, the *Post* will be barred from the governor's office."

"Were you misquoted?" asked the puzzled reporter, conscious of no error.

The governor astonished the reporter by saying, "Absolutely not. You quoted me exactly, word for word."

"Then," asked the bewildered newsman, "what in the world are you crabbing about?"

"You also quoted the floor leader of the opposition, and everything he said was a lie!" exploded Sweet.

The relieved reporter couldn't repress a chuckle. As a boy he had been one of Sweet's Sunday School pupils at Plymouth Congregational Church, and felt free to give a word of advice.

"Governor, you're new in public life, and you've had no experience in dealing with the press. Every newspaperman will quote you exactly as you wish, even though your statement isn't in line with the policy of his sheet. But when you try to forbid a newspaper to quote someone else, you're biting off more than you can chew."

"We'll see about that," stormed the raging governor. "What I said still goes."

When Tammen and Bonfils were informed of the governor's ultimatum, they issued orders to open up on him again. *Post* reporters were barred from Sweet's office, and he was defeated at the next election.

A departmental editor used his life savings of $10,000 to buy a one-third interest in one of Denver's leading retail clothing stores. A few years later Tammen, noting that his editor seemed to be in low spirits, made a tactful inquiry as to the cause of his depression.

"The clothing business is in bad shape," the employee explained dispiritedly. "My partners want to squeeze me out. They've offered me $2,500 for my $10,000 interest. I'm in a tight place, and I need the money, so I have to sell."

"Hold everything," the little Dutchman advised cheerily as he reached for the phone and called one of the clothing store partners.

"Hello. This is Harry Tammen of the *Post*. One of my boys here has just offered to sell me his one-third interest in your business for $12,500, and I've decided to buy. You know I'm in the circus business, and man, have I got some promotional ideas that'll knock your eyes out! I'll hitch an elephant to the fire plug in front of your joint, and fill your show windows with boa constrictors and monkeys. I'll sure make business boom!"

"But you can't do that!" cried the horrified clothier. "We cater to a high-class clientele, and circus methods would ruin us!"

"Well," said Tammen, winking at his editor, "I've offered $12,500 for his one-third interest, but I don't go a cent higher. If you want to meet my offer, it's all right with me."

Within fifteen minutes the clothing store partners paid the editor $12,500 for the interest they previously had valued at $2,500.

A reporter who had incurred the enmity of a wealthy and politically powerful friend of the *Post* publishers learned that the tycoon was exerting every influence to get him fired. He went to Tammen to present his side of the case.

"Listen, son," said Harry. "When you're working for the *Post* you're always in the right, and no one has influence enough to get you fired."

Next payday the reporter found his salary increased five dollars a week.

Tammen was vacationing in Honolulu when the publishers of the *Post* were cited for contempt of court. Bonfils was found guilty, was fined $5,000 and sentenced to five days in jail—which he never served.

Upon Tammen's return to Denver he was haled into the district court. The evidence was identical with that in the Bonfils case, and there was every reason to believe the sentence would be identical.

"Have you anything to say," the judge asked sternly, "before sentence is passed upon you?"

Tammen's attorney, John T. Bottom, read a lengthy, previously prepared legal statement. Then the little Dutchman lost his temper, leaped to his feet, flung the attorney's stand aside, and shook his fist at the court.

"Listen here, you!" he screamed. "This is nothing but a goddamned cat and dog fight, and you know it, and I know it. You can toss me in jail for twenty years, but by God, I'll get you yet!"

For a moment a pin could have been heard to drop in the courtroom. The judge's face went white. His jaw dropped. Finally he whispered, "Case dismissed."

The *Post's* account of the contempt hearing omitted reference to this passage. Unexplainably, the rival *Times* likewise omitted it. Only the now defunct Denver *Express* published a full account of the proceedings.

A Corsican by descent on his father's side, Bonfils was said to have traced family kinship to Napoleon.

"Fred thinks the spirit of Napoleon comes to him and gives him tips," Tammen once told a *Post* reporter. "He told me he was sitting on the coping of the courthouse grounds in a small Missouri town debating entering the real estate business at Kansas City when Napoleon's spirit first visited him.

"Napoleon told him, 'Listen, Fred. This is your chance to get in on the ground floor and make a lot of dough. Grab it.' He took Napoleon's tip and cleaned up $800,000. After that he never made an important decision without asking Napoleon's advice. Got so Fred and Napoleon were real chummy."

The truth of this yarn is not guaranteed, since it bears the earmarks of an attempt by Tammen to kid his partner about his claim to relationship with the noted Corsican.

Bonfils has been depicted as a hard, cold, driving, utterly vindictive person, and the more human facets of his character have been neglected. No one will believe that he was too softhearted to fire an employee. He, of course, employed only the department heads, but when he wished to get rid of an editor, he would cut his pay in half. The indignant employee would promptly quit—which was precisely what Bonfils wanted; to be in a position to say the employee had left of his own volition.

One editor, his pay thus halved during the depths of the 1929 depression, was unable to find another job. Swallowing his humiliation, he continued to work at half pay for nearly a year, but Bonfils could not muster nerve enough to fire him.

In only one instance was Bonfils known to have fired an executive, and in that case it was a matter of placing him on notice so he fired himself. The employee was in the habit of going on periodical benders, which always wound up in a fist fight with another executive whom he disliked.

Bonfils notified him that the next time he got drunk on duty he could consider himself fired. All went well for some weeks until a Saturday night when he was taken unexpectedly bourbonated and resumed his fist feud.

Sunday morning, considerably hungover, he sat in his home debating his plight while his wife was at church. He had earned an excellent salary but had saved nothing. Now he was an old man, jobless, and the future seemed bleak. Determined to end it all, he wrote a farewell note addressed to his wife, left it on the living room radio, got a pistol, and went to the basement to kill himself.

He seated himself in a chair and, while nerving himself to the point of pulling the trigger, fell asleep. Meanwhile his wife returned, found the farewell note, and dashed to the basement. Finding him slumped in the chair, she leaped at the conclusion he already had killed himself.

Her screams awoke the befuddled husband. Startled, his finger closed convulsively on the trigger. The weapon was discharged and the bullet inflicted a slight flesh wound on his wife's *empennage*. Shocked out of his suicidal impulse, he presently found as good a job as the one he had lost.

Despite the circumstances of his departure from the *Post*, Bonfils remembered him in his will.

During elections it was customary for the *Post* editorial staff to remain on duty all day, all night, and the following morning until the returns were all in and the final edition had gone to press. About five o'clock in the morning, there was usually a lull which permitted a weary worker to snatch an hour or two of sleep stretched out on a table.

The softest sleeping place was the leather couch in the holy of holies, Bonfils' office. Counting on the publisher's habit of appearing at the office promptly at eight-thirty each morning, a dog-tired reporter bedded himself down on the couch at dawn on an election morning.

But this time Bonfils, eager to learn the election returns, appeared much earlier than usual. Discovering the reporter on his couch, he pressed a finger to his lips, whispered, "Take it easy, son. Get a good rest," and tiptoed out.

In later years he was sensitive about his age. A standing rule prohibited anyone being described in the *Post* columns as "aged" unless he was at least five years older than Bonfils.

He was generally regarded as a nonsmoker, although he occasionally smoked a pipe while on a fishing trip. He did, however, enjoy a "secondhand smoke" that gave rise to an astonishing custom.

For some years he retained Volney T. Hoggatt, an immense man built like a gorilla, as a bodyguard and smoke-blower. In the midst of important conferences Bonfils would turn to Hoggatt with the curt order, "Blow," whereupon the bodyguard would blow a cloud of cigar smoke in his employer's face. Bonfils would inhale deeply of the secondhand smoke with evident satisfaction. The command "Blow" would be repeated at intervals of perhaps ten minutes.

Bonfils was deeply attached to his pet poodle and was grief-stricken when the dog died. Hoggatt consoled him with, "But, Fred, you've still got me."

If Harry Tammen caught a sucker when he induced Bonfils to finance the purchase of the *Post*, Bonfils was the most fortunate of suckers, for the deal brought him power, prestige, and riches. It is doubtful if either could have succeeded without the talents of the other. Together they constituted a team that provided a sensational brand of journalism admirably suited to the lusty taste of young and virile Denver.

(18)

The Last of the Penroses*

$\mathbb{A}$ NEW stampede was born when Spencer Penrose, four years out of Harvard, joined the Cripple Creek gold rush in 1891, wearing the riding costume of a dude. All the bearded boys who had failed to strike pay dirt in Poverty Gulch abandoned their sluices and made a rush for the bar of Wolfe's plank hotel to take this soft-spoken young pilgrim. Trimming tenderfeet was more profitable and easier than panning.

Young Spencer was delighted by the evidences of Western hospitality. Everyone seemed eager to buy him drinks. They nicknamed him "Spec." Each was quite willing to let him in on the ground floor of a hot proposition for—well, how much did he happen to have with him?

The callow pilgrim drank their liquor, listened to their high-pressure sales talk, and entered the real estate business with a kindred soul, Charles L. Tutt. Tutt, like young Penrose, came from an old Philadelphia family.

Spec had turned down a job in a bank to seek gold and adventure. He found plenty of adventure, but no gold, in the Yaqui Indian country of Mexico. He was in Las Cruces, New Mexico, when Tutt invited him to Colorado Springs, Colorado. Young

* This chapter originally was published July 25, 1937, as an article by the author in the *Saturday Evening Post*.

Penrose came, decided it was the most beautiful spot he had ever seen, and discovered that the mile-high elevation gave liquor an extra kick. Such a combination seemed almost too good to be true. Just as he settled down to serious cultivation of the delights of this paradise at the eastern base of Pikes Peak, the town was electrified by the news that Bob Womack, a cowpuncher, had discovered gold in Poverty Gulch on the Bennett and Myers ranch, just on yon side of the peak. This was Cripple Creek. Spec, in his dude riding costume, hopped into a buggy and joined the stampede, but halted for refreshments so frequently en route that when he arrived he found every available inch of ground staked out. The whole camp chuckled when the pilgrim real-estaters, Tutt and Penrose, bought the Cash on Delivery claim, across the gulch from the Womack discovery claim.

Spec promptly wired the oldest of his three brothers, Boies Penrose, then a member of the Pennsylvania state senate, offering to let him in on the ground floor of a red-hot proposition for only $10,000. Boies replied, in effect: "Don't be a sucker, kid. Am sending $150 for living expenses."

Without capital to operate their property, the pilgrims leased it to Joe Troy and Pete Burke for $20,000. The lessees sank a new shaft and hit squarely on the apex of one of the best-defined veins in the district. Tutt and Penrose shared in the dividends.

Congress repealed the purchase clause of the Sherman Act in 1893. Colorado, a silver state, was left prostrate. Banks collapsed on every hand. Troy and Burke went panicky. They persuaded Tutt and Penrose to buy back the lease on the C. O. D.

Miners from the demoralized silver camps flocked to Cripple Creek. Within a year, the new gold camp boasted a population of 20,000. Tutt and Penrose sold the C. O. D. to a French syndicate for $300,000. The Frenchmen deepened the shaft and ultimately went bust trying to unwater it.

Meanwhile, Spec had hopped a train for Philadelphia. He planked down $75,000—reputedly in gold coin—on the desk of brother Boies. "Your share of the grubstake," he explained.

"But I didn't stake you!" protested the bewildered Boies. "I refused to advance the ten thousand dollars!"

"You sent me one hundred and fifty dollars, didn't you?" asked Spec. "Well, then!"

The following year brother Boies was elected to the United States Senate.

Now Cripple Creek began to sit up and take notice of the young pilgrim who was beginning to make history both in mining circles and in the kerosene hot spots of the day—or night.

He still wore his dude riding clothes but adopted the broad-brimmed Western hat. Seldom was his voice pitched much above a whisper. He wore his face in the dead-pan style. It was unreadable, but not expressionless. Rather, its expression was always the same—one sardonic eyebrow cocked high and handsome. He stood more than six feet and he could, and did, use his fists.

His famous white horse, Rabbit, could be found nightly hitched at the tie rail in front of the Ironside dancery or Johnny Nolan's place or the Topic theater-saloon-dance hall. Rabbit cultivated a taste for lump sugar soaked in gin.

Young Penrose set a pace few except Charles M. MacNeill, youthful mill owner, could equal. The boom town's most accomplished single-jack drinkers regarded the two with awe. Those were the days when one who bellied up to the bar and demanded less than "a gallon of rye and two fingers of water" was considered a big sissy.

The town boasted almost as many speculatoriums as saloons, but at poker Penrose was a sucker and knew it. He spent money lavishly on entertainment, but in a business deal he was as shrewd as a pawnshop uncle.

In 1894 Penrose and W. H. Leonard were baching in a log cabin. There the so-called Cripple Creek smelter trust was born. Together with Tutt and MacNeill, Penrose built a chlorination mill and set about gaining control of the smelting business of the district.

Within a few years they owned almost every mill in the region, and most of the mines were paying them tribute. Penrose, becoming rich, was a headache to those who once had pegged him as a pilgrim. With his associates he built or bought the Cripple Creek Sampling & Ore Company mill, the National Gold Extraction Company mill at Goldfield, the Standard Milling & Smelting Company mill, and the Colorado-Philadelphia Reduction Company mill at Colorado City, which now is a part of Colorado Springs. They built a famous scenic railroad, the Cripple Creek Short Line, from the gold field to Colorado City.

They had cleaned up millions before the Western Federation of Miners, of which W. D. ("Big Bill") Haywood was secretary, called the strike designed to close all mines shipping ore to the smelter-trust mills.

Friends say Penrose at that time expressed the guiding philosophy of his life as follows:

"Any man who works after noon is a damn fool." Another way of saying, "A time for work and a time for play."

Today he brands this report a libel. In proof he directs attention to the testimony of Harry Orchard at the trial of Haywood for complicity in the bomb murder of former Governor Frank Steunenberg, of Idaho. Orchard had confessed twenty-six murders—mostly in the Cripple Creek region, the dynamiting of the Vindicator mine, and the assassination of Steunenberg. In his published confession he charged Haywood had employed him in his career of terrorism.

Questioned by William E. Borah, then a state senator and special prosecutor in the Haywood case, Orchard admitted he had lain in wait outside the home of MacNeill night after night in an effort to murder, under cover of darkness, the archenemy of the strikers.

"But you didn't kill him, did you?" thundered Clarence Darrow, counsel for the defense. "Why?"

"How could I get a chance at him," complained the witness, "when he and Penrose never rolled in till after daylight?"

From which it may be inferred that Penrose believes one should begin at noon to have a good time—and continue until the following noon.

All through his turbulent, polychromatic career, he has revealed himself a hedonist with one eye on the main chance. He has rolled up an immense fortune, and he has had a gloriously swell time doing it.

He has made mining history. He has helped make presidents. If he has been a playboy whose quips have sometimes left a continent chuckling, he likewise has helped build up two huge industries. None will deny he has made his particular corner of the world a more beautiful place in which to live.

The superintendent of the smelter-trust mill at Florence, Colorado, was gigantic young Daniel C. Jackling, a mining engineer with an idea, but little cash. Jackling went to the Mercur Gold Mines in Utah, where he evolved a plan for the treatment of low-grade porphyry copper ores, bought an option on a low-grade copper property in Bingham Canyon, Utah, and sought to interest the Cripple Creek crowd of mining millionaires.

Included in the party he took to Utah to investigate his proposition were the brilliant MacNeill, the unpredictable Penrose, their partner, Tutt, and Clarence C. Hamlin, a young lawyer recently a member of the Wyoming legislature.

Many yarns are told about the night-long conference on the veranda of the old Knutsford Hotel at Salt Lake City, where the Utah Copper Company, greatest low-grade copper property in North America, was born. They differ in details, but the substance follows:

With every round of drinks, MacNeill, noted for the uncanny accuracy of his snap judgment, became more enthusiastic over Jackling's proposal. At dawn he pledged the first $100,000 of the needed capital.

He pointed out that Penrose had won a $100,000 bet with W. S. Stratton, Cripple Creek gold king, on the election of McKinley, and kidded Penrose into risking his winnings on this new mining deal. Both turned upon Tutt and convinced him Now $300,000 was pledged—enough to launch the venture. Jackling was cut in for a $100,000-stock interest for his option, idea, and experience, Hamlin for an equal amount for his legal ability.

The remaining capitalists were pikers—a term, by the way, born of Zebulon Pike's failure to climb Pikes Peak. They lost the opportunity to participate in an undertaking that proved fabulously profitable.

Again Spec offered to let brother Boies in on the ground floor. This time the senator did not pooh-pooh his kid brother's offer. When Boies died, it was found that his estate consisted of $250,000 in gold coin and stocks in his young brother's mining properties.

Spec interested another brother, R. A. F. Penrose, noted mining engineer, in Utah Copper. Each of the four Penrose brothers —Boies, R. A. F., Dr. Charles B., of Philadelphia, and Spencer— achieved a place in *Who's Who*, it may be said in passing.

Utah Copper stock knocked around the market at next to nothing in the early days. Most of the Cripple Creek crowd would have nothing to do with it.

Here is a yarn told about a business associate concerning the transfer of a good-sized block of the supposedly doubtful stock:

"A friend who had bought Utah Copper on Spec's suggestion remained lukewarm. He was more interested in a Colorado gold-mining venture, in which he tried to interest Penrose.

"The two stocked a Manitou hack with liquor and set out to inspect the mine, far back in the mountains. But they made an error in cutting the driver in on the liquor. The hack overturned, and every bottle was smashed, except one.

"Spec refused to stir another step without refreshments. The friend was in tears at the prospect of losing the Penrose backing. Desperate, he offered to swap his Utah Copper holdings for funds to finance the gold mine.

"Penrose refused. The friend had an inspiration. He offered

to throw in the remaining bottle. This was something else again. The deal was made. Penrose acquired stock that in a few years was worth a fortune in itself."

As it became apparent that the new process was proving successful, the stock began to soar. The organizers had staked everything on their ability to handle 5,000 tons of ore a day—an unheard-of amount at that time. If they could treat this volume successfully, they could earn a profit, they believed.

They surpassed this upset figure. They doubled their goal and quadrupled their profits. They set out to tear down an entire mountain, using steam shovels and trains on stepladder levels. Volume was doubled again, then redoubled.

Finally, the Guggenheims became interested in this vast project that had been started on a shoestring. Utah Copper was merged with Kennecott at a price that left the organizers multimillionaires.

Immediately the same group started all over again. They organized Chino Copper, built it to huge proportions, and sold out to the Guggenheim interests at an immense profit.

A third time they tried—this time with Ray Consolidated—and a third time they cleaned up, although in this instance the profits were measured merely in single millions instead of multiple millions.

Then Jackling conceived the idea he could apply the same process successfully to low-grade gold ores. Alaska Gold was organized, and sold at twenty-five cents a share before it started to sky-rocket. When the stock reached twenty-seven dollars a share, the canny Penrose served notice on the other members of the pool that he was selling out. He advised them to do the same.

The stock zoomed to thirty-five dollars. They gave him the needles for getting cold feet. Then the operators struck a horse—a huge area of barren rock—and the stock collapsed. Later Jackling's process was proved successful, and is being used today. However, so far as the other members of the group were concerned, it was a case of "the operation was a success, but the patient died." They had dropped part of their copper winnings, but Penrose now possessed an immense fortune. His spectacular plunging days were over.

Like his brother Boies, Spencer Penrose was a staunch Republican. Colorado likes to brag that Spec's generous campaign-fund contributions maintained the senator as political dictator of Pennsylvania almost two decades.

Spec placed bets totaling $175,000 on Charles Evans Hughes. On that memorable election night, it will be remembered, early returns indicated the election of Hughes. Spec threw a victory party which will be long remembered, because it lasted on and on and on and on, until the final returns changed it into a consolation party. Hughes lost the election and Spec lost his $175,000, but it was a swell party while it lasted—and man, how it lasted!

Spec Penrose was one of the thirteen Republican leaders in the smoke-filled hotel room where the nomination of Harding was decided upon. In 1928 he boiled over on the Prohibition issue and bolted to Al Smith.

Just prior to the beginning of Prohibition it was rumored Spec had bought a trainload of bonded liquor to last him through the drought. Presently it was noised about that he had stored this immense stock in one of his Cripple Creek mines.

Immediately there was a rush of liquor prospectors that threatened to eclipse the gold stampede of the 90's. The prospectors became so troublesome that it was necessary to place guards about the Penrose mining properties. Which, naturally, appeared to confirm the suspicions.

Then, so goes the story, a group of Colorado's most distinguished bootleggers formed a syndicate to hijack the "million-dollar liquor lode" by buying an adjoining worked-out mine owned by Penrose and drifting through into the supposed hiding place.

When approached, Spec suddenly became coy. He was not a

sentimental man, but he wished to retain this property for old times' sake. But of course, if the price were right—.

The ending seems a little too good to be true, but the syndicate is said to have bought the abandoned property, carried through its plan, and found nothing. The liquor had been stored in a bonded warehouse, to be withdrawn in small quantities—carload lots—as needed.

The befuddled bootleggers were left "holding a sack containing a hole in the ground." One even voiced his resentment in the obviously untrue charge that this was the first time in history a mine had ever been "salted" with a million dollars' worth of liquor.

Leader of the repeal forces in Colorado, Penrose was the target of constant denunciation from the pulpit. Consequently he detests most clergymen.

Penrose has always entertained a sincere dislike for personal publicity. He is flooded with letters whenever his name appears in print. He knows how to handle the blackmail letters, and he ignores the begging letters, but he is utterly bewildered by the poets. He can comprehend why the beauty of the Pikes Peak region inspires visitors to burst into verse. But why, he asks, oh, why must they wish their efforts on him?

His dislike of publicity is no pose. Years ago, the Colorado Springs Evening *Telegraph* was accustomed to print laudatory articles about the city's leading citizen. Despite his protests, invariably he was described as a multimillionaire civic benefactor.

Penrose, MacNeill, and Hamlin bought the newspaper. Next morning Spec walked into the city room and announced:

"The next condemned so-and-so that prints my name in this sheet is fired!"

For years thereafter Penrose's name was barred from his own newspaper. MacNeill died and willed his share to Hamlin, who, in control, thought it a swell joke on his pal to resume the "multimillionaire public benefactor" articles.

Penrose fumed and ranted—he is the only living man who can

rant in a voice scarcely above a whisper—but it required months
of argument to persuade Hamlin. Now the name of Penrose is
handled as straight news, and never, never, never is he described
as a multimillionaire or civic benefactor.

Since the turn of the century he has spent much of his time
abroad. In 1906, at London, he and Mrs. Julie Villiers (Lewis)
McMillan, of Detroit, were married.

Penrose and MacNeill spent $500,000 building the famous
automobile highway to the 14,106-foot summit of Pikes Peak,
and later bought the equally famous cog railroad up the peak.
The highway was operated as a toll road for years, but recently
was turned over to the federal government and now is free. The
annual automobile races up the world's most widely advertised
mountain were originated and sponsored by Penrose.

Some years ago MacNeill occupied the top floor of a Colorado
Springs hotel. When the manager was fired, MacNeill remarked,
"Don't worry, Billy. I'll give you a job."

He found himself with a hotel manager on his payroll and
no hotel to manage. So he and Penrose built a hotel for their
friend to manage, and set out to make it the most beautiful hotel
in the world. This was the beginning of the Broadmoor, upon
which Penrose has spent, and is still spending, millions of dollars.

Maxfield Parrish went into raptures over the Broadmoor and
its gorgeous setting at the base of Pikes Peak. Unknown to Penrose, he painted a picture of the hotel. When Spec returned from
abroad and heard about it, he procured permission to use the
painting to exploit his pet project. It is one of the artist's most
widely known works and has helped make the Broadmoor
known throughout the world.

As a playground for the children, Penrose bought Cheyenne
Mountain, which rises to an elevation of 9,200 feet almost at the
door of the Broadmoor. Upon its slope he established the world's
most elaborate private zoo. Most of the animals he collected
himself, in the course of world tours.

His friend the maharajah of Nagpur, in 1926 presented him with an immense elephant. To the public she was known as the Empress of India, but Penrose and his pals of the Cripple Creek days called the ponderous creature Tessie, in memory of a pink-tighted and buxom dance-hall gal of the camp.

Tessie was to be used as a caddie on the Broadmoor Hotel golf course, but her feet created so many new hazards she finally was assigned to carry children, twelve at a time, up the slope to the zoo.

Recently Penrose noted Tessie perspiring excessively after her climb, so, to spare her further effort, he ordered a railroad built to the zoo. Tessie died before the railroad was completed. She has been replaced by a baby elephant named Shirley Temple.

Penrose believes nothing he has seen in his world travels equals the splendor of a sunrise viewed from the top of Cheyenne Mountain. To make this superb spectacle accessible he built "the ladder to the sky"—a switchback automobile road up the 3,000-foot almost sheer granite face of the mountain. The road cost $500,000. Penrose declares he'll get more than half a million dollars' worth of fun out of it.

In 1920 he staged at the Broadmoor what newspapers tagged "the Arabian Nights Party," the most costly affair of its kind ever held. He brought thirty-two guests from the Atlantic seaboard on special cars for a week-long jamboree. After the first night of the party he routed out his astonished guests before daylight to show them the sunrise.

At seventy-two Penrose swims and rides daily and is still a skilled boxer. A few years ago a burglar invaded his home in the Hotel Miramare, Genoa. Penrose beat him to ribbons. Taking pity on his plight, he helped him escape police by tossing him out the window, twenty-four feet from the ground.

In 1927 newspapers announced the ramshackle old log cabin where the second Colorado territorial legislature met in 1862, at Colorado City, was to be torn down. Histories reveal that the majority members lured the minority into a wagon with a keg of whisky and kidnaped them, taking them to Denver and there establishing the permanent seat of the state government. Penrose bought the log capitol building and removed it to the Broadmoor grounds.

When Colorado is not laughing with or at Penrose, it is applauding or cursing him, but it will never understand him. Friends say no one will ever get behind that dead-pan expression with the sardonic cocked eyebrow, to discover the real Penrose. Mrs. Penrose concurs.

But ask him if his passion for the beautiful is the result of boyhood yearning to become an artist, and the poker pan vanishes and he blushes as he denies the charge, shy and self-conscious as a school-girl.

He detests being called a prominent citizen. If you must label him, call him a sportsman. He is exquisitely but almost inaudibly profane. Like Boies Penrose, he possesses the gift of whiplash sarcasm. Yet he is a woeful orator.

Business associates say his predominating characteristic is his keen, cold intellect. Friends say he is a dreamer who puts up a front of cynicism. All agree he possesses a fantastic sense of humor.

Recently he ordered photographs of one of the most magnificent of his building projects. The best shot revealed, in the foreground, two standard, government-type outhouses of the kind known in the Nice Nellie days of Cripple Creek as necessaries.

"Of course," explained the artist, "we can paint them out."

"Paint 'em out?" protested Penrose indignantly. "Have you no soul? The Government designed 'em, and I dedicated 'em to President Roosevelt!"

The New Deal has replaced Prohibition as his favorite hatred.

"Roosevelt helped us replace Prohibition," he declares in what he maintains is the first direct quotation he has ever authorized for publication. "Except for that, I am against everything he ever did, or ever will do."

He dislikes those who whisper in his presence. He detests dial telephones, which he cannot master. He distrusts New York capitalists because they ruined his pal, MacNeill, and because they trimmed Dave Moffat, who made a fortune in Cripple Creek and lost it in an attempt to build a railroad over the Rockies, counting on the verbal pledge of assistance from Wall Street financiers.

This line, known as the Moffat Road, instead of climbing over the continental divide, now burrows beneath it, passing through the seven-mile Moffat tunnel.

Penrose warned MacNeill against "the New York crowd."

"Stick with the Guggenheims," he advised. "They're not only smart but they're honest. Which is more than you can say of the Wall Street highbinders."

But MacNeill was confident in his snap judgment. It had never failed him yet. A few years later he dropped $8,000,000 in one day, his friends say, and died shortly thereafter.

Colorado mining camps have made many millionaires. Tabor made a fabulous fortune and lost it within a few years. Moffat, who entered the banking field to add to his mining fortune, ultimately went broke. MacNeill was taken to the cleaner's. Canny Spec Penrose is one of the few to keep what he made in mining, and add to it through investments in other fields.

For years the Broadmoor has claimed his first interest. At the slightest excuse he will burst into a panegyric on Colorado scenery and climate. He is a member of more than two dozen clubs, including some of the most exclusive in Paris, New York, and Philadelphia, but his favorite is the Cooking Club. With five other Cripple Creek gold kings, he organized it years ago. Its one aim is conviviality.

At the annual meeting, they say, the member last to go under the table is elected president for the ensuing year. Spec has been president since its organization.

The Cooking Club, which is housed in a building on the slope of Cheyenne Mountain, now includes many of the millionaire

colony at the Broadmoor. It has entertained many celebrated
guests.

Penrose was a friend and admirer of Will Rogers, a frequent
visitor at the Broadmoor. The story is told that he called Rogers
to a window during a thunderstorm, promising to show him an
unforgettable spectacle. Clouds rolling down the slope of Cheyenne Mountain parted on either side of a promontory, which
projected above them like a rocky island in a billowing sea.
Abruptly the sun broke through above Pikes Peak. The pink
granite crag jutting up through the clouds was spotlighted in
blazing sunlight. Rogers was speechless.

Immediately after the airplane crash that ended the life of
the humorist-philosopher, his friend Penrose began construction
of the Will Rogers Shrine of the Sun on this granite buttress of
Cheyenne Mountain.

It is a hundred-foot spire, built to last 1,000 years. Five thousand cubic yards of pink granite were quarried from a single
boulder for its walls. With glasses one can look from its top into
the westernmost end of Rogers' native state of Oklahoma, 150
miles away. It cost a fortune to build—how much, Penrose will
not reveal.

The shrine will contain an immense bronze bust of Rogers by
Jo Davidson. Interior walls bear frescoes by Randall Davey,
Santa Fe artist, depicting phases of life in the Pikes Peak region
from the earliest days: the discovery of gold at Cripple Creek
by Bob Womack; the interior of a saloon, dance hall, and
gambling establishment; and an exterior of the frame shack occupied by Tutt and Penrose, with big shots of the boom days in
the foreground.

Spencer Penrose died December 7, 1939 and his ashes were
placed in a crypt in the Will Rogers Memorial on Cheyenne
Mountain. Penrose deeded the promontory to a perpetual-care
association which he named the End of the Trail Association.

BOOK FOUR

Scarlet Lady

(19)

Mattie Get Your Gun

THIS is the story of lovely Mattie Silks, the fastest woman in all the West, and her knight in tarnished armor, Corteze D. Thomson, who tried hard to be the fastest man.

It deals also with their bizarre friends, their extraordinary contemporaries, and their strange bedfellows.

It begins with an account of the only known formal pistol duel ever fought between women. This duel was fought on the night of August 25, 1877, in the Olympic Gardens at Denver. The principals were Mattie Silks and Katie Fulton. Feminine marksmanship being what it is, Mattie missed Katie, and Katie missed Mattie, but Cort was shot in the neck.

Denver was proudly a "wide open" town. That is the reason Mattie Silks chose Denver for the practice of her profession. It is among the reasons why foot racer Cort Thomson, the "handsome-made" man, cherishing the delusion he was an accomplished gambler, became a resident of the Queen City of the Mountain and Plain. However, the compelling reason Cort was a Denverite was because Mattie Silks was making money hand over fist, the twenty-dollar gold pieces burned a hole through the coin pocket of her de Medici frock, and he could always depend on her to make good his losses at faro bank.

Twenty-nine years old in 1877, Mattie looked like a vest-pocket edition of lovely Lily Langtry. Her eyes sparkled, blue, challenging, impudent. With her clear and creamy complexion she scorned to use rouge. There was a gold-dust sheen to her blond curls, piled atop her head in the fashionable Langtry hair-do. Her full underlip projected just enough to give an impression of petulance and impudence and daring.

Though not receding, her chin was delicate, and the flesh beneath it slanted down at an angle that left the merest suggestion of frogginess. At her throat she wore a cross of blazing diamonds.

Slightly under medium height for a woman, in her early days Mattie inclined to soft plumpness. She bought her clothing in Kansas City shops, and if her taste bordered a bit on the lurid, her apparel was always in the latest fashion and very, very expensive.

All her dresses were made with two pockets. The pocket on the left was for gold coins—Denver was a "hard money" town. Mattie used to say, "the sweetest music in all the world is the jingle of gold coins," recalls Charley Nolan, in 1950 proprietor of Jiggs' Buffet, Eighteenth and Larimer streets, Denver. In the other pocket she carried a pistol with an ivory grip. Cort had bought it for her—with her money. She claimed Wild Bill Hickok had taught her marksmanship when he was marshal of Abilene in '71 and she was operating the principal sporting house in that rip-roaring frontier cow town. She thought herself a better shot than she really was.

Mattie was an accomplished hell-raiser. She loved life, enjoyed every minute of it, and drank nothing but champagne, according to her former Negro maid, Hattie Green, who was still living in Denver in 1950.

She was just beginning to build up her famous stable of racing horses. She had an unfortunate passion for playing the races—horse and human.

Her laugh was low and throaty, and most of the time she was

laughing, but when it was necessary she would be steel-hard with everyone but Cort. Cort was her man.

Cort was a year younger than Mattie and in those days not a great deal larger. He was a Texan, his talk slurred with a soft Southern accent. He claimed that, while still in his mid-teens, he had served with the James and Younger boys in Quantrell's guerrillas during the closing year of the Civil War. While with Quantrell he had learned to carry two pistols in twin holsters sewed inside his hip pockets.

Like most foot racers, Cort was lithe and slender and, when he wanted to be, lightning fast in his movements. He told a friend, Will Toner of Wray, Colorado, that he had acquired his speed as a boy "running down wild turkeys in Texas." He boasted that he won his foot races because he was a "fast starter."

"I always gain a head start of twenty feet because my first jump is twenty feet long," he bragged.

Cort's hair was a sandy blond. In his twenties he wore his off-pink mustache in tight, twin bartender upcurls. He was a sporty dresser, writes Judge Irving L. Barber of Yuma County in his reminiscences, and he walked with a swagger, arms slightly akimbo.

Cort was a proud man, too proud to work. "In the South, where I come from, nobody works but niggers," he explained. He won a little money foot racing, lost a lot gambling, and most of his life preserved what he believed to be the workless status of a Southern gentleman by living on Mattie Silks's earnings.

Stripped for racing, he was a sight to set any woman's pulse aflutter. He wore pink tights and star-spangled blue running trunks. Across the breast of his quarter-sleeve striped racing jersey were pinned rows of gold medals, some won legitimately.

He trained rigorously on the choicest bourbon. Perchance for this reason, or possibly because an athlete reaches his prime in his late twenties, Cort was beginning to slow down slightly when, on the afternoon of August 24, 1877, he raced the noted Sam Doherty in a 125-yard winner-take-all match at the Denver fair grounds. Among the spectators were Mattie Silks, who had bet $2,000 on Cort, and Katie Fulton.

Somewhat younger than Mattie, Katie was one of the lesser madames of Holladay Street and an ardent admirer of the sandy-haired young ex-guerrilla athlete. She operated a house at 449 Holladay Street. At that time, Mattie's establishment was at 501 Holladay.

Cort Thomson shaded Sam Doherty by a nose, touching off prolonged home-town alcoholic rejoicing among Denver's sporting element. Mattie, coin pocket weighted down with her winnings, invited all present to be her guests at an evening champagne victory jubilee at the Olympic Gardens.

Sometimes called the Denver Gardens, the resort was a beer garden operated by George Bartholomew and owned by the Denver Brewing Company. Opened in 1872, it was situated on the west bank of the South Platte River, near what today is the west end of Denver's Colfax-Larimer viaduct. At that time the river marked the western limits of the city, so Mattie's victory celebration—perhaps with the law in mind—was to be staged just beyond the boundary limiting the jurisdiction of the Denver police. The Gardens included a pavilion, a grove of cottonwood trees, a museum of freaks, a museum of Rocky Mountain ores, and a zoo of Rocky Mountain beasts. Like the modern night club, it entertained its guests with a variety show.

All the elite of pioneer Denver's sporting world were Mattie's guests; monte throwers, short-card artists, faro-bank buckers, chuck-a-luck sharps, cappers and shills and shell men; many of the sports and rounders and speculators from the Central City and Blackhawk and Georgetown mining camps; all the leading Holladay Street madames—including Katie Fulton—and their gentlemen friends; rakehells and rascals and renegades.

Belle Siddons, the Civil War spy, who operated in Denver under the name of Madame Vestal, had just departed from booming Deadwood, confident there was more gold in them thar Black Hills. But the guest list included many other outstanding tenderloin personages. There was Minnie Clifford of 451 Holladay Street; Lizzie Preston, cigar-smoking Anna Gouldie Gould, Belle Bernard, Gussie Grant, Jennie Caylor, Belle Jewell, May Smith, Anna Guy, Minnie Palmer, Clara Hayden, and Emma Lewis.

Exotic Jennie Rogers with her emerald earrings had not yet come to Denver to challenge Mattie's supremacy as queen of the courtesans. Nor had college educated Verona Baldwin, ex-paramour of millionaire Lucky Baldwin. Nor had Lillis Lovell, mistress of the silver camp of Creede, nor Rosa Lee, Faye Stanley, Annie Ryan, or Leona de Camp. But it is reasonably certain that every madame of Denver's thriving Holladay Street drank Mattie's champagne that night.

Posterity has been denied details of what quite possibly was one of the wildest parties ever staged in one of the wildest eras of one of the pioneer West's wildest towns. The Rocky Mountain *News*, August 26, 1877, confined itself largely to blistering criticism of the authorities for their failure to curb such goings-on.

Both Mattie and Katie had been setting their caps for the handsome, swaggering foot racer and former Quantrell guerrilla. What touched off the pistol duel between the green-eyed scarlet ladies must remain a matter of conjecture. Possibly Katie was paying too much attention to Cort to suit her hostess, Mattie. Or perhaps Cort was paying too much attention to Katie. It was quite within character for reckless Mattie, who cherished the delusion that she was a crack shot, to force the pistol duel on Katie.

The belligerent damsels were out for blood, even though it is highly probable that the menfolk felt that neither was sufficiently skilled with firearms to hit the broad side of the Rockies. The broad side of the Rockies, snow-capped and glistening in the moonlight, lay only a few miles to the west, stretching from snowy Long's Peak eighty miles northwest to snowy Pikes Peak eighty miles south.

Mattie selected Cort as her second. Katie chose bearded Sam

Thatcher, a gambler. While the coyotes in the zoo howled mournfully and were answered by their wild kin on the highlands to the west, the party adjourned from the pavilion to the cottonwood grove on the bank of the Platte, where thirty paces were stepped off, formally and probably solemnly.

Since the assemblage included the outstanding figures in the sporting fraternity, it is likely that someone was making book on the outcome; someone like Tinhorn Bill Crooks, the diamond biter.

The pistol-packing madames were marched to their respective positions, and at the count of three turned and fired. A scream of pain splintered the August night. Cort Thomson fell to the ground. Blood spurted from between his fingers as he clutched at the back of his neck. Mattie pocketed her pistol with the ivory grip and knelt by his side, dabbing at his wound with her lace kerchief.

In its account of Denver's—and perhaps the world's—first formal pistol duel between women, the morning paper, the Rocky Mountain *News*, waxed bitterly indignant. The city's fair name had been sullied. The newspaper demanded an end to such disgraceful revels but pointed out that municipal law-enforcement authorities were powerless to act, since the duel had been fought just outside the city limits. It called upon the Denver Brewery, owner of the Olympic Gardens, to prevent a repetition of the duel.

After a doctor had patched up the flesh wound in Cort's neck Mattie hired a hack and took him back across the wooden bridge to his bachelor chambers on the second floor at 403 Larimer Street, on gamblers' row, just around the corner and a block away from Mattie's Holladay Street establishment.

Had jealous Katie Fulton, convinced that her attachment for the swaggering young foot racer was hopeless, deliberately aimed at Cort instead of at Mattie? Had she sought to kill him so her rival couldn't have him?

For four decades the question was good for an argument anywhere in Denver's underworld. The patrons of Ed Chase's temple of speculation said it was a five-to-one shot that Katie aimed at Mattie and winged Cort by mistake.

Resenting this reflection on feminine marksmanship, the young ladies of the commercial boudoirs generally held to the opinion that Katie all along intended to shoot Cort.

He survived to become, along with Mattie, a principal in a years-long tempestuous love affair that put to shame the fabled amours of Frankie and Johnny.

(20)

Scarlet Sister Mattie

AT the close of the Civil War Springfield, Illinois, a city of 17,364, was in the grip of war-born inflation, but the high cost of living was less remarkable than the cost of high living. It was a community where "crime found safe refuge," and it was accustomed to rowdiness and brawls among soldiers.

"The street walks and corners were so infested by gay and flashing damsels, brazen-faced courtesans and their parasites, that the newspapers set up a howl of protest," writes Arthur C. Cole in the *Centennial History of Illinois*.

"In 1865 matters came to a climax when the soldiers were being mustered out at Springfield. The city was so 'overrun with blacklegs, burglars, garroters, and harlots (male and female) who have congregated to rob the soldiers . . . of their hard-earned wages that General John Cook detached two additional companies to act as a provost guard.' "

Among the "gay and flashing damsels" was Martha A. Silks. Only nineteen years old, already the young sophisticate was "madame" of a notorious "boardinghouse for young ladies," according to the story she later told Denver friends.

Virtually nothing is known of Mattie's girlhood. For a time,

she lived in a small town in Indiana, according to the story she
told her Negro maid, Hattie Green, and members of her family
were unaware that she had dedicated herself to pursuit of the
oldest profession.

Friends believe that Mattie in her early teens is shown in an
unidentified family group photograph found under the floor of
a house at 1942 Market Street when it was being converted into
a warehouse in the summer of 1948. The premises had been
owned and occupied by Mattie after the turn of the century.

The picture shows a group of seven, ostensibly the parents and
their children, three girls and two boys. The plump, blond
mother bears a striking resemblance to Mattie as she appeared
in later years, and might be of Bavarian descent. The father with
piercing eyes and a severe expression might have been a Prussian.
In one of the older daughters, a girl of perhaps fourteen, friends
profess to see Mattie's petulant mouth, impudent eyes, delicate
chin, and froggy throat.

Like most women of her calling, she was reluctant to talk
about her family. Upon crossing the Missouri on their way to the
frontier West, real names customarily were left behind by the
bad men—and bad women.

"I never was a prostitute," she liked to tell her Negro maid.
"Except for a brief period when I was in the freighting business,
I was a madame from the time I was nineteen years old, in
Springfield. I never worked for another madame. The girls who
work for me are prostitutes, but I am and always have been, a
madame." She was inordinately proud of this fine class distinction.

After leaving Springfield, Mattie, at one time, operated a
sporting house at Olathe, Kansas. In fact, say those who later
lived near the Colorado ranch where she kept her racing stable,
she was "run out of Olathe." She spent her winters at Kansas
City, and devoted her summers to working the boom towns.

Olathe, county seat of Johnson county, had been sacked by

the Quantrell gang in September, 1862, along with the adjoining
towns of Spring Hill and Squiresville.

In his autobiography, *Cow by the Tail* (Houghton Mifflin
Co., 1943), Jesse James Benton describes a boyhood adventure
in Olathe at the time Mattie operated her parlor house in that
place.

> I walked up to the dance hall and looked in. What a
> sight to anyone, the prettiest gals from all over the
> world, dressed like a million dollars, was all there. If
> you did not come in to dance, they would grab you
> and pull you in, whether you wanted to dance or not.
> All the girls acted glad to see you. Round after round of
> drinks, then all hands would dance.

Could it have been Mattie Silks's establishment that seemed
so glamorous to the emigrant boy?

Westward expansion of the railroads in the sixties and seventies gave birth to some of the toughest frontier boom towns
known to history. Known as railroad "end towns," each of these
lawless, turbulent frontier communities in turn marked the spot
"where rails end and trails begin." In turn each marked the
shipping point for hundreds of thousands of cattle driven north
from Texas over the famed Chisholm and other cattle trails.

Abilene and Hays City were the principal hell-roaring end
towns as the Kansas Pacific Railroad was built westward from
Junction City, across Kansas into Colorado. Dodge City, "cowboy capital of the West," was the outstanding Kansas boom
town on the Santa Fe.

Craving excitement and always seeking locations where
money was plentiful and freely spent, Mattie operated houses in
all three of these boom towns, her neighbors of later years say.
Still in her twenties, she probably was the youngest madame on
the frontier.

Each spring, just before the arrival of the first longhorn herds
from Texas, these towns were invaded by a horde of desper-

adoes, gamblers, saloonkeepers, and filles de joie, mostly from the underworlds of St. Louis, Kansas City, and Memphis.

One of Mattie's most intimate friends, then and for many years after, was a leading Kansas City madame. At the beginning of her professional career, Mattie in all probability was financed by and was operating branch houses for this Kansas City courtesan.

Abilene originally was a station on the Overland stage line. It reached its zenith as a shipping point on the Texas cattle trails after the Kansas Pacific Railroad was extended west from Junction City in the spring of '67.

Consisting before the coming of the railroad of a dozen log cabins on Mud Creek near the Smoky Hill River, it soon blossomed into a rip-roaring frontier cow town and railroad end town.

When Abilene was still a cluster of log cabins it was served by a single saloon, known as "Old Man Jones's place." Within a short time after the coming of the railroad, it boasted thirty-two licensed saloons.

Chief of these was the Alamo. Inside its three double glass doors such rugged frontier characters as Wes Hardin, Ben and Billy Thompson, Phil Coe, and the Clements boys—and perhaps lovely young Mattie Silks, the vest-pocket edition of Lily Langtry—made merry and played poker, faro, chuck-a-luck, and Spanish monte. Orchestras played day and night. The walls were decorated with nudes in imitation of the work of the Venetian Renaissance painters.

The Alamo was the favorite gathering place of the wealthy Texas cattlemen. The hundred-room Drovers' Cottage was their favorite hotel. Trail hands preferred the Applejack Saloon; the Bull's Head, operated by Phil Coe and Ben Thompson, and the other lesser saloons. "Tanglefoot" whisky sold at fifty cents a drink. Champagne brought twelve dollars a bottle.

By common consent the settlement of all personal quarrels arising on the trail from Texas was postponed until the cattle drive ended. Arrival of a trail herd at the Great Western stockyards frequently was the occasion for settlement, by gunplay, of feuds begun on the trail. Boot Hill cemetery literally was the end of the trail for many a Texas cowhand who died facing the blazing muzzle of a "Navy," as the Colt Navy revolver of that day was known. The trail hands spent their time and their wages in the saloons, the gambling houses, and the maisons de joie, seldom ending their sprees until they were broke—or dead.

The town's leading parlor house dominated a principal corner on Texas Street, across from the schoolhouse. Since it was the policy of Mattie Silks to operate the leading sporting house wherever she established herself, it is possible and even probable that she at one time was the madame of this house, catering chiefly to the cattle owners.

The trail hands sought entertainment and relaxation in the red-light district, restricted to a colony of some twenty rambling frame buildings a mile north of the railroad tracks. Each of these buildings contained from ten to fifteen rooms, indicating the presence of from 200 to 300 girls.

Tom Smith, a hard hombre from Kit Carson, Colorado, was the first town marshal. Tough as he was, Tom was a man of character, modest, strong, and efficient. Only as a last resort did he use his gun. His pay was $150 a month, plus two dollars for each conviction.

When the town built a jail the cowboys promptly tore it down. When it was rebuilt they dedicated it with a jail delivery, freeing the first prisoner. Abilene was rugged. Lovely Mattie Silks was in her element.

While attempting to make an arrest in 1870 Tom Smith was killed. As his successor the town fathers employed six-foot, long-haired J. B. Wild Bill Hickok. Fearless, attractive Wild Bill, who wore an embroidered sash, drew $150 a month plus twenty-five per cent of all fines. He was overly quick on the trigger, played favorites, and permitted lawlessness when it did not interfere with his own interests.

If true that he taught Mattie how to shoot, her duel with

Katie Fulton was no credit to his tutelage. Hickok departed from Abilene after shooting and mortally wounding Phil Coe in the Bull's Head saloon.

The Abilene boom burst in 1872 when members of the Farmers' Protective Association, indignant because the great Texas trail herds were swarming over their lands, adopted a resolution asking the cattlemen to kindly take their business elsewhere. They did—to Hays City and Dodge City.

This period marked Mattie's only departure from her chosen profession. Later she told many friends that at one time she had engaged in the freighting business, financing and accompanying a shipment of a wagon train of merchandise from St. Joseph to Denver. The nature of her merchandise, and the possibility that she was accompanied by a number of her girl boarders, must remain a matter of speculation.

The first railroad reached Denver in 1870, virtually ending long-distance freighting by wagon, which indicates Mattie's freighting venture was undertaken before that year. Subsequent litigation to which she was a party fixes the year of her first visit to Denver as 1869.

At the time of her freighting venture she was still in her early twenties, and the plains were still infested with hostile Indians. If she took the Republican River trail to Denver instead of the Platte River route, she passed within a few miles of the ranch she was to own in later years, near the spot where the boundary between Kansas and Nebraska ends at the Colorado line.

In its earliest days Denver's commercial boudoir area lay on the south side of Cherry Creek facing the spot on the north bank where Denver's gray stone City Hall Building was to be erected. It has been replaced by a modern Municipal Building facing the Civic Center. Several blocks distant on the north side of the creek stood a stable, originally owned by the Leavenworth City & Pikes Peak Express Company. In later years this was to be the site of Denver's most magnificent sporting house, a place famed for its glittering parlor of mirrors, owned and operated by Mattie Silks.

The cream of the profits from the Pikes Peak gold rush had been skimmed away by earlier arrivals, but the end towns in Kansas were still on the boom.

Presently Mattie was setting up shop at Hays City. It was much like Abilene, and populated largely by the same boomers. Every other building was a saloon or sporting house. The principal parlor house displayed a sign, "GENERAL OUTFITTING." Ablaze with light throughout the night, the Santa Fe was the leading saloon and gambling resort, where the roistering cowboy could lose his money at keno, poker, *rouge-et-noir*, or horsehead. In 1867 Hays boasted twenty-one saloons, three dance halls, one grocery and one clothing store. The proportion had not changed materially by the time of Mattie's arrival.

Here she again encountered Wild Bill Hickok, who killed five men at Hays while acting sheriff of Ellis County. He made his headquarters at Tommy Drum's saloon, where the town's first church service was conducted in 1873 by the Reverend Leonard Bell, Methodist minister. Drum's place became the headquarters of Generals Sheridan and Custer and of Buffalo Bill Cody.

Women as well as men carried guns in Hays, and occasionally used them. An exception was Poker Alice, a skilled gambler but a rather mild character compared to others of her sex.

It is likely that Mattie spent only her summers in the Kansas boom towns, returning to Kansas City or possibly Denver for the winter. It is known that during these years she was in Chicago, for it was there she met Cort Thomson. He was matched against one of the leading sprinters of the Central West. She liked the looks of the sandy-haired young Texan and placed a sizable bet on him. Cort won.

"She won so much cash that the only way she could carry it was by lifting her skirt as if it were an apron and letting the stake holders pour it in," Cort later told "Gyp" Shafer, one of the cowpunchers on Mattie's ranch. "She looked like a wash lady carrying a bundle of laundry."

At the close of the Civil War the band of guerrillas operating along the Kansas-Missouri border under Charles W. Quantrell, alias Charles Hart, disbanded and scattered through Texas, Oklahoma, Kansas, and other Western states. Quantrell had been killed in Kentucky shortly before the end of the war. Some, like Frank and Jesse James and the Younger boys, took to the outlaw trail.

Swashbuckling Cort Thomson, the "handsome-made" man, who packed his two guns in specially tailored hip pockets and was too proud to work, was capitalizing on his prowess as a foot racer and aspired to win quick riches by gambling. Already he was one of the wise gamblers who played nothing but faro, considered to be the one gambling game that could not be braced, or fixed. The wise players shunned the brace games.

Neighbors of their later years say the meeting of Cort and Mattie was a case of love at first sight. The fact that Cort was married and the father of an infant daughter in no way interfered with their torrid romance.

From Cort's viewpoint there may have been other considerations. Mattie was rolling in money and, being soft of heart in matters concerning Cort, was always good for a touch when his luck ran out on him at faro bank. To his credit, it may be said that he always promised to repay her loans, and was quite generous with her money, always spending part of it on her. To her dying day she thought of Cort as her knight in shining armor, and was strangely blind to the smudges of dirt, the tarnish, and the streaks of rust with which that armor became defiled.

It is doubtful if he accompanied Mattie when the Hays boom burst, and she moved on to Dodge City. At about this time he departed for San Francisco, where the pickings were said to be rich, indeed.

On the Santa Fe Railroad, Dodge City was a major cattle-shipping point for a decade. Texas longhorns milling in the corrals and loading pens kept the town in a constant cloud of dust. Front Street reeked with the odor of buffalo hides stacked in front of the trading posts which were, naturally, less numerous than the saloons, gambling halls, and sporting houses. In '72, the first year after the coming of the railroad, fourteen men were killed in gun fights and twice as many were wounded.

Jack Bridges was the town's first marshal. Succeeding marshals included Billy Brooks, Ed Masterson, Wyatt Earp, Billy Tilghman, Ben Daniels, "Mysterious Dave" Mathers, T. C. Nixon, Luke Short, Charley Bassett, and the Sughrue brothers. Bat Masterson, who wore a pearl-gray derby and a diamond scarf pin, served as sheriff, but not until after Mattie had departed for the bonanza towns of the Pikes Peak gold region. Pals of Bat at Dodge City included Lou Blonger, who became Denver's underworld czar, and his brother, Sam, who always wore blue glasses.

Marshal Ed Masterson, Bat's brother, was killed in the Lone Star dance hall while battling a group led by Bob Shaw. Later Bat killed four of the men he considered responsible for his brother's death, according to the story Bat told "Colonel" W. S. (Billy) Thompson, Denver bartender and a close friend.

Wyatt Earp, whose reputation has been greatly exaggerated, was a gunman and gambler, generally considered to be merely an outlaw operating under the protection of a badge. He preferred to team up with his brothers, Virgil and Jim, and with "Doc" Holliday, the dentist-gunman-gambler. After the Dodge City boom subsided, the Earps transferred their activities to Tombstone, Arizona, where they served as city marshal, deputy sheriff, and United States marshal.

Eastern newspapers called Dodge City "The Wickedest City in America." Robert M. Wright, in his book, *Dodge City* (Wichita *Eagle* Press, 1913), described the wild end town as follows:

Her principal business is polygamy without the sanction of religion, her code of morals is the honor of thieves, and decency she knows not.

Her virtue is prostitution and her beverage is whisky. She is a merry town and the only visible means of support of a great many of her citizens is jocularity. No restriction is placed on licentiousness. The town is full of prostitutes and every other place is a brothel.

Its citizens boasted that "all they raised around Dodge City is cattle and hell."

Doc Holliday, a native of Charleston, who contracted tuberculosis and went West for his health, was one of the delightful characters of Dodge City. He was a dentist, an immaculate dresser, a deadly gunman, and a genius at cards. He died in Colorado "without his boots on."

Another was the Honorable Skunk Johnson, lawyer, preacher, farmer, and blacksmith, who, on the day he prepared to take the state bar examinations, crossed the path of a polecat with the unfortunate result that he was arrested by Bat Masterson and ordered to leave town until the atmosphere cleared. He was widely known in later years and highly respected, but never lived down the name of the Honorable Skunk Johnson.

Nothing in Dodge City cost less than twenty-five cents. The town's first jail was a well fifteen feet deep, for drunks. The north side of the railroad tracks was kept respectable, but there was no law south of the tracks. Gambling ranged from games of five-cent chuck-a-luck to thousand-dollar poker pots.

In the hot spots of this "Beautiful, Bibulous Babylon of the Frontier" could be found "nice men with white neckties, the cattle dealer with his good clothes, the sport with his well-turned fingers, smooth tongue, and artistically twisted mustache. The mayor, cigar in a corner of his mouth, but talking to one side, indulges in the giddy dance with the girls." Dodge City was a paradise for gamblers, cutthroats, and girls.

Acting Assistant Town Marshal Brooks shot yardmaster Browne through the head over a girl named Captain Drew. The girl and Browne lived at the Dodge House, the principal hotel during the winter of '72. Browne recovered.

As a protection against fire, barrels of water were kept on porch roofs and street corners. Cowboys coming into town were required to check their guns at the Wright & Beverly Store.

A cattleman, considering himself insulted by the mayor on a drinking party, shot up his house. His honor was absent, but Miss Dora Hand, an actress who chanced to be occupying his bed, was killed. Sheriff Bat Masterson, with a posse including Earp, Bassett, and Tilghman, took out after the cattleman, wounded him, and placed him under arrest. He lived to kill several other persons, and finally himself became a victim of "lead poisoning."

Tappan's store was the headquarters for Wild Bill Hickok, California Joe, Apache Bill, and Bill Wilson. Other noted characters were Cherokee Bill, Prairie Dog Dave, Fat Jack, Cockeyed Frank, and Dutch Henry.

A noted resort was the Lady Gay Theater and dance hall. Here it was customary to "try" tenderfeet for imagined offenses. A pilgrim wearing the fashionable linen duster of the day was certain to find its tails set afire by some practical joker, doubtless the progenitor of the perpetrator of the modern hot foot.

A medicine-show "doctor" rented the Lady Gay Theater to make his pitch. The cowboys shot it up and the lecturer fainted from fright. Believing him dead, a narcotic addict, who accumulated dream money by robbing drunks and corpses he chanced to find on the street, set about rolling the distinguished doctor. When the "corpse" suddenly came to life, it was the drug addict who fainted from fright.

Lap jacket was the favorite contest of the freighters. Standing toe to toe, they would lash each other with their bull whips until one quit or passed out.

Doc Holliday sold a gold brick to a Leadville businessman. Later a confederate, posing as a government agent, staged a fake arrest aboard a train, charged the victim with possessing "a counterfeit gold brick," and extorted an additional $15,000 from him.

In 1875 Mattie Silks shook the alkali dust of Dodge City from her dainty slippers and moved to Georgetown, Colorado. The only dust in this mining camp was gold dust, which was all right with Mattie.

(21)

Knight in Tarnished Armor

FIRST Mattie Silks and then the railroad came to Georgetown. Tall, dark, magnetic George W. Silks, a professional gambler with cavernous eyes and marvelous longhorn mustaches, was already a resident. After San Francisco adopted its antigambling laws in '73 handsome, young Cort Thomson found it expedient to depart from the coast city, and since he could always "borrow" a fresh stake from Mattie, he too, showed up in the mountain-rimmed Colorado mining camp. She operated one of the five parlor houses on Brownell Street, center of Georgetown's red-light district.

In 1859 the red-haired Georgia mule skinner, John H. Gregory, washed four dollars worth of "color" from his pan and touched off the Pikes Peak gold rush.

Actually the discovery was nearly one hundred miles from Pikes Peak, but the entire region then was known as "the Pikes Peak country." The news spread like wildfire. Presently thousands of excited gold-seekers were hurrying across the plains by covered wagon, on horseback, even afoot.

In the forefront of the stampede were as many expecting to ning gold and without growing calluses working a "Long Tom." accumulate secondhand riches without soiling their hands pan-

These were the desperadoes, the gunmen, the short-card artists, the gamblers, the saloonkeepers, the ladies devoid of virtue. With a few notable exceptions these camp followers ultimately accumulated the lion's share of the gold dust from the new diggings, sometimes by the devious method of "subtraction, division, and silence."

Nearby Central City and Blackhawk boomed into prominence as center of "the Richest Square Mile on Earth." Ores from the sluices and mines of "the Little Kingdom of Gilpin" poured their riches into frontier Denver, forty miles away at the eastern base of the mountains.

The gold fever was epidemic. Fortunes were being sluiced from the sandbars and later blasted from the mines. Gold was the source of everyone's prosperity. Gold enriched the miner, poured into the greedy fingers of those who preyed upon him. One thought was uppermost in every mind—gold, gold, gold!

George F. and D. T. Griffith, brothers, had panned the sands of Spanish bar, but luck wasn't with them. A few years later, searching for the mother lode, they followed the "float" up a nearby tributary of Clear Creek. One sample that assayed only a trace of gold proved to be rich in silver. And so the Griffith lode proved that gold was not the only precious metal to be found in the gulches of the Pikes Peak country.

The boom town of Georgetown came into being almost overnight when the new stampede began in 1865. Nearby Silver Plume was born of another stampede in 1870. The famous Pelican and Dives mines produced fortunes for their owners and fortunes for the lawyers who handled their endless litigations. Wealthy Jacob Snider, Denver banker and one of the principal owners of the Pelican, was murdered by desperado Jack Bishop in '75.

One of Georgetown's few brick buildings was the Hotel de Paris, built by an eccentric Frenchman who called himself Louis Dupuy, but whose real name was Adolphus Francis Gerard. After squandering an inheritance of $50,000, he joined the

United States Army as a cook, deserted, changed his name, and went to work in the Georgetown mines where he was horribly mutilated by a delayed shot. He was a misogynist until he fell in love, after which he wrote his inamorata a series of love letters that are considered masterpieces. He possessed one of the finest libraries in the West, claimed to be an anarchist, refused to pay his taxes, and got away with it. He died of pneumonia in 1900. The Hotel de Paris, which still stands, was operated for many years as a tourist resort.

Most of the business houses and dwellings in Georgetown were built of logs or of lumber sawed on the spot from the thick timber on the mountainsides. They were little better than fire-traps. In '74 fire virtually destroyed neighboring Central City.

Consequently the local volunteer fire department was always of the utmost civic importance. Only the huskiest and fleetest of foot were recruited to draw the two-wheeled hose carts, hooks, and pumpers. Races between the volunteer fire department crews of the frontier mining towns were frequent and spirited. Every holiday celebration was marked by a race between these fire laddies.

As a sideline to his gambling activities Cort Thomson became a member and trainer of a Georgetown volunteer fire depart-ment crew.

At an earlier date, H. H. Honoré, father of Mrs. Potter Palmer, owned a half interest in a mill at Central City. Palmer was the multimillionaire Chicago department store and real estate tycoon. He and Mrs. Palmer were leaders in New York, Newport, and Chicago society. The trails of Mattie Silks and the Potter Palmers were soon to cross in as zany an episode as ever graced the pages of the most lurid Western fiction.

In 1860-61 George W. Pullman was operating a mill at the junction of Russell and Leavenworth gulches. He lived in a log cabin and rode an old mule. He soon departed for Chicago and later invented the Pullman-car berth, inspired, according to an unauthenticated story, by the hinged bunk in his Colorado cabin, which folded against the wall.

Georgetown lay in a narrow valley between towering mountain walls. At best it could never be anything more than a small mountain town. More and more the miners sought diversion in Denver. Already a metropolis of some 25,000 population, the Queen City of the Mountain and Plains could not be strangled by mountain walls. Foreseeing Denver's promising future, Mattie left Georgetown flat in the spring of '76.

Cort Thomson and George Silks either accompanied or followed her to Denver. Most of the city's gamblers lived in the block adjoining the Holladay Street tenderloin. Here, a stone's throw from Mattie's parlor house, both Cort and George occupied rooms.

Some years earlier gold had been discovered in California Gulch, on the headwaters of the Arkansas. But it was not until the rich carbonate strike of '78 and '79 that the fabulous Leadville boom began at about the time the Central City-Blackhawk-Georgetown mines were beginning to play out.

George Silks joined the Leadville rush. In 1881 he became cashier of the famous Board of Trade Saloon, one of the three leading gambling places. It specialized in stud poker.

On May 8, 1882, the Rocky Mountain *News* published the following item:

> A LEADVILLE OFFICER IS LOOKING FOR MR. SILKS, WHO LEFT THAT PLACE UNDER A CLOUD. MR. SILKS, IT IS AFFIRMED, COULD BE FOUND JUST NOW IN NEW MEXICO.

So George W. Silks passed out of the life of Mattie Silks forever. Were the two ever man and wife? Possibly, although the preponderance of evidence indicates the contrary. Friends say Mattie was known as "Madame Silks" in her Kansas days, long before she ever met George Silks. They say she assumed the name merely because of her predilection for wearing garments of silk.

The early-day records, such as they are, reveal no evidence of their marriage or divorce, or of Silks's death. He seems to have vanished into thin air and cuts no further figure in the strange life story of Mattie. A George Silks operated a gambling establishment in Colorado's San Luis Valley, dealt faro at Pueblo, and as late as 1902 was following the same calling at Albuquerque, but he was blond and fat, unlike the lean, dark Leadville gambler.

For a short time after Mattie came to Denver to stay, she operated a rented establishment on Holladay Street near the corner of F, now Fifteenth, Street. Presently, she bought the property at 501 Holladay, which she was to occupy for some years.

It was the first of several houses she was to occupy on The Row, the rallying place of the wicked and unholy. Later, she acquired several additional Holladay Street houses which she rented to other madames.

Denver was on the eve of its third mining boom. The first, following on the heels of the discovery at Gregory Diggings, was based on placer mining. The gold that could be panned or sluiced from the streams was speedily washed out, and the first boom subsided.

The hills were full of gold-bearing quartz, but with the crude refining methods of the day only a small proportion of the gold could be recovered from the quartz. Crude Mexican drag-stone mills called *arrastres* proved sadly inefficient.

Construction of the Boston & Colorado smelter at Blackhawk marked the beginning of a new era, for its improved methods made possible the recovery of a far greater amount of gold from the refractory ore. Riches began to pour in from the mines—and there was no income tax. Mattie reached Denver shortly before the discoveries at Leadville brought the wealth of the mines again pouring into the city.

A few weeks before her famous duel with Katie Fulton, Mattie first broke into the Denver news columns. The Rocky Mountain *News* of March 28, 1877, reports:

MADAME SILKS WAS FINED $12 FOR DRUNKENNESS, AND
PAID IT LIKE A LITTLE WOMAN. SHE OUGHT TO PLAY IT
FINER WHEN SHE GETS ON A SPREE.

In 1879 she borrowed twenty-five dollars from Emma Lewis.
When Emma suggested repayment, Mattie flew into a rage and
beat her with a parasol, inflicting inconsiderable injuries to
Emma's arm.

Emma brought suit against Mattie in the Arapahoe County
Court and won her case. Mattie appealed, lost, and was compelled to repay the loan, plus interest.

She paid A. W. Waters & Company $14,000 in cash for her first
Holladay Street property. To accommodate her carriage clientele she built a $3,000 carriage shed in the rear of her place.

In 1880 she bought a home at 2635 Lawrence Street, then in the
heart of a fashionable residence district. She began to buy the
string of twenty-two race horses that was to make her a leader in
regional horse-racing circles.

By this time she was recognized as Queen of the Red-light
District. On January 15, 1880, she sold a small Holladay Street
house to tall, brunette, personable Leah J. Fries, who used the
professional name of Jennie Rogers.

At the time Mattie dueled Katie and Cort was shot in the neck
he was a foot racer willing to meet all comers.

The volunteer fire departments were producing scores of fleet
runners. Of necessity every town possessed at least one crew of
volunteer firemen. The fastest man on each crew competed with
the best other departments could offer at county fairs and state
meets.

Before he came to Denver with Mattie, Cort was the best man
of the Silver Queen volunteers at Georgetown. During the
seventies and eighties foot racing was more popular than horse
racing in the mountain and plains states. The races attracted huge
crowds, willing to back their favorites with hard cash and plenty

of it. Mattie won—and lost—many thousands backing her man Cort.

He first broke into print in Georgetown in 1875 as one of the horsemen in a lance-tilting contest. His mount was named Corteze.

After achieving a local reputation as a sprinter while a member of the Silver Queen volunteer fire department, Cort was challenged to a fifty-yard foot race in 1876 by a stranger named Gilbert, for a bet of $200. The race was staged on Argentine Street near Church's mill. After Cort lost, the stranger was recognized as "a Mr. Crandall, of Niles, Michigan, one of the best runners in the Union, who, under the name of Wallace, had 'scooped' Colorado Springs." The *Miner* commented that "Mr. Thomson is a handsome-made man and a good runner."

Cort challenged Tony Garry to a race on July 15, 1876, for $300 and the championship of Clear Creek County. By "post time" the purse had been upped to $1,000, and $4,000 in additional bets were wagered on the outcome. This time Cort won by eighteen inches—and the chances are good that Mattie Silks cleaned up in the betting.

On November 19, 1880, he lost a race at Greeley, Colorado, for a $250 side bet. The newspapers described him as "late of California." Shortly afterward he won a thousand-dollar purse at the Denver fair grounds. On March 26, 1881, he won another thousand-dollar stake.

Meanwhile he turned promoter. The following August he promoted a race in the Denver fair grounds for a $1,000 purse and $9,000 in side bets. He placed $2,000 on the racer he himself had trained. Contemporary newspaper accounts report that an additional $3,000 was bet on Cort's choice by "a woman of the demimonde."

This time there was no champagne victory celebration. Cort's runner lost. Someone disappeared with the stakes and the "take." Cort was jailed. Mattie bailed him out. He was her man.

Following are excerpts from the sports news of 1882:

January 9. Thomson, who lost the recent foot race at Leadville, has been arrested through the complaint of the Carbonate Camp sports, whom his alleged sell fleeced out of $2,000.

January 30. Campbell, the Leadville runner, won close to $1,000 on his recent foot race with C. D. Thomson, and is consequently "flush."

February 20. C. D. Thomson is in training for next Saturday afternoon's race with Kittleman, of Kansas. The distance is sixty yards. Considerable money is staked on the outcome.

February 27. The Thomson-Kittleman foot race for a purse of $1,000, to have been held at Pueblo yesterday, was postponed by consent until Campbell of Leadville is in condition to run, as Thomson may put him in the race instead of running himself.

June 26. C. D. Thomson is now manager for Wood Thompson, the Hugo Trade Wind.

Himself a victim of a "ringer" at Georgetown, it was not long before fleet-footed Cort found this was the surest way to easy money, and presently he, too, was racing as a ringer in rigged matches.

Foot races of the period were frequently "rigged." Teamed with a confederate, some runners made more money trimming the home-town suckers than they made in the widely publicized match meets.

Using an assumed name and dressed in working clothes, a runner drifted into a small town, began boasting of his prowess, finally challenged the local champion.

"All I've got is twenty-five dollars," he'd say, "but I'm willing to lay that on myself, even Steven."

All the local sports turned out to witness the race. Of course the local runner won by a wide margin. The loser burst into tears.

"I'd saved up that twenty-five dollars to get married on," he'd sob. "Now I haven't got a dime. Will somebody lend me two bits to buy a square meal?"

This was the cue for the confederate to do his stuff. "I just got into town last night and I don't know either runner from Adam, but this young stranger did his damnedest, and I'm willing to give him a dollar so he can eat." He'd pat him on the back condescendingly and begin to feel of his arm and leg muscles.

"Why, this kid's a born athlete!" he'd exclaim. "No wonder he lost, wearing these brogans and ditch-camp overalls! Give him running shoes and trunks and a head start of three paces, and he'd stand a good chance to win. I hate to see him lose his girl because he's dead broke, so I'm willing to help him win back his twenty-five dollars. How about another match?"

To build up the odds, the confederate permitted himself to be argued out of the advantage of a head start. Confident that they were betting on a sure thing, the local sports would lay their last dollar on the home-town boy—and oddly enough, the lone backer of the loser of the first match always had plenty of cash to cover their bets. The outcome was, of course, a foregone conclusion. The ringer and his confederate split their winnings and moved on to greener fields.

At one time the flying start was preferred, as in horse races. When a standing start was used, it was actually a standing start—the runners did not crouch with their knuckles on the ground, as do modern sprinters. The starter always turned his back on the runners when he fired his gun.

"Silverheels" was the nickname of a noted Eastern runner, who later became a justice of the United States Supreme Court. According to one report, Colorado's Mount Silverheels was named in his honor by a group of his admirers. More commonly accepted is the story that it was named after a legendary courtesan who risked her life to nurse the residents of the mining camp at Buckskin Joe through a smallpox epidemic. Variations of the Silverheels legend have been attributed to many mining camps in the Rockies and the Klondike, and each may have some factual basis, for all women served as volunteer nurses during epidemics.

The popularity of foot racing began to decline when horse-drawn equipment replaced the hand-drawn hooks and pumpers of the volunteer fire departments. Bicycle racing presently became a more popular sport.

Long before this shift in popular favor Cort Thomson began to fade from the picture as a runner, perhaps because his early youth was fading, perhaps because of his habit of training on bourbon. For a few years he was a promoter, until his many arrests led the sporting fraternity to take a dim view of his activities.

But he possessed other sources of revenue. He "bucked the tiger" in McAvoy and Dale's gambling saloon on the floor above Murphy's Exchange Saloon at 403 Larimer Street. When he won he was flush, and when he lost he could always tap Mattie for another stake. He was a lavish spender, whether the money was his own or Mattie's.

When short of cash he had a weakness for riding his horse up the steps of Mattie's Holladay Street house and through the front door.

"Money!" he'd demand arrogantly, whipping forth a pistol and pointing it toward the crystal chandelier. "Cash money—shower down or I'll shoot up the joint and wreck the ballroom floor!"

It was never necessary for Cort to shoot or to ruin the floor with the sharp caulks of his horse's shoes. His little pleasantry was always good for all the gold Mattie carried in her coin pocket. Why shouldn't she shower down? He was her man.

Cort's favorite hangout was Murphy's Exchange Saloon at 1617 Larimer Street, known as "the Slaughterhouse" because of its many killings. Its walls were covered with mirrors, its floors with velvet carpets, its fixtures with silver plate. Its proprietor was Johnny Murphy, who lost seven thousand dollars in 1881 betting on foot-racer McComb to beat Floyd.

"Cort Thomson was an unusually handsome fellow, slightly under medium height," says Colonel W. S. Billy Thompson, of Denver, former bartender at the Exchange; "he was what you'd call a 'swell' dresser—the best of everything, trim and neat, and not much jewelry.

"Because of the similarity of our names he always called me 'Cousin Bill.' When he was sober you couldn't want to meet a pleasanter fellow, but when he wasn't, it was time to look a little bit out. He could be poison mean.

"One night when Cort had a few too many George Watrous, the head bartender, tried to give him the bum's rush. Cort reached for his hip. I knew he carried two pistols in his hip pockets, so I grabbed him from behind and said to George, 'Get behind the bar and let me handle this. Cort will do what I say, because we're cousins. Aren't we, Cort?'

"Cort said, 'Sure, Cousin Bill,' I took him outside and called a hack and sent him home."

Murphy's Exchange was headquarters for the California Gang, so-called because it was made up largely of gamblers run out of San Francisco in '73.

(22)

Wide, Wide Open Spaces

DURING his prime as a foot racer Cort had basked in the adulation of the admirers of his athletic prowess. As a former member of Quantrell's guerrillas he had enjoyed a reputation as a two-gun man, feared and even respected. All this was understandingly stimulating to his ego and contributory to his swagger.

But once his racing days were o'er, so was this pleasant aura of adulation. His foot-racing promotional activities so often led him to jail that his reputation suffered sadly, even among those of the sporting fraternity. The once-dashing athlete and Quantrell raider was becoming known merely as a cheap crook, and not overly bright at that.

He found it comparatively easy to maintain his workless status as a Southern gentleman, for softhearted Mattie was more than generous with the gold pieces that found their way into the coin pocket of her de Medici gown. He was living with her at her Lawrence Street home without benefit of clergy, for the wife he had deserted would not agree to a divorce. Since her infancy he had never laid eyes on his daughter and was startled when he learned she had married in her late teens.

More and more Cort turned to gambling in an effort to boost

his sagging ego, but he lacked the mental acuity to become a proficient gambler. When he made a killing, he always bought Mattie a diamond or a fur, or perhaps a horse to add to her racing stable, and spent the rest on a bender.

When he lost, he could always "borrow" a fresh stake from Mattie. He kept a record of these borrowings, which subsequent court records indicate totaled from $45,000 to $50,000 within a few years, and always promised to pay them back when he could afford it. In the beginning it is probable that he had every intention of keeping these promises. As a matter of fact, he liked to cite the incident of the diamond cross as evidence of his good faith.

Originally the cross that Mattie wore at her throat contained but a single jewel. Cort's repeated "borrowings" had bled her of her ready cash, so while she slept he "borrowed" the cross and pledged it at a Larimer Street pawn store as security for a loan.

With this fresh stake his luck turned and he won and won and won. He failed to redeem Mattie's cross, but with a portion of his winnings he replaced it with the cross of blazing diamonds that she wore until the day of her death.

To Mattie the gift evidenced a touching bit of sentiment on Cort's part. Of course, she had been the source of the stake upon which his winnings were based, but aside from this inconsequential fact, the money he had paid for the magnificent gift had been his own. That was the reason she so cherished the cross, for every other gift he had made her had been paid for with her own money.

The "wise" boys and girls of Cort's social circle always held that one man's money is as good as another's. Yet every now and then he encountered a nonunderworld gambler who refused to sit at the same table with him, and there were many who refused to drink with him.

Ruled by a rigid caste system, the underworld includes those who would cheerfully slit a throat or crack a safe or skin a sucker, but who would not dream of associating with a man who lives off the earnings of a woman.

Seeking to buy a drink in a Curtis Street saloon, Cort was told contemptuously by the bartender, "This is a respectable place. We don't cater to the likes of you. Go back to Holladay Street and your women, you pimp!"

Cherishing the delusion that he was living the workless life of a Southern gentleman, Cort became increasingly aware of these social distinctions. In respectable bars and restaurants where he was known he found himself *déclassé;* his activities were restricted more and more to the underworld establishments of Holladay and Larimer streets.

A sensitive soul, he sought escape in alcohol. A modern psychologist would relish the study of his record as a case history of the steady development of an inferiority complex.

A woman of Mattie's profession is subject to much more rigid class distinctions. And yet, in a way, they troubled her less than they did Cort. Having once taken the step across the border of respectability, a woman realizes it is virtually impossible to regain her lost status and resigns herself to the inevitable.

Unlike Cort, Mattie had been born to no tradition of aristocratic pretensions. In choosing her professional career, she had nothing to lose but her reputation, and a great deal of cash to gain. To her simple way of thinking she was just born lucky.

While not wholly satisfied with her lot, as she confided to friends in later years, she was not of the temperament to brood. Rather, she made the best of a bargain into which she had entered with open eyes. She had plenty of money to spend on her racing stable and on her man. In her own way she was enjoying life. No one ever heard her complain.

In Denver, where they were known, Cort and Mattie found themselves prisoners of convention, rigidly restricted to their own substratum of society. But elsewhere, where they were not known—ah! That's where travel promised escape for both. And so, as was the case with so many madames and their males, they made frequent trips together—to California, to Kansas City, to Hot Springs, to Chicago, and New York, and even to London.

These trips permitted Cort to recapture something of the illusion of life as a gentleman. Not as a Southern gentleman, for he always posed as a prosperous Colorado mining operator. In the role of his wife, Mattie gloried in the attention attracted by her soft Lily Langtry type of beauty, set off by glittering diamonds and the most costly apparel. But at best, these periods of escape necessarily were but temporary. There was no permanent escape for them from Holladay Street.

On the morning of July 2, 1884, Cort received a telegram telling of the death of his wife.

Now he and Mattie were free to become man and wife, legally and with benefit of clergy. The arrangements offered inducements for both. To Cort marriage meant he would have a legal claim upon the fortune she was accumulating. Marriage would wipe out his financial debt to her. No longer would he be forced to "borrow" from her to meet his gambling debts. He could lawfully claim a share of her assets as his own. It is doubtful if any emotional considerations governed his decision in favor of wedlock.

Not so with Mattie. She loved her man deeply, devotedly, and was blind to the tarnish with which the shining armor was becoming dimmed. Moreover, marriage implied a certain degree of respectability. After all, it was not every man who would bestow his name upon a woman of her profession. But Cort was kind, Cort was considerate, Cort was generous.

Two days later they departed for Peru, Indiana. On July 5 they obtained a marriage license in Miami County. The following day they were married by the Reverend H. W. Daniel at the home of W. A. Gibney.

Why did they choose the little Indiana town for their wedding? Because they wished to keep it secret? Or because Mattie wished to impress someone—possibly friends of her childhood, friends who may have predicted she would come to no good

end, friends who perhaps had suspected something of her mode
of life in the years since she had left home?

And yet, there is no actual evidence to indicate that Peru was
her childhood home.

Knowing the pretense put up by Cort and Mattie on their
travels, it is safe to assume that the wedding guests were led to
believe that the dapper bridegroom was a prosperous Colorado
mining operator. Certainly the bridal couple would have put up
an imposing front. Thirty-six years old at the time, Mattie was
still a remarkably attractive woman, and her soft loveliness must
have been set off by a most expensive bridal costume. A year
younger, Cort was but a trifle heavier than in his racing days,
and still was regarded as very much of a dandy.

Less than two years later, the lives of Cort and Mattie, now
Mr. and Mrs. C. D. Thomson, were changed by the receipt of
another telegram.

"It's about my daughter," Cort reported soberly as he studied
the yellow telegraph blank. "She's dead. Died in childbirth."

He was not greatly affected, for he had not laid eyes on his
daughter since she was an infant. So far as he was concerned,
the emotional impact was much less than the economic problem the message posed.

Mattie asked, "How about the baby?"

"The baby?" repeated Cort blankly. "Oh! The kid's father
has pulled out, and there are no living kinfolk—except me. The
neighbors have the gall to ask me what I'm going to do about
supporting the kid." He glanced at the telegram again, and
added, "It's a girl."

"Well," inquired Mattie curiously. "What are you going to
do?"

Irritably he demanded, "What can I do? Put her in an orphan
asylum, I reckon. I'm going to see a lawyer. I don't see how
they can make me pay for her keep. I'm only her granddaddy.
Her daddy's people ought to do the paying."

"There's one thing sure," observed Mattie, toying with the

diamond engagement ring Cort had bought her. "You can't bring her here, Cort." She couldn't repress a smile as she pictured Cort caring for an infant child. "Holladay Street is no place to bring up a kid. Especially a girl."

"They can put her in an orphan home, but they can't make me pay. Why, I've never even seen the brat!"

"After all," mused Mattie, studiously regarding her wedding ring, "an orphan asylum is no place to raise a kid, Cort. Half the girls on Holladay Street are from orphans' homes. Give her a break. She's your own flesh and blood."

"Give her a break? How?"

"A farm is the place to raise a kid, Cort. Farm kids grow up healthy. They grow up clean." She paused long enough to breathe a little sigh. "She's got to grow up on a farm, Cort."

"How you talk!" He was puffing his cigar furiously. "You know I can't afford to pay for her keep on a farm. Besides, why should I—"

Mattie was laughing at him now. "Go buy a farm, Cort. I'll pay for it. We've got to give that tike a break. By the way— what's her name?"

Cort shrugged. "Telegram doesn't say. Listen, Mattie. You really mean that I should—"

"My racing stable is getting so big, I really need a place to keep my horses." Mattie's air was quite businesslike. "Besides, it would do you good to live on a farm. You're drinking too much."

So, to provide a suitable environment for rearing the grandchild of her husband—child of his child by another woman, an infant she had never seen, whose name she didn't know—the Scarlet Lady of Holladay Street put up the money for a purchase of land that was to have a decided bearing on her life, and Cort's.

Why? Because the telegram had aroused a starved maternal instinct? Because she hoped Cort could be induced to live in the open, and abandon his drinking and gambling? Or because she hoped the child would prove a bond between them?

Their marriage had failed to draw them closer together. The underworld grapevine had brought to Mattie rumors about Cort and a henna-haired young Holladay Street wench named Lillie Dab. Would the presence of the child bind him closer to Mattie, lead him to forget Lillie? If he made his home on a farm, would the wench drift out of his life?

She faced the same problem Augusta Tabor had faced in striving to hold her man. She succeeded where the wife of the bonanza king failed, probably because she was the one who held the family purse strings.

Doubtless Mattie's proposal brought Cort visions of a Southern plantation, where the idle master could recline on the veranda sipping juleps. But the raw pioneer West was no region of lush plantations. The nearest approach were the cattle ranches.

Cort could settle for that. He would become a cattle baron. The prospect stiffened his flabby ego. No longer would he be a creature scorned for living off the earnings of a woman. He would become a cattleman, a personage, a respected leader in the community. His feeling of inferiority vanished as he permitted his imagination to run riot.

But all his adult life Cort had lived in an underworld atmosphere where legitimate enterprise was regarded with scorn. His world was peopled by two groups—the suckers and those who preyed upon the suckers. Characteristically he could not bring himself to consider an enterprise that would yield him an honest living.

Only suckers work. It was inconceivable that he should turn a hand to honest toil. No, he would become a cattle baron, all right—but there were means by which a smooth operator could get rich quick at this range racket.

In the seventies and early eighties, when the lush grass ranges were free to the first comer, vast herds of cattle were trailed northward from Texas into Wyoming and Montana. These decades saw the rise of the cattle kings, marked the golden age of the cattle business.

First of the region's cattle kings was John Wesley Iliff, a graduate of Delaware College, Ohio, who turned down his father's offer of a $7,500 farm to seek adventure and fortune in the Indian country. Reaching Colorado in '59 he discovered that, while it was true that in this new country there was gold from the grass roots down, it was equally true that lush profits were to be had from the grass roots up.

By the early seventies he had parlayed a $500 stake into a sizable fortune. The 50,000 cattle bearing his *Backward L. F. Connected* brand ranged over northeastern Colorado and parts of Wyoming and Nebraska on lands inhabited by the warlike Kiowas, Comanches, and Ogallala Sioux. His brand originally was the trail brand of a Texas herd brought north by Captain D. H. Snyder.

Iliff owned nine ranches in three states. He could ride for a week over his tristate cattle kingdom, sleeping each night at a different Iliff ranch. The devout cattle king used no liquor, carried no gun, but was a middling good man with his fists. After taking a terrific beating at the hands of an enemy he shook hands with the victor, slaughtered a steer, carved two steaks from the carcass, and applied them to his moused eyes.

At the close of the Civil War steers weighing from 600 to 800 pounds could be bought in Texas for from three to six dollars each. Every summer Iliff would pay from eleven to fifteen dollars a head for from 10,000 to 15,000 of these trailed-in longhorns. After double-wintering them on the 65,000 acres of lush grassland under his control he sold them, principally to Indian agencies and army posts, for from thirty to thirty-seven dollars a head. Animals bred from his Iowa and Illinois shorthorns brought from thirty-eight to fifty dollars.

Iliff made his home on Wildcat Creek in northeastern Colorado. He was only forty-eight years old when he died in 1878. Captain Snyder rebought his brand from the estate, and the Iliff cattle empire was broken up into smaller holdings. Members of the cattle king's family founded and partially endowed the Iliff School of Theology, Denver. Some of the Iliff lands were bought by English capitalists, who were investing heavily in American mining, railroad and livestock enterprises. English capital was behind the $500,000 *See-Bar-See* Land & Cattle Company, incorporated December 10, 1884.

The searing drought of '86, followed by an Arctic winter that left the ranges strewn with bleached bones and destroyed up to sixty per cent of all the cattle in the region marked a new epoch. It was possible to walk from Wray, Colorado, to Haigler, Nebraska, on the carcasses of frozen cattle, according to one account of the "big freeze." Many cattlemen literally were frozen out.

The *See-Bar-See* Company rounded up and sold the remnants of its herds and went into the real estate business. Some of its range was broken up into small farm units and sold to settlers. Wray, which in 1885 had been nothing but a section house and a frame depot on the Burlington & Missouri, now the Chicago, Burlington and Quincy Railroad, was surveyed by the company as a townsite. On the Colorado-Nebraska border the name of the station known as *See-Bar-See* was changed to Laird, after Congressman James Laird of Nebraska.

The company employed "locaters" to sell farm tracts to the settlers who swarmed into the country. The choicest locations were on the flatlands south of Wray—where the descendants of the early settlers were destined to reap fortunes from wheat acreage during and after World War II. North of Wray lay a desolate sand-hill section, where buffalo still could be found in dwindling numbers.

On a spring day after the big freeze, buffalo hunters Kellogg and Cole had just brought a load of buffalo meat to Haigler, Nebraska, which is only a mile north of the Kansas boundary and some six miles east of the Colorado line. There was little demand for the meat, which was threatened with spoilage.

The two buffalo hunters were seated at a lunch counter, bemoaning their luck to C. M. Webster, then a liveryman at a Haigler stable and today a prosperous retail grocer of Wray.

"Reckon I'll go back to our buffalo camp and spend the summer," Cole remarked glumly. "Got a nice pond and a patch of wild grass for my horses, and I can eat buffalo meat and it won't cost me a dime to live."

"Just a moment, Mister," broke in a customer straddling an adjoining stool. "I'll give you a hundred dollars if you'll take me to that place." Plainly the stranger was a city man, for his face was city-white, and he wore a pearl-gray derby canted on one side of his head and a vest embroidered with Texas bluebonnets. His expressionless eyes were blue, and his sandy mustache hung straight down over his lips. He said his name was Corteze Thomson.

(23)

Pigs' Feet and Whisky

THAT was how I met Cort," said Webster sixty-three years later. "At the time I didn't know he was a gambler. I had never heard of Mattie Silks. I didn't know he was Mattie's man, nor that the one hundred dollars he offered to pay was Mattie's money."

The buffalo hunter omitted explaining that the best farming land lay well to the south. If this city fellow wanted to pay a hundred dollars for a buffalo wallow, that was his own lookout. They packed food sufficient for two days, for there were no roads across the sand hills, and twenty miles a day was good mileage in Webster's rig, fighting sand and sagebrush.

"When we stopped for lunch, we discovered we'd left our food behind us," Webster said. "But toward evening Cole shot a buffalo, and we managed to get along on unsalted buffalo meat for two days."

Cort said he expected to run a few cattle and raise race horses. The patch of grass surrounding the pond at the buffalo camp would provide grazing for only a few head, but in those days few questions were asked of strangers. Fewer were answered.

Cort made casual inquiry about his neighbors and their cattle brands. He learned that the buffalo pond was only two miles

from the Nebraska border, and fifteen miles from the Kansas
border. He filed a homestead claim on the apparently worthless
land, and later bought two adjoining tracts—paying for them
with Mattie's money but recording the property in his own
name. He carted in materials from Haigler and built a frame
ranch house that was much more pretentious than the ordinary
homesteader's shack. Later he added an adobe ell, used as a
kitchen. For miles around his was the only ranch house with a
basement. He stocked the place with a small herd of cattle and
employed a foreman known as Dirty-face Murphy and two or
three cowpunchers. One of the cowhands was married, and his
wife was hired as cook and housekeeper and was made responsible for the care of Cort's granddaughter, a chubby, broad-
faced child whose identity shall be concealed here under the
name of Rita, since she grew to be a respected woman.

Presently Cort registered his brand, the H X X. The brand
aroused no suspicion until neighboring ranchmen found some
of their calves strangely missing. Then it was discovered that
Art Armstrong's *H Double-Open-A* brand and Tom Ashton's
Ч X brand could be converted into Cort Thomson's H X X
brand with a few strokes of a running iron. The Open A's of the
Armstrong iron were like inverted V's, and could be converted
into X's merely by extending the tops of the upside-down V's.
Ashton's Ч X brand could be changed by adding a second X and
by extending downward the left side of the figure 4. H X̌ X̌
H X X

Suspicion redoubled when it was rumored that Cort had
chosen this location because, if a Colorado sheriff's posse took
after him, he was only two miles from the safety of the Nebraska
border and fifteen from the Kansas border. They recalled that
the strategic location of Ladore Canon in northwestern Colorado made it an ideal location for cattle rustlers and other law-
breakers, since it was so near the intersection of the Colorado,
Utah, and Wyoming boundaries that a few miles would permit
a fugitive from the law to hop into an adjoining state beyond
the jurisdiction of pursuing officers of the law.

When neighbors sought to screen Cort's cattle for strays, they were warned away at the point of a rifle. They found him to be a tough customer, mean as a tail-tromped badger when he was drunk, and seldom sober. He liked to brag of his skill with a gun, and was fond of establishing deadlines which he challenged neighbors to cross at the peril of their lives.

Armstrong, who was no great hand with a gun, hired Harry Cox, a tough cowhand and accomplished gun slinger who had ridden the Chisum trail from Texas, to accompany him to the Thomson ranch to search for strays. Upon their arrival they offered Cort a drink. Then Cox tossed the empty pint flask into the air and shattered it with a bullet. Only after this display of marksmanship did they announce the object of their visit. "Go ahead and take a look," Cort told them, impressed by the display of marksmanship. They found none of Armstrong's missing calves, but discovered in a barn a calf with a half-healed brand that had been worked over from Tom Ashton's 4 X into Cort's H X X. They said nothing to Ashton of their find. Why should they? Let him trace his own missing calves!

Cort was constantly feuding with his neighbors. After threatening to kill a Nebraska cattleman if he caught him west of the Colorado boundary, he came upon him unexpectedly in a surrey driving his daughter into Wray.

Whipping out one of his pocket-holstered revolvers, Cort covered his enemy and barked gruffly, "Get out of that rig and get down on your knees and pray. You know what you're going to get. You asked for it."

Screaming, the cattleman's daughter flung herself in front of her father. "Think of your granddaughter, Cort," she begged. "If you kill pa, what will become of me?"

"All right," grumbled Cort, holstering his weapons. "I'll let him go this time. But if I ever catch him this side of the dead-line, you're going to be an orphan, ma'am."

Old-time residents of Wray still chuckle over another incident in which Cort figured. Encountering an enemy cattleman on his range, he whipped out a gun and forced him to dismount. "Start legging it for home—fast!" he ordered. Hour after hour Cort, on horseback, followed the running man, urging him to greater speed by firing into the ground at his heels. As evening neared the exhausted man halted, panting, "I'm plumb tuckered out, Cort. I haven't had a bite since breakfast, and I can't move another step without something to eat."

"Eat grass," Cort ordered gruffly and at gun-point forced the cattleman to get down on all fours and nibble a bunch of grass.

Prior to 1902 the county seat was at Yuma, twenty-seven miles west of Wray. Only once did a neighboring cattleman file a formal complaint against Cort. A deputy sheriff arrested him in "Pigfoot" Grant's speakeasy in Wray, and together the two set off on horseback for the county seat. Presently Cort let his mount lag a few steps behind. He uncoiled his lariat, dropped the loop over the deputy's shoulders, and jerked him from the saddle. After disarming him and hog-tying him like a calf, Cort rode back to his ranch. The deputy finally freed himself of his bonds but, unable to capture his horse, walked back to the county seat.

Soon after the Burlington Railroad was built through Wray, the cowpunchers of the *See-Bar-See* and other ranches developed a pastime guaranteed to provide boisterous merriment for the off-duty hours they spent in town. Westbound passengers were in the habit of getting off the train at Wray to stroll up and down the platform for their first breath of rarefied Colorado air. Suddenly an unsuspecting male passenger would feel a lariat drop about his shoulders and would be dragged across the dusty street to Pigfoot Grant's resort, where a pint of raw whisky would be forced down his throat and his face would be smeared with soot from the stove. Black of face and full of whisky, he would be deposited aboard the train just as it pulled away from the station. One passenger who proved to be exceedingly unco-operative was nailed inside a packing box and dragged behind whooping horsemen up and down the main street. Still boxed, he was pitched aboard the train as it pulled out.

Cort felt that he was a pretty good hand with a lariat. Objecting to an item about him published in the weekly newspaper, the Wray *Rattler*, he lay in wait until the editor emerged from his one-story frame building and then, from the saddle, cast his rope. The editor flattened himself against the side of the building so the loop could not drop over his shoulders. Three times Cort, on horseback, chased the editor around the building, trying to lasso him, but the newspaperman thwarted him at each cast by shrinking against the wall. Finally Cort rode away, shouting, "If you ever print my name in your dirty sheet again, I'll rope-drag you from hell to breakfast!"

An acquaintance of the nineties—Cort's only friend in Wray appeared to be Pigfoot Grant—says he never saw Cort smile.

"He walked with a swagger, and one side of his mouth was always twisted in a sneer," he said. "He was the kind of a man who, if he encountered a group of folks on the sidewalk, wouldn't walk around 'em, but would bull his way right through them, elbowing 'em this way and that. I was in Pigfoot Grant's place one night when Cort was having a drink. A farmer came into the place and greeted him with a boisterous slap on the shoulder. Cort whirled about, struck him in the face with the back of his fist, sent him reeling across the floor, and then turned to finish his drink and never gave him another look."

In his reminiscences Judge Irving L. Barber wrote: "[Cort Thomson] was noted as being a sport, a spender, and a gambler, and he always wore the latest clothes. He was also noted for being a cattle rustler. He is supposed to have killed a number of men, but nothing was ever proved on him. Mattie Silks financed most of the money for his different ventures, including the ranch."

Presently neighbors began to repeat strange rumors to the effect that the bodies of two men were buried in the cellar of the Thomson ranch house. These reports may have arisen from the fright of one of Cort's youthful cowpunchers. After Cort threatened to kill him, he fled from the ranch afoot without drawing his pay. Then it was recalled that two of the Thomson cowhands had disappeared without leaving a trace. However, since few cowboys left forwarding addresses when they quit a job but simply rode away across country until they found a berth elsewhere, too much credence cannot be placed in these sinister rumors of corpses buried in the cellar. It is entirely possible that Cort's threats may have driven some of his hands to quit without drawing their pay. It is wholly within character for him to boast of imaginary killings to frighten employees and neighbors and to bolster his ego.

It is highly probable that Cort, looked down upon by all respectable Denver citizens, suffering from a deep feeling of inferiority at the time he located the ranch at Wray, sought to pose as a bad man in an attempt to regain his self-respect.

It was not long, however, before everyone in the vicinity of Wray learned that he was Mattie Silks's man. It was his custom to pay his employees only once every three months. On these quarterly paydays Mattie would come from Denver with two or three of her girls and a case of whisky. Between the girls, the whisky, and Cort's skill with cards, it was only a day or two before most the H X X payroll was back in the hands of the boss.

One of his cowpunchers, in 1949 a retired cattleman living at Laird, Colorado, has no fault to find with Cort as an employer.

"He paid good wages and set a good table," he says. "I never tried to put anything over on him, so we got along all right. Although he was a heavy drinker and put on weight as he grew older, he was a fine physical specimen, though not very tall. I recall that once when he gathered an armful of kindling at the woodpile, the wind slammed shut the gate behind him. With his arms full of wood, he jumped that four-foot gate without half trying."

During the winter months Mattie kept her stable of race horses at the Wray ranch. She was inordinately proud of her best horse, named Jim Blaine. This horse is said to have won many races on Texas tracks.

While visiting the ranch she practiced marksmanship, shooting at tin cans on fence posts. Cort continually bled her for money. Months after she had given him several thousands of dollars to buy cattle, she learned he had sold them the next day and had gambled away the proceeds.

"That man is ruining me," she told L. S. Watson, conductor on the Burlington Railroad.

Cort's granddaughter attended classes in the brick schoolhouse at Laird. The high school consisted of a room in the basement.

His only friend at Wray, Charley Pigfoot Grant, was proprietor of an establishment where liquor was retailed in shoe boxes. Pigfoot became one of Wray's greatest civic benefactors, for he is credited with winning the county seat away from Yuma in an exploit which won him his nickname.

When Cort located his ranch, it was in Washington County. Three years later Yuma County was established from the eastern part of Washington County. The town of Yuma, west of Wray, was chosen as the county seat by a vote of 477 to Wray's 315.

Thirteen years later a movement was begun to change the county seat to Wray, and the proposal was submitted to the voters in 1902. Since the county extends some seventy-five miles north and south, it became a problem to induce indifferent voters to make the long trip to the polls.

Charley Grant advertised in the *Rattler* that he would provide free whisky and a pigs' feet dinner to all voters who came to Wray on election day. Thus induced, the voters of the eastern half of the county swarmed to the polls in sufficient numbers to carry the election. Grant led a nighttime foray in which the county records were seized at Yuma and brought to Wray in a wagon. After he changed the county seat by means of pigs' feet, Charley was known as Pigfoot Grant.

Following the discharge of Dirty-face Murphy as foreman

of the Thomson ranch, Cort hired John Dillon Handsome Jack
Ready, alias Jack Kelly, a railroad telegrapher employed at
Haigler. Handsome Jack was a huge Nova Scotian with red hair
and an attractive grin. Friends say he weighed 240 pounds in
his stocking feet, 253 in his shoes. When Jack discarded his
range clothing for a trip to Denver, he dressed in a Prince Albert
coat and striped trousers, wore a curl-brim derby and lemon-
colored chamois gloves and swung a cane. He claimed to have
been a prize fighter at one time, but in his go-to-town regalia he
looked more like a prosperous banker. He never carried a gun
and liked to boast that the man didn't live whom he couldn't
whip with his fists.

Handsome Jack, the king-sized dude, was destined to play a
leading part in the life of Mattie Silks.

(24)

Sentimental Journey

IMBUED with civic pride and the good old chamber of commerce booster spirit, Denver was accustomed to crown the entertainment of distinguished guests by taking them for a midnight tour of her leading Holladay Street temples of sin.

In the middle eighties the ebullient civic boosters were angling for a new railroad, expecting to add millions of dollars to the local payroll. Nothing was too good for the St. Louis railroad president who came out in his private car to look over the ground. The official reception committee provided him with the keys to the city, which gave access to unlimited free entertainment at Mattie Silks's famed establishment.

Charmed by Denver's openhanded hospitality, the rail tycoon dallied several days longer than he originally had planned. However, once he had visited Mattie's place, he could find no time to meet with the committee to consider Denver's manifold business advantages. Members of the group were most unhappy.

Mattie's place was widely known for the youth, beauty, and vivacity of its young lady boarders. But the charms of these delectable houris were wasted on the distinguished visitor. He had eyes for no one except the plump and impudent young madame, who had yet to reach the shady side of forty. Presently he proposed that she accompany him in his private car for a thirty-day holiday in California.

"Sorry," she told him coyly. "I'm afraid my husband wouldn't like it. Besides, I must stay here and attend to business, for I must meet a $5,000 note which comes due the first of the month."

Dismay spread through the members of the committee when they learned of Mattie's decision. How could they appeal to her civic pride? Couldn't she see what a new railroad would mean for the Queen City? The high-pressure sales talk prepared for the rail magnate they delivered instead to Mattie.

They directed her attention to the fact that railroad workers were free spenders, that a sizable proportion of the anticipated payroll would be spent on Holladay Street. If Mattie would but accept the invitation of the distinguished visitor and make use of her charms during the California vacation trip to persuade him to extend his line to Denver, she would be numbered among the city's outstanding benefactors.

"Sorry, boys. I'd like to oblige," she told them. "But I'm a businesswoman, and business is business. After all, I have a $5,000 note to meet on the first of the month."

When she told Cort of her decision, he was anything but pleased. He hurried to the chairman of the committee, prepared to turn a fast trick.

"If Mattie wins the railroad for Denver," he bargained, "will you take care of the $5,000 note?"

After grave consideration the committee informed him it was a deal. But Mattie's feelings were cruelly hurt when Cort reported the offer to her. She had never ceased to love him, and it shocked her to learn that he not only approved but actually urged that she sell herself to another man.

"So that's the way it is, is it?" she queried cynically. "All right, Cort. Send the boys around. I'll close the deal, but not on your terms. You never had a lick of business sense anyway."

So when again the members of the committee called upon

her, she put it to them, cold. The ethics of her profession precluded contingent fee deals. Her terms were cash in advance,
win, lose, or draw, and she would guarantee nothing except to
do her best for dear old Denver. The deal was sealed when
they handed her the note, marked "Paid in full." The next day
she departed for California with the magnate in his private car.

Together the two toured the Pacific coast hot spots of the
eighties. Everywhere the rail official introduced Mattie as his
wife. For her the best was none too good. He showered her
with every luxury, every attention, bought her a wardrobe suitable for a millionaire's wife.

The trip was extended for an additional thirty days, which
they spent together as house guests of the Potter Palmers on the
palatial Palmer ranch on the Laramie plains, north of Laramie,
Wyoming. The multimillionaire Chicago merchant prince and
Mrs. Palmer, leader of Newport and New York society, accepted Mattie without question when the railroad president
introduced her as his wife.

Potter Palmer made his start in 1858 operating a small dry-
goods store in Chicago. During the Civil War his profits totaled
$2,500,000. He took into partnership Marshall Field and Levi
Z. Leiter, selling out to them in 1867. Not many years later
Field and Leiter used part of their profits to buy stock in the
Chrysolite mine at Leadville, Colorado, on a tip from H. A. W.
Tabor—an investment from which they reaped immense profits.

Meanwhile Palmer bought a mile of State Street frontage in
Chicago and constructed a dozen large buildings, all destroyed
in the Chicago fire of 1871, in which the first Palmer House
went up in smoke thirteen days after it opened. The second,
completed in 1873, was replaced in 1927 by the present Palmer
House.

In 1882 the Palmers built their mansion at 1350 Lake Shore
Drive. The entrance hall rose, tier on carved tier, three floors
to a glass dome. The great fireplace was copied from an Italian
palazzo, complete to andirons of smoked silver. There was a

Louis XVI salon, a Spanish music room, an English dining room, a Moorish room where the rugs were impregnated with rarest perfumes.

Mrs. Palmer brought big-time Society to gawky, brash Chicago. She chartered a yacht, set off for Moscow for the coronation of Czar Nicholas II, and returned triumphantly with a shipload of Russian princelings and princesses to waltz in her velvet-lined ballroom.

Presidents Grant, McKinley, and Garfield ate off Mrs. Palmer's golden plates, and Grant offered her husband the cabinet post of Secretary of the Interior, which he refused. Other guests at the Chicago mansion or the Wyoming ranch were the duke and duchess of Veragua, the prince of Wales, who was later to become Edward VII, the Infanta Eulalia of Spain, and Mattie Silks.

The Palmers bought their Wyoming ranch in 1886 and built an immense rambling log ranch house, constructed in tiers against a hillside. When they were occupying the house an American flag was flown on the towering pole in front of the main door.

Here they entertained lavishly the leaders of New York, Newport, and Chicago moneyed aristocracy—and Mattie Silks and her traveling companion. The Potter Palmers never dreamed that the beautiful blonde they believed to be the wife of the visiting railroad tycoon was actually one of Denver's leading Holladay Street madames.

Her identity unsuspected, Mattie spent a delightful thirty days mingling on equal terms with the nation's social leaders. All the rest of her life she boasted about this venture into the loftiest circles of high society.

"I showed those Newport society dames I was as good as any of 'em," she bragged. "But not a one of 'em could make the grade as a boarder in my parlor house."

No one seems to know what brought the sentimental journey to an end. Perhaps the rail magnate simply tired of his blond mistress. Perhaps Mattie's business responsibilities brought her back to Denver. More likely, she simply became lonesome for Cort.

A fitting ending to the story of the sentimental journey would relate the successful conclusion of Mattie's endeavor as a civic benefactor. The actual conclusion is anticlimax, for she failed to win the new railroad, and the Chamber of Commerce committee was left holding the sack. One is left wondering how the committee accounted to the chamber for the disbursement to Mattie. Was it charged up to entertainment? Traveling expense? Good will? Sleeping accommodations?

Had success crowned her efforts perhaps the name of Mattie Silks could be found today among the names of those who have made notable contributions to the city's progress, in letters of bronze on the stone wall of the Court of Civic Benefactors in Denver's beautiful and imposing civic center.

The Potter Palmers sold their ranch in 1894. The following year the magnificent log ranch house burned to the ground. Palmer died in 1902 and his wife in 1918. For years the Chicago mansion with its eighty-foot crenelated towers stood empty. In 1950 it was torn down to be replaced by an apartment building.

Mattie was not the only madame who rivaled her boarders in attractiveness. A gentleman visitor became enamored of one of her contemporaries and kept forcing his unwelcome attentions upon her. The exasperated madame consulted her lawyer.

"Next time he lays hands on me, I swear I'll kill him," she announced angrily.

"You do, and you'll hang for it," warned the attorney.

"What sort of a law is it," she demanded indignantly, "that won't protect a girl defending her honor?"

The exterior of Mattie's two-story red brick house at 501 Holladay Street was not particularly imposing. The interior, however, was furnished lavishly. The windows were high and narrow and were always curtained, day and night. During daylight hours the interior was gloomy and forbidding—but then, guests never came a-calling until after dark.

At one time or another approximately two million dollars, largely in gold coin, passed through the special money pocket that balanced the special pistol pocket in Mattie Silks's dazzling de Medici gown.

The Rocky Mountain *News* of April 16, 1883, carried the following report of a meeting of the board of aldermen:

> The clerk read a petition from one Mattie Silks requesting the change of a liquor license. He began, "A petition from Mattie Silks—" Alderman Armstrong, who was busily employed fixing up some papers, raised his head when the name was read and exclaimed, "What?" Everybody laughed while the mayor pounded with his gavel and Alderman Armstrong bent to his work on the papers with an energy both surprising and praiseworthy. But he blushed.

Strangely parallel to the struggle of Augusta Tabor of Capitol Hill to hold the man she loved, was the struggle of Mattie Silks to hold the love of her ne'er-do-well Cort Thomson.

By 1891 Mattie Silks no longer was the alluring vest-pocket Lily Langtry. She was forty-three years old and buxom rather than plump. Cort, a year younger, had added "tomcatting" to his drinking and gambling. Mattie was well aware of his affair with the henna-haired wench, Lillie Dab, who was young enough to be her daughter. Like Augusta Tabor, Mattie was ready to fight for her man. The bonanza king's lady and the bawdy-house biddy were sisters under the skin.

But Mattie, who some years earlier had won Cort from Katie Fulton in a pistol duel, believed in direct action. On the night of March 13, 1891, she carefully cleaned and loaded the pistol with the ivory grip and set out to eliminate one side of her domestic triangle.

Surprising Cort in the arms of the siren, Mattie wasted no

words. Her first shot snipped off a hennaed curl. Her marksman-ship had not improved over the years. Lillie barely beat the sec-ond shot through the door.

There was no third. Cort closed with her, wrenched the pistol from her fingers, and beat her unmercifully. One of her eyes was blackened for days. The last seen of Lillie Dab, she was speeding, screaming, in the general direction of Cheyenne, Eve on the loose from Eden, clad in openwork black silk stockings.

Early the next morning the raging Mattie filed suit for divorce in the Arapahoe County Court. She set forth in her complaint that they had been happily married until Cort became addicted to the excessive use of alcoholic liquors and a year after their marriage beat her in a barbarous manner. In spite of repeated solemn promises to reform he had failed to mend his ways, she said.

Since their marriage at Peru, Indiana, in 1884 she had given him from $45,000 to $50,000 above his legitimate living costs, she maintained, charging that he had squandered it all in gam-bling and riotous living. She said he had lived openly with Lillie Dab for six months and at other times with other women, but insisted that she had forgiven him.

Mattie herself was in no position to come into court with un-soiled hands, for in charging Cort with unfaithfulness, she was risking his countercharge that she had spent sixty days as the mistress of the railroad president. In an evident effort to answer such charges in advance, she insisted that any acts she had com-mitted inconsistent with her marriage vows had been sanctioned and condoned by Cort, and claimed she had conducted herself so he could find no real fault with her. She sought the divorce on the ground of cruelty and asked the restoration of her maiden name, Martha Silks.

The complaint likewise set forth that he was the owner of three separate tracts of ranch land in Yuma County, paid for with money furnished and earned by her solely, and that all the improvements, horses, and cattle on the property had been purchased with her money. She said she had reason to believe he intended to sell the ranch property, and asked the court for an injunction restraining him from taking such action. Mattie's complaint said the plaintiff had been a resident of Denver for fifteen years.

The court granted a temporary restraining order enjoining Cort from selling the ranch property.

Faced with the loss of his meal ticket, the knight in tarnished armor apparently was contrite and filled with remorse. He agreed that the ranch property be transferred to Mattie's name. He swore solemnly that he would never so much as look at Lillie Dab again and would keep free from entanglements with other women. So, on March 25, 1891, eleven days after the divorce suit was filed, softhearted Mattie ordered her lawyers to ask the court to dismiss it. Success crowned her struggle to hold her man. Augusta Tabor failed under somewhat similar circumstances. Perhaps the reason Mattie succeeded where Augusta failed lies once more in the fact that the former held the family purse strings.

For many years Mattie reigned unchallenged as empress of the underworld. The house she herself operated, known after the change of street names as 1916 Market Street, was much the most pretentious on the Row.

Queen Victoria's diamond jubilee, June 27, 1897, brought to London one and one-half million visitors, including Cort Thomson and Mattie Silks.

Preparations for the jubilee began six months in advance. Tickets for seats along the six-mile course of the procession were sold all over the world for from five dollars to $500 each, and thousands turned out to be fraudulent. A chair on a roof top was priced at fifty dollars—and the purchaser took his chance on rain. A room facing St. Paul's cathedral, where the ceremony was to take place, was marked at $2,500 for the one day.

One entire building was torn down to provide room for a temporary grandstand, and was rebuilt later. Churches built grandstands over their churchyards. Tenants of rooms facing the route of the procession were evicted by the hundreds, that their quarters might be rented for jubilee day. Scaffolding supporting tiers of seats covered the fronts of theaters, hotels, and restaurants.

One American paid $10,000 to rent a house in Piccadilly for one week. It might have been Cort Thomson, for nothing was too good for Mattie—so long as she paid for it.

Business had been good in Denver. The city had recovered from the paralyzing effects of the panic of '93. Bob Womack had discovered gold at Cripple Creek in 1891, and once more the Queen City was enjoying the benefits of another mining boom. Mine owners had been spending their gold liberally in the parlor houses of Denver's Market Street.

Cort Thomson had put Lillie Dab out of his life forever, and once more he and Mattie were happy together. They were nearing middle age, and their journey to London was something in the nature of a long-delayed honeymoon.

London newspapers published stories of a fabulous character called Diamond Jem of Colorado. There is no actual evidence that this was Cort Thomson, but no other known resident of Colorado attended the jubilee. Cort had always been a show-off, and it was wholly in character for him to bedeck himself with diamonds—Mattie's diamonds—and strut the streets telling wild tales about Colorado's riches and assuming the name of Diamond Jem.

It is known, however, that Cort bought Mattie the finest mink cloak in England—with her money. She brought the cloak back to Denver and wore it everywhere, boasting of Cort's kindness. She wore it to the horse show in the winter, where her prize high-school horse won many blue ribbons. She even wore it to the Overland Park races in the summer. Her London cloak was the envy of every madame on Market Street—and probably of many Capitol Hill women, as well.

In London Cort took her to dinner at the Savoy, where they

both stood and let their dinners grow cold as they joined in
the singing of "God Save the Queen." Together they admired
the royal coachmen in their red and gold liveries; the Chinese
police from Hong Kong, with their soup-plate hats; the bearskin
shakos of the Buckingham Palace guards; the Negro soldiers
from the Gold Coast of Africa; the head-hunters from Bor-
neo; the Mohammedans from Cyprus; the members of the Rho-
desian Horse; the troops from India with their turbans and
fezzes. They were among the three million spectators who witnessed the widow of Windsor in her sober black dress, shielded
by an ivory lace parasol, drive from Buckingham Palace to St.
Paul's and back. Sixty years earlier, a month after her accession
to the throne, Victoria had become the first English sovereign
to use Buckingham Palace for a residence.

Together Cort and Mattie drove down Pall Mall, and halted
at the spot where Nell Gwynne had leaned across her garden
wall to talk to the king. The Honorable Whitelaw Reid, in
evening dress, rode in a carriage with the Spanish ambassador
behind the United States ambassador the Honorable John Hay.

Mattie saw many women of royal blood in splendid gowns,
but none was more splendid than her own Market Street working costume, her collared de Medici gown.

Rubens' painting of Marie de Medici shows a virtually identical costume. It consists of a cloak with a long train, worn over a
tight bodice with a broad, flaring turned-up collar which produced what was known to women of fashion as "the Medici
effect." During working hours, with just such a cloak and bodice,
Mattie wore a skirt with tiers of lace flounces, and white gloves.
Her sleeves lacked the rows of "cabbage" puffs shown in the
Rubens painting.

Seen driving her famous buggy at the Overland Park race
track, where she backed her judgment of horseflesh with abun-
dant cash, she carried a huge lace parasol, and a lace kerchief to
wave at friends.

At one time Overland Park, in South Denver, was owned by

Henry Wolcott, brother of United States Senator Ed Wolcott. He acquired it from a group of capitalists, including Tabor, who had established it as an amusement resort, under the name of Jewell Park, in 1883.

The ball held during the running of the Colorado derby was a leading event of the Denver social season. Walls and ceiling of the ballroom were draped with bunting and lavishly decorated with tulips and daffodils.

Former gambling house manager Ed Gaylord owned Agnes Lee May, one of the fastest harness mares to race at Overland, and the gelding, Billy Duncan. Prince Henry was the 1892 derby favorite. The most famous sulky horses of the nineties were Carbonate, a gray stallion, and Sulphide, a bay stallion. Famous pacing mares were Laura Spurr and Maxine.

Except for Jim Blaine, the names of Mattie's horses remain unknown. Entered under the name of Mrs. C. D. Thomson or of her trainer, Frank W. Nott, they may be included among the following outstanding animals racing at Overland: Commonwealth, The Major, Harry Logan, Miss Logan, Topgallant, Birchtwig, Mary Hall, Master Delmar, Donami, John C. King, and Lero.

Leading bookmakers at Overland included Phil Archobald of San Francisco, Texas Jones of Dallas, and Connors of Chicago.

Denver's social leaders went to the races in such vehicles as the English Kensington, Victoria, and Park Wagon. The *hoi polloi* used the Denver & Rio Grande narrow gauge excursion trains.

In 1900 the first automobiles appeared at Overland Park. In an exhibition time trial, one of the horseless carriages covered one mile in what a newspaper described as "the terrific time of 1.57 ¼."

Betting on horse racing was outlawed in Colorado in 1908. For many years thereafter, the Gentlemen's Riding and Driving Club staged betless Sunday afternoon harness races at City Park.

No longer used for racing, Overland Park was the scene of Denver's first flying machine flight. In February, 1910, Louis

Paulhan, French pilot, flew a Farman biplane through a light snowstorm, taking off and landing at the race track.

In 1948 pari-mutuel betting in Colorado was legalized by adoption of a constitutional amendment, but Overland Park had been converted into a municipal golf course long since. Centennial Park, located a few miles away, was one of many racing plants opened in Colorado in 1950.

(25)

Red Northern Lights

MATTIE and Cort returned from London in the summer of 1897 to find Denver's tenderloin almost depopulated. Discovery of gold in the Klondike had given birth to a new boom. Soapy Smith and his Soap Gang had pulled out for Dyea, which had just been renamed Skagway. The gamblers of the California Gang, who had once packed Murphy's Slaughterhouse, had answered the call of the northern wild. The nymphs had deserted the cribs and parlor houses in droves. Wyatt Earp, the former two-gun marshal of Dodge City passed through Denver with wild tales of the enormous profits to be gained in the far North. His saloon at Nome later cashed in handsomely on these profits.

Gold from the Cripple Creek district had helped Denver recover from the disastrous panic of '93, brought about by the repeal of the Sherman Act which almost wrecked Leadville's silver-mining industry. But now the output of the Cripple Creek mines was slowing down.

Mattie and Cort decided to join the gold rush to the Klondike. With a dozen of their most attractive boarders they left Denver for Seattle in the spring of '98.

They steered clear of Skagway, where Soapy Smith ruled the underworld, for Cort and Soapy had been bitter enemies since the shooting affray in Murphy's Slaughterhouse saloon. They decided that the merchandise Mattie had to offer was in far greater demand at Dawson City, in Yukon Territory. Few women had braved the rigors of the trail over Chilkoot pass into the Yukon. But the railroad had just been completed from Skagway to White Horse, and steamboats were plying the Yukon from White Horse to Dawson City. No longer was it necessary to mush over Chilkoot on foot.

Mattie and Cort found Dawson City not unlike the boom towns of the prairies and of the Rockies. Built on a flat in a bend of the river, it was a collection of hastily erected log and frame shanties somewhat larger than the neighboring camp, Lousetown.

From a man named Jenkins, proprietor of the Sour Dough Saloon, Mattie rented a good-sized frame building on Second Street for $350 a month, one block from Front Street. Her leading competitor was Beatrice Larne.

Mattie had been accustomed to pay protection money to the police, usually in the form of cash passed out to a collector for city officials, sometimes in the form of periodical fines paid in police court. Here she found Dawson City was run by the Canadian Northwest Mounted Police.

"The protection money I paid in Denver was penny-ante stuff alongside what the redcoats of the Mounted Police demanded," she later told her Denver friend, Charley Nolan. "I had to pay them fifty dollars a day for every day I operated at Dawson City, but I'm not kicking. It was worth it."

After paying Mattie her fifty per cent and board, each of her girls was earning from thirty to fifty dollars a day. Her expenses were high, but her total receipts were enormous, and she could afford to pay fifty dollars a day to the Northwest Mounted. Her sales of liquid refreshments brought huge profits. She sold champagne for thirty dollars a quart, and the boarder's cut on each sale was five dollars. Whisky was fifty cents a shot. There was no beer, no gin, in Dawson City. A large proportion of the whisky was of the moonshine variety, made from alcohol that cost sixty dollars a gallon.

The miners paid a dollar for a drink and a dance, and danced in their dirty mackinaws, muddy boots, and mukluks. The dance-hall music never stopped, day or night. The wages for common labor were from ten to twenty dollars a day. Lumber cost $250 a thousand feet. Eggs were ten dollars a dozen. Oysters brought a dollar each, in cans. Potatoes from the Stewart River were fifty dollars a sack. Condensed milk was four dollars a quart. Moose meat, dark and coarse, was comparatively reasonable in price. Caribou meat, sweet and tender, brought premium prices.

Mattie had brought with her the old gold scales she had used at Georgetown, and the little square of carpet that caught the dust spilled from the scales. The money pocket in her de Medici gown contained, instead of gold coins, a buckskin poke filled with gold dust. She still packed her pistol in the other pocket.

As usual, Cort was no help with the business. He spent most of his time playing faro at Joe Cooper's Dominion Saloon.

Almost all her life Mattie had lived in the dry, almost rainless climate of Kansas and Colorado. She detested the constant downpour that left Dawson streets ankle-deep in mud. Many miners were suffering from scurvy and pneumonia.

Late in the summer Cort developed a heavy cold and treated it with his favorite remedy, whisky. All around her Mattie saw evidences of colds that had developed into pneumonia. Dawson City boasted a population of 4,000, but no hospital. Mattie dreaded the approach of the long Arctic winter. She feared Cort would not survive. She wanted to go home. She squared up his gambling debts and booked passage on the outbound steamboat *Susie*.

"How did you make out in the Klondike, Mattie?" asked Charley Nolan upon her return to Denver.

"After all expenses were paid, including the passage both ways, the protection money, and Cort's gambling debts, I have a net profit of $38,000 for my ninety days at Dawson City," she told him. "It's more than I ever made in such a short time before, but I wouldn't spend a winter in the Klondike for a million dollars!"

The dry atmosphere of the eastern Colorado plains speedily cured Cort's cold. He was almost fifty years old when he returned from the Klondike. Since his foot-racing days he had put on quite a bit of weight. He was still drinking heavily and spent much of his time in Pigfoot Grant's resort at Wray, with occasional benders in Denver. He left the operation of the ranch almost entirely to the foreman, the 240-pound Nova Scotian redhead, Handsome Jack Ready, alias Jack Kelly.

Seepage resulting from the growth of irrigated farming had caused the original buffalo wallow to become a twenty-three-acre lake, which threatened to inundate the dwelling. It was, and still is, known as Thomson's Lake.

"Cort liked to tell us about his experiences in the Klondike," says Gyp Shafer, at that time one of Thomson's cowboys and in 1950 a retired cattleman living at Laird, Colorado. "He'd chuckle about the way they'd get the miners drunk and roll them of their gold dust.

"He told us that two Swedes who had been parted from some $50,000 worth of dust made so much trouble with the authorities that it was necessary to get rid of the loot. They buried it somewhere out in the timber country, but the officers kept such a close watch on them that they were scared to take it with them when they left for the States. He said it was still buried, just as safe as if it were deposited in a bank, and sometime he was going back and dig it up."

Early in April of 1900 Cort went to Denver and demanded that Mattie give him $5,000 to buy cattle. Suspicious, she refused his demand, claiming she had no money.

"This is too good a deal to pass up," he argued. "If you haven't the ready cash, I know where we can raise $2,000 by selling the race horse, Jim Blaine."

Fearful that he would sell her favorite horse, Mattie gave him a check for $1,500. He immediately cashed the check, taking payment in twenty-dollar gold pieces.

But instead of buying cattle, Cort plunged into another drinking spree, with a one-legged drug addict known as Peg-leg Murphy—no kin to the former ranch foreman, Dirty-face Murphy. It was two days before word reached Mattie that Cort and Peg-leg had scattered gold coins in every saloon and gambling joint of Denver's tenderloin and then boarded a train for Wray.

Suspecting that her husband had spent all the money she had given him and was headed for the ranch to sell the race horse, Jim Blaine, she telegraphed the sheriff of Yuma County to keep him in custody until she reached Wray.

The sheriff found it unnecessary to arrest Cort, who was suffering from intense stomach cramps in a room at Grandma Simpson's old Commercial Hotel, since destroyed by fire. Murphy had departed on horseback—his peg leg proved no handicap to horsemanship—for the Thomson ranch.

When Mattie reached Wray she found Cort in a rocking chair in his hotel room, writhing in agony. He told her he was suffering an attack of ptomaine poisoning from eating spoiled oysters. She sent for a doctor and for Will Toner, a cowpuncher. Toner, a farmer now living near Wray, gives the following account of the ensuing events.

"Mattie told me she was afraid Murphy had gone to the ranch to steal the horse, Jim Blaine. She asked me to ride out to the ranch, get the horse, and bring it back to the livery stable at Wray.

" 'Do you carry a gun?' She asked me. When I told her I didn't, she gave me money to go down to the hardware store and buy one.

" 'This fellow Murphy is a snowbird, and dangerous when he's full of cocaine,' she told me. 'His nerves will be on edge and he'll be likely to shoot first and ask questions afterward.'

"While we were talking the doctor came into the lobby. He handed Mattie a half-pint bottle and said:

" 'Put some of this laudanum in his whisky as needed, Mattie, and it will ease the pain of his cramps.'

"After I had bought the gun at the hardware store I came back to say 'Howdy' to Cort. He offered me a drink from a whisky bottle, but Mattie, who was standing behind him, shook her head, like she was trying to tell me that there was painkiller in the whisky. So I only took a little sip, and it had a queer, bitter taste.

"I rode out to the Thomson place, and didn't have the slightest trouble with Peg-leg Murphy. I told him Mattie had sent me to bring Jim Blaine back to Wray. He said that was all right, but asked if I'd just as leave wait until tomorrow, as he'd figured on riding Jim Blaine to Haigler to catch a train. I told him I'd ride with him to Haigler and lead Jim Blaine back to Wray after he caught his train. And that was the way it was."

Exactly what happened that night in Cort's room at the old Commercial Hotel will never be known, although Wray old-timers accept as true an account that has passed from mouth to mouth for many years. In an attempt to ease his pain, they say, Mattie kept dosing him with a mixture of laudanum and whisky. Along toward morning Cort, still seated in the rocking chair, became convinced he was about to die.

"Damn you, Mattie," he groaned through gritted teeth, "you poisoned me to get rid of me. If I had a gun I'd kill you!"

"All right, Cort," she agreed, drawing from the pistol pocket of her skirt the ivory-handled revolver she always carried. She pressed it into his stiffening fingers. "If that's the way you feel about it, go ahead and kill me, darling. If you're going to die, I don't want to live."

He was her man.

Later in the morning Will Toner rode into Wray, leading behind him the riderless race horse, Jim Blaine. A friend told him:

"Cort Thomson died at sunup, sitting bolt upright in a chair.

Five minutes after he was dead his face was the color of a storm cloud over the plains: blue-black."

Just what powerful emotions struggled for mastery of Mattie Silks during the long hours of that night, as she sat by his rocking chair and plied him with laudanum and whisky?

Few women had endured more from a man than Mattie had suffered from Cort Thomson. For years he had bled her for money to fritter away over mahogany bars and the green baize of gambling tables—$45,000 to $50,000 in seven years, according to her divorce complaint, and no one knows how much more during the ensuing years. He had been unfaithful to his marriage vows in his affair with Lillie Dab and other women, if the charge in her divorce suit could be believed. He had condoned, if not urged, her affair with the railroad president, because it meant money in his pocket. He had beaten her, had never done an honest day's work, and had lived on her earnings. If any woman ever had reason to loathe and detest a worthless wastrel husband, and wish to be rid of him, that woman was Mattie Silks.

And yet—

In the days of her youth she had risked her life for Cort in the famous pistol duel with Katie Fulton in Denver's Olympic Gardens. Later, when she had the opportunity to rid herself of him, she had dismissed her divorce suit as soon as the ranch property was saved from his profligate grasp. Why? Because she still loved him in spite of his unfaithfulness and abuse?

When the dying Cort had accused her of poisoning him, why had she pressed her pistol in his hand and invited him to kill her? If his charge were true and she knew she was about to be rid of him at last, why should she take such a chance with her own life? Was she simply bluffing, secure in the knowledge that Cort was at heart a fourflusher, a characterless weakling who loved to bluster and threaten but who never could muster the courage to carry out such a threat?

Or—

Did she mean what she said? Did she really feel that life was no longer worth living without the man she loved? After all, he had "done her wrong," but he was her man. Though all the rest of the world could see nothing but the tarnish, it is possible that in her eyes he was still her knight in shining armor, the handsome-made athlete she had first met at the foot race in Chicago, whom she was fated to love, not alone till the parting of death but through time and eternity. Some women are like that.

Twenty-nine years were to elapse before anyone could know, with certainty, what emotions ruled Mattie's heart during that long night.

There was no investigation of the circumstances surrounding Cort's death. It was taken for granted that he died of ptomaine poisoning caused by eating spoiled oysters.

He died April 12, 1900, as he had lived: at Mattie's expense. She paid for his funeral and for his burial at Fairmount cemetery, Denver.

Cort's death left her faced with another problem. What was to become of Rita, his granddaughter? Now she was left, a child in her early teens, without a living person she could call blood kin.

And so Mattie went into court and legally adopted Rita, child of Cort's child by another woman.

Following his death, Mattie operated the ranch at Laird under the management of foreman Handsome Jack Ready until Cort's granddaughter married, and then sold it. When horse racing was outlawed in Colorado, she sold her racing stable but retained her favorite horse, Jim Blaine, stabling the animal at trainer Frank Nott's livery in Denver.

Handsome Jack had developed arthritis in his fingers, so he could no longer go back to his occupation of telegrapher. Mattie therefore brought him to Denver as bookkeeper and bouncer at her Market Street house. There was little difference in his job as foreman of a cattle ranch, he insisted, and his job as foreman of a seraglio.

In the ballroom of Mattie's house, Handsome Jack was a principal in Denver's longest and most savage bare-knuckle fight, his opponent an obstreperous livestock dealer who objected to being bounced. As Mattie and her young ladies cheered and made side bets, Ready and his foe slugged it out without respite for one solid hour. Perhaps the handsome bouncer's arthritic fingers proved a handicap. The livestock dealer almost beat Handsome Jack to death.

The author, then a cub police reporter on the Denver *Post*, met Mattie Silks just once, on a bitterly cold night in 1913. He accompanied the police to her house in response to a call for the police surgeon to aid a boarder who had swallowed poison.

Downstairs in the ballroom at 1942 Market Street, behind the parlor of magnificent mirrors, the roistering guests danced to the thumping of the piano. Upstairs Stella, wearing nothing but a pair of openwork black silk stockings, lay sobbing and praying and retching and writhing and dying, alone. In the reception hall Madame Silks, in her regal silken de Medici costume, impatiently fingered her cross of diamonds as she awaited the arrival of the police ambulance.

Outside, the cop on the tough Market Street beat hunched his head low in his greatcoat collar to protect his ears from the twenty-one-below-zero midnight cold. High above him, her ample rose stone bosom covered with snow, seductive Jennie Rogers smiled sardonically, as for thirty years she had smiled down from the gray stone façade on the males thronging Denver's street of the houris.

Just below her the four sculptured rose stone faces winked and scowled and smirked and mourned, jealously guarding their fantastic story of scandal and blackmail and possible murder.

The ambulance was responding to another emergency call, so the police machine that skidded up to the snowy curb was an open touring car. There were few sedans in 1913.

"Another bichloride case," muttered the cop on the beat wearily as the three men hopped from the police car—the uniformed police driver; Diedrick Franz Stackelbeck, the veteran

Times reporter; and a cub reporter. A few years later, as a reporter for the *Post*, Stackelbeck was to win the thanks of the United States Senate for unearthing the Teapot Dome scandal.

"Look, kid." Stack was showing the cub reporter the rose stone sculpture on the doorpost—the horseshoe in a bed of lotus leaves. "Horseshoe's upside down. Somebody's luck has run out." The faint, sweet odor of opium smoke drifted across the street from Hop Alley.

The three stamped the snow from their feet on the white tile doorstep, inlaid with the name "M. Silks." Madame Silks took Stack to be a police surgeon. "I gave her an emetic, doctor." She gathered up the flounces of her skirt and led the way up the narrow staircase to the second floor. The cub reporter wanted to snatch a look at the parlor of mirrors, the famous "ice palace," but the door opening from the reception hall was closed.

So this fat, grandmotherly woman who was nearing seventy was Mattie Silks, queen of the courtesans, madame of Denver's most luxurious and notorious sporting house! The cub reporter couldn't picture her as the bold and alluring siren who had fought a formal duel with Katie Fulton for love of a fancy man, as the gorgeous blonde who had played such a lusty part in the turbulent life of pioneer Denver.

The door to the ballroom was closed, too, but the thump-thump of the piano was still audible. Cupping his hand to his mouth, Stack whispered over his shoulder, "The virgin daughter." The cub reporter nodded knowingly, for he had heard the yarn about the virgin college-graduate pianist whom Mattie guarded so jealously from the attentions of male guests.

Lacking a stretcher, the four men carried the naked Stella down the narrow staircase and rolled her in a blanket.

Diamond rings glistened on the fingers of both the madame's hands. The cub reporter noted the diamond cross at her throat.

As the girl was lifted into the tonneau of the open car Stack said, "That bichloride gnaws the lining right out of your stomach. You're better off if you die."

Mattie was standing in the doorway, giving the cop on the beat the information for his report. The car pulled away from the curb to the thump-thump of the ballroom piano.

The cub reporter sat beside Stella and kept the blanket wrapped about her during the ride in the open car to the county hospital, and her retching ruined his coat sleeve. She died the next day, perhaps from the poison, perhaps from the sub-zero ride to the hospital. Her suicide rated a three-line story in the *Post.*

(26)

The Tumult and the Shouting

SOMETIMES the aging Mattie Silks would weep softly into her champagne and tell her Negro maid, "If I had to live my life over again I'd go into some other line, Green. What with the police pay-off and everything, running a sporting house is a very uncertain line of business."

The maid, her hair now white, still lives in Denver. She was a sensitive soul, with a burden of guilt on her conscience, and strove to conceal from the madame the fact that she was a "gamblin' woman." Under her first name she was known in the gambling joints of Hop Alley as one who enjoyed considerable luck at games such as fan tan and Chinese lottery.

"Madame Silks would not have liked it if she knew I was 'playing the Chinaman,' " she says, "so I wouldn't ever tell her my first name. So she wouldn't know who I was, I only told her my last name—Green.

"She was an awful kind and generous lady. Never drank anything but champagne, 'cept sometimes somebody was buying a round of beer she would take a sip, just out of politeness.

"She told me about her gun duel with Katie Fulton—said it was over a man, but didn't tell what man. She claimed to be a crack shot. Every once in a while she would take a week's vacation and go to the ranch to practice shooting. Said the ranch was in the San Luis Valley, but she was just funning. She just said that 'cause she didn't want the folks near Wray to know she was a sporting lady. She used to shoot at tin cans on fence posts.

"She fed her boarders real good meals, twice a day—ham and eggs, and steak, and things like that. She had two or three 'call girls' that lived at the toniest uptown hotels and never did come to the Market Street house at all; just kept appointments that she made for them. She made her boarders dress real pretty, and most of 'em were always in debt to her for clothes. They all hated the iron bars on the windows—said it made 'em think they were in jail.

"A rich gentleman from upstate wanted to marry one of the girls named Dollie, but Dollie told me she didn't think she'd do it because she wasn't sure she loved him. I told her, 'Honey, you got a chance to grab a permanent man, you do it,' so she did. She is a middle-aged lady now, but every four, five years she comes to Denver and visits a spell with me.

"Madame Silks, she told me she'd made a million dollars, maybe two million, but she didn't have much left account she taken too many chances. She was a bettin' lady and lost lots and lots of money backing her string of horses at the Overland Park track. She told me she would have been better off if she hadn't been such a fool for good-looking men.

"She always wore diamond rings and a diamond cross, but as she got older she didn't dress as elegant as some of the younger madames. She talked a lot about her adopted daughter, who didn't live in Denver. I think she gave this daughter a lot of her jewelry. Once she told me the daughter was going to have a baby soon.

"Every once in a while she would tell us she was going to an uptown hotel for a day or two, because her daughter was coming to Denver for a visit. I never saw her daughter. If she ever played the piano in Madame Silks's house, it was not while I worked there.

"Madame couldn't write very good, and used to get the girls to write her letters for her. But after Mister Jack came to work at the house he took care of everything for her. My, but was he a handsome man! Big, red-haired, always smiling, a sporty dresser and a lot younger than Madame Silks.

"After he'd been there a while he began to get awful bossy with her, but she didn't seem to mind being bossed around. He told me he had to take care of her, 'cause she was getting old.

"She told me she had run away from home and was operating her own boardinghouse when she was only nineteen years old. Said her family didn't know what business she was in and probably thought she was dead. When she got sick, she wouldn't let anybody but Mister Jack cook for her."

When Mattie had bought the house at 1942 Market Street from the estate of Jennie Rogers she failed to note that the carven horseshoe in the bed of lotus leaves was upside down. A year earlier the voters of Colorado had defeated a constitutional amendment calling for state-wide prohibition. District Attorney Willis Stidger made a valiant attempt to dim the red lights of Market Street with a series of raids, but within a short time the Row was operating full blast once more.

After holding office for many years, Mayor Robert W. Speer was ousted in a reform wave and was succeeded by Henry J. Arnold. Arnold appointed as police commissioner George Creel, editorial writer for the *News*, and later World War I wartime censor. Creel had his own ideas about cleaning up Market Street, theorizing that the girls could be reformed by committing them to a municipal farm. He ordered a certain number to be arrested every night. His idealistic scheme reduced the population of the street temporarily, but strangely enough the young ladies failed to see eye to eye with him. They didn't want to be saved. Before long Market Street was operating again, full blast, still the West's most wicked thoroughfare.

In 1908 only two states had laws prohibiting traffic in women. By 1918 all forty-eight states had such laws, and the passage of the Mann Act still further discouraged the practice of the oldest profession. Between 1912 and 1917 twenty-nine cities closed their segregated districts.

Another attempt to close Denver's district of wine, women, and wrong was made in 1913.

In 1914 the people reversed themselves and voted the state bone dry. Just before the prohibition amendment became effective in 1915 Sheriff Glen Duffield clamped a chastity belt on the tenderloin and closed all the Hop Alley gambling dens and opium joints.

This time the red lights were dimmed forever. The year 1915 saw the tumult and the shouting die, the madames and the pimps depart.

The author took part in the closing raids, accompanying a squad of patrolmen cleaning up Hop Alley's opium dens. The officers were instructed to arrest all persons actually found in the act of smoking opium, but were too fat to boost one another up to peer through the transoms of the tiny cubicles. So the lightweight young police reporter was hoisted up for this purpose. If an addict was found to be merely sleeping off the effects of his pill, his roseate dreams were left undisturbed. If actually found in the act of smoking, he was placed under arrest. The raid netted a number of white men and Negroes, but no Chinese and no women. Few women were opium addicts.

Confident that the "good old days" would return, Mattie closed the doors of 1942 Market and permitted the premises to stand vacant. She still owned the building at 1916 Market. Here, for a time, she operated the Silks Hotel. But the district had become a blighted slum area, and her guests were largely penniless flophouse bums. For a short time she operated a hotel on Broadway near Thirteenth Avenue, but it, too, was a failure.

Finally Mattie abandoned hope that The Row would ever reopen. She was in her middle seventies, living on borrowed time, ready to retire with her memories. The value of her Market Street property had depreciated tremendously. Her house at 1942, standing vacant, was merely piling up taxes. She removed part of its gorgeous furnishings to her home at 2635 Lawrence Street and ordered the rest sold at auction.

Among the auctioned articles was a coffin found in the wine room in the basement. Some believed Mattie had been keeping it for her own funeral. Others held that it had been used to frighten inebriated gentlemen guests, who were laid out in the casket when they passed out from overindulgence. Best bet is that it had been used by rum runners operating from the premises during Prohibition. Coffins were frequently used as containers for transporting illicit liquor, as few persons suspected a hearse of being used for rum running.

The old Row was no more, but the oldest profession had not been stamped out. Its practitioners were scattered through the city, operating from establishments that were ostensibly rooming houses. During the depression years the "maid system" came into existence. Under this plan, police permitted each hotel to keep two girls who were listed on the payroll as "chambermaids."

On November 18, 1919, the premises at 1942 Market Street were acquired by T. Ono, a Japanese. In 1929 the property was purchased by the Buddhist church and was maintained as a place of worship for many years. Over the course of years the old Row became a street of warehouses.

After World War II many Japanese flocked to Denver from the relocation centers to which they had been removed from Pacific Coast states. This shift in population impelled the Buddhist church to seek larger quarters. In 1948 an imposing new church was built at Twentieth and Lawrence streets, and the premises at 1942 Market were sold and remodeled into a warehouse.

In 1921 Mattie still owned the property at 1922 Market, which the city directory listed as the address of John D. Ready, telegrapher.

The 1923 directory lists Ready and Mattie Silks as living at 2635 Lawrence Street. The 1924 directory changed the listing to show that John D. Ready, livestock dealer, and his wife, Martha, lived at the Lawrence Street cottage. The name "Mattie Silks" never again appeared in the directory. She was seventy-seven years old when she married Handsome Jack so she might have someone to care for her in her declining years.

In 1926 she incurred a fractured hip in a fall, and thereafter spent most of her time in a wheel chair. At a Christmas party in 1928 she rose from her wheel chair to drink a toast, fell again, and once more suffered a fracture of the same hip.

She was removed to the Denver General Hospital, where the following day she made out a holographic will on a hospital letterhead. She died January 7, 1929, at the age of 83.

So it was that the Scarlet Lady lived, and loved, and died.

Funeral services were held at the Hofmann undertaking parlors without benefit of clergy—because, pallbearer Charley Nolan was informed, it was a Quaker service. It lacked music and flowers, and there were few mourners—but among the few was one of Denver's leading and wealthiest industrialists.

Three or four friends followed the hearse to Fairmount cemetery. Without prayers Mattie was buried beside the unmarked grave of Cort Thomson, the sweetheart of her youth, her knight in tarnished armor. He was her man.

The name on her modest stone is Martha A. Ready.

At one time worth half a million dollars, Mattie left an estate consisting of $4,000 in real estate and $2,500 worth of jewels. By the time the public administrator got through with the estate its net value was only $1,922.

The only real estate Mattie owned when she died was the

cottage on Lawrence Street. Her humble Negro maid, Green, owns three houses in the same block.

The estate was divided equally between Handsome Jack, the second husband, and the adopted daughter, then married and residing in another state. Ready died, penniless, May 23, 1931. His burial expenses were paid through a collection taken up in the barrooms of Larimer Street. He is buried at Fairmount cemetery in an unmarked grave far from the stone bearing the name "Martha A. Ready."

The jewelry Mattie kept until her death consisted of her diamond cross and two diamond rings. Of all her jewels, why had she retained to the last only the cross and the rings? Had her knight in tarnished armor given her one ring, and Handsome Jack the other?

Was the cross a symbol of something life had withheld from the scarlet lady?

Nineteen years after her death the following story appeared in the Denver Daily *Journal* of July 8, 1948.

DENVER LANDMARK WILL BE REMODELED INTO WAREHOUSE

One of Denver's oldest and most famous buildings is soon to be remodeled into a warehouse, according to Royal Judd, of Judd & Co., general contractors.

Little remains of the original edifice to remind one of the fabulous past of the 1942 Market Street building, but that little still gives an impression of its once beautiful architecture.

Worked into the front of the building are five faces sculped from rose stone. A look inside reveals its famous parlor of mirrors framed with blond, bird's-eye maple.

Remodeling will include tearing out all wood floors and partitions and replacing them with concrete slabs and steel. The top of the building will be removed and replaced with a flat roof and the basement will be filled with dirt and covered with a concrete slab.

Plans call for an overhead door and loading dock at the front. The new owners will also have the building sandblasted.

The Buddhist Church of Denver, occupants of the building since 1919, sold the building to Judd. Remodeling will begin as soon as the Buddhists move to their new temple on Lawrence Street between 19th and 20th streets the latter part of July.

When workmen began dismantling the old house, the author, prowling through the low, dusty attic, came upon a gilded chair and two player-piano rolls. The rolls contained—of all things to find in such a place—recordings of Beethoven's *Fifth Symphony!*

A few days after the remodeling operations were begun, Denver newspapers were filled with stories concerning a ghost seen flitting about the rooftops in the neighborhood of Mattie's old home at 2635 Lawrence Street.

"It was an old woman in a white dress," a twelve-year-old Arapahoe Street boy was quoted as saying. "When you got close to her you could still see her dress, but her face disappeared."

For several nights crowds numbering as many as 500 persons gathered to see the ghost. Hundreds of automobiles jammed the streets, creating a serious traffic problem. A police cruiser equipped with a loudspeaker patrolled the neighborhood, begging the members of the crowd to "go home."

The once fashionable neighborhood had been taken over in recent years by a population consisting largely of Mexicans and Negroes. These newcomers never heard of Mattie Silks. The newspapers passed up a bet when they failed to connect the appearance of the ghost with the destruction of the famous house of Denver's long-dead queen of the courtesans. What a newspaper yarn it could have made!

Mattie Silks was beautiful and bad. She sinned prodigiously. She lived dangerously. She loved extravagantly but unwisely. Her love for a man who was unworthy of any woman's love brought her little but misery. She reared and educated the daughter of his child by another woman, which not all women who hold themselves her betters would have done. A bad woman, but not altogether bad.

The year 1915 marked not only the end of Denver's old tenderloin, but the end of an era. It was the year Denver passed from its hell-roaring pioneer youth and settled down to smug respectability. Like the man of middle age trying to forget youthful indiscretions, Denver today is trying its best to forget the old Market Street "Row." In achieving respectability, the city has lost much of the color of its youth—and the color is scarlet.

NOTES

P. 5. The story of Belle Siddons is taken largely from an interview with her in the San Francisco *Examiner* in October, 1881, and quoted by W. B. Thom in the Leadville *Herald-Democrat*, August 19, 1937; from Agnes Wright Spring, *Cheyenne and Black Hills Stage and Express Routes* (Arthur H. Clark & Co., 1949); and from the New York *Tribune*, January 3, 1878.

P. 52. For a complete account of Verona's lawsuits involving Baldwin, see C. B. Glasscock, *Lucky Baldwin* (Bobbs-Merrill, 1933), pp. 220-232.

P. 87. Material in this chapter is largely from contemporary newspaper files, and from William Ross Collier and Edwin Victor Westlake, *The Reign of Soapy Smith* (Doubleday, Doran, 1935).

P. 97. Material in this chapter, except for that part resulting from the author's own experience and observation, comes largely from Philip S. Van Cise, *Fighting the Underworld* (Houghton Mifflin Co., 1936).

P. 171. From Charles Kingsley, *Poems* (London and New York: The Macmillan Co., 1889). Also published in an earlier edition, 1859. Quoted by permission of publishers.

BIBLIOGRAPHY

ANDERSON, GALUSKA. *A Border City during the Civil War.* Boston: Little, Brown & Co., 1908.

ASBURY, HERBERT. *Sucker's Progress.* New York: Dodd, Mead & Co., 1938.

BARBER, JUDGE IRVING L. "Reminiscences." Unpublished Manuscript, Colorado State Historical Society.

BENNETT, EVE. "Shady Ladies of the Eighties," *Rocky Mountain Life* Magazine (April, 1947).

BENTON, JESSE JAMES. *Cow by the Tail.* Boston: Houghton Mifflin Co., 1943.

Biographical History (Colorado). Denver: Linderman Co., Inc., 1927. Vol. V.

BRADLEY, LIEUTENANT JAMES H. *Montana Historical Society Contributions,* 1923, Vol. IX.

BURCH, J. P., as told by Captain Harrison Trow. *Charles W. Quantrell and His Guerrilla Band.* Kansas City: Privately printed, 1923.

BURNLEY, JAMES. *Millionaires and Kings of Enterprise.* London: Harmsworth Bros., Ltd.; Philadelphia: J. B. Lippincott Co., 1901.

CODY, WILLIAM F. "Famous Hunting Parties of The Plains," *Cosmopolitan* (June, 1894).

COLE, ARTHUR C. *Centennial History of Illinois* (Springfield), Vol. III, 1919.

COLLIER, WILLIAM ROSS, and EDWIN VICTOR WESTRATE. *The Rein of Soapy Smith, Monarch of Misrule.* New York: Doubleday, Doran & Co., 1935.

Colorado Handbook, 1880.

COOPER, ARTHUR. *Visitor's Pocket Guide to Denver.* 1896.

COUTANT, C. G. *History of Wyoming.* Vol. I.

CREEL, GEORGE. *Rebel at Large.* New York: G. P. Putnam's Sons, 1913.

CROWLEY, ELMER S. "The History of the Tabor Grand Opera House." Unpublished thesis, Western History Collection, Denver Public Library, 1940.

CUMMINS, JIM. *Jim Cummins' Book, Written by Himself* (Life Story of the James and Younger Gang). Denver: Reed Publishing Co. 1903.

CUSHMAN, GEORGE L. "Abilene, First of the Kansas Cow Towns," *Kansas Historical Quarterly,* Vol. IX, 1940.

CZERNIN, COUNT FERDINAND. *This Salzburg.* New York: Greystone Press, 1938.

DAVIS, RICHARD HARDING. *Queen's Jubilee, in a Year from a Reporter's Handbook.* New York: Harper & Brothers, 1903.

Debrett's Peerage.

(DENVER) City Directories, 1877-1929.

(DENVER) *History of the City of Denver.* Chicago: O. L. Baskin & Co. 1880.

(DENVER) *Polly Pry's Magazine* (December 26, 1903).

(DENVER) *Post.* Files, 1892-1948.

(DENVER) *Republican.* Files, 1882-1904.

(DENVER) Rocky Mountain *News.* Files, 1868-1948.

(DENVER) *Times.* Files, 1881-1910.

Denver City and Auraria in 1860 (Maps). Colorado State Historical Society, 1936.

FISK, CAPTAIN JAMES L. *Expedition to the Rocky Mountains.* Senate Document, 38th Congress, 1864.

GANDY, LEWIS CASS. *The Tabors*. New York: Press of the Pioneers, 1934.

GARDINER, ALEXANDER. *True Story of the Greatest Gambler*. New York: Doubleday, Doran, 1930.

(GEORGETOWN) *Miner* (Colorado). Files, 1873, 1878.

GLASSCOCK, C. B. *Lucky Baldwin*. Indianapolis: Bobbs-Merrill, 1933.

HALL, FRANK. *History of Colorado*. Chicago: Blakely Printing Co., 1889-95.

HAMBLETON, CHALKEY J. *A Gold Hunter's Experience*. Chicago: Privately printed, 1898.

HASKELL, THOMAS NELSON. *Young Konkaput, the King of the Utes*. Denver: Collier & Cleaveland, 1889.

HAYS CITY, *Kansas Historical Quarterly*. Vols. VII, IX.

HEADLEY, J. T. *Napoleon and His Marshals*. New York: Baker & Scribner, 1847.

HELDT, F. GEORGE. "Interview with Henry Bostwick," Montana, *State Historical Society Contributions* (1876). Vol. I.

HILL, W. A. *Historic Hays*. Hays, Kansas: News Publishing Co., 1938.

HORNER, JOHN WILLARD. *Silver Town*. Caldwell: Caxton Printers, Ltd., 1950.

HOWARD, SARAH ELIZABETH. *Pen Pictures of the Plains*. Denver: Reed Publishing Co., 1902.

JENKINS, MALINDA, as told to Jesse Lilienthal. *Gambler's Wife*. Boston: Houghton Mifflin, 1933.

JOHNSON, J. H. *The Open Book*. Kansas City: Privately printed, 1927.

Kansas Historical Quarterly (1937). Vol. VI.

KENT, L. A. *Leadville*. Denver: Daily *Times* Steam Printing House, 1880.

KINGSLEY, CHARLES. *Poems*. London and New York: The Macmillan Co., 1889.

——*Lectures Delivered in America in 1874*. Philadelphia: Joseph H. Coates & Co., 1875.

KRAUSER, MINNIE HALL. Article, *Colorado Magazine* (March, 1947).

(LEADVILLE) City Directories, 1881-83.

(LEADVILLE) Daily *Herald*. Files, 1883.

(LEADVILLE) *Herald-Democrat*. Files, 1901, 1936, 1937, 1940.

LOUNSBERRY, CLEMENT A. *History of North Dakota*. Chicago: S. J. Clarke Pub. Co., 1917.

LOWTHER, CHARLES C. *Dodge City*. Kansas: Dorrance & Co., 1940.

MAYER, JOSEPH. "The Passing of the Red Light District," *Social Hygiene Magazine* (April, 1918).

McLAIN, JOHN SCUDDER. *Alaska and the Klondike*. New York: McClure, Phillips & Co., 1905.

McMECHEN, EDGAR G. "Baby Doe Tabor—Epilogue," *Monthly Brand Book*, the Westerners (February, 1949).

MORRIS, JOHN (pseud. for John O'Connor) (ed.). *Wanderings of a Vagabond*. New York: Privately printed, 1873.

O'SHAUGHNESSY, EDITH. *Marie Adelaide*. New York: Harrison Smith, 1932.

(PERU) Indiana *Republican,* Files, 1884.

(PUEBLO) *Chieftain* (May 28, 1944).

RICHARDSON, ALBERT D. *Beyond the Mississippi*. New York: American Publishing Co., 1867.

Rocky Mountain Directory and Colorado Gazetteer, 1871.

ROMBAUER, ROBERT J. *The Union Cause in St. Louis in 1861*. St. Louis: Nixon-Jones Press, 1909.

(SAN FRANCISCO) *Call* (January 5, 1883).

(SAN FRANCISCO) *Examiner* (October, 1881).

SCHOBERLIN, MELVIN. *From Candles to Footlights*. Denver: Old West Publishing Co., 1941.

SCHOFIELD, LIEUT.-GEN. JOHN M. *Forty-six years in the Army*. New York: Century Co., 1897.

SEMPER IDEM. *A Bibliographical Attempt to Describe the Guide Books to the Houses of Ill Fame in New Orleans as They Were Published There*. Privately printed, 1936.

SMILEY, JEROME C. *History of Denver*. Denver: Times-Sun Publishing Co., 1901.

SPRING, AGNES WRIGHT. *Cheyenne and Black Hills Stage and Express Routes*. Glendale, California: Arthur H. Clark Co., 1949.

STRAHORN, ROBERT E. *Wyoming, Black Hills and Big Horn Region*. Cheyenne, Wyoming: Western Press, 1877.

TABOR, AUGUSTA (Mrs. H. A. W.). Scrapbooks. Unpublished, Western History Collection, Denver Public Library.

THOM, ARTHUR. Letters in Leadville *Herald-Democrat*, January 1, 1936, August 19, 1937, March 11, 1940.

THORP, MARGARET FARRAND. *Charles Kingsley*. Princeton: Princeton University Press, 1937.

VAN CISE, PHILIP S. *Fighting the Underworld*. Boston: Houghton Mifflin Co., 1936.

VESTAL, STANLEY. *Jim Bridger, Mountain Man*. New York: William Morrow & Co., 1946.

WESTRATE, EDWIN VICTOR. See COLLIER, WILLIAM ROSS.

WHARTON, J. E. *History of the City of Denver*. Denver: Byers and Dailey, Printers, 1866.

Whitaker's Almanack.

WISTER, OWEN. "How Lin McLean Went East," *Lin McLean*. New York: Harper & Brothers, 1903.

WRIGHT, ROBERT M. *Dodge City, the Cowboy Capital*. Wichita: Wichita *Eagle* Press, 1913.

(YUMA COUNTY, COLORADO) "Reminiscences." unpublished manuscript, Colorado State Historical Society.

INDEX

Abilene, Kans., 208, 216-20
Adair, Lord; see Dunraven, Earl of
Ah Lee Pang, 114
Ah sing, 110
Aiken, Jenny, 29
Airlie, Earl of; see Ogilvy, David Graham Drummond
Aladdin Theater, 69
Alamo Saloon, 217
Alaska Gold Mining Co., 196
Albany Hotel, 71
Albuquerque, N.M., 230
Alcazar Theater, 20
Alexis, Grand Duke, 37, 139
Allen, Lizzie, 153
American Fur Co., 130-31, 136-38
Amethyst vein, 54
Anaconda, Mont., 113
Anderson City; see Storyville
Anderson, Tom, 22
Annunciation Church, Leadville, 150

"Apache Bill," 224
Applejack Saloon, 217
Arcade, The, 17, 82, 93, 112
Archobald, Phil, 265
Argyle, Jeff, 92
Arkansas River, 229
Arlington, Josie, 22
Armstrong, Alderman, 260
Armstrong, Art, 248
Armstrong, Hamilton, 26, 118, 120
Arnold, Mayor Henry J., 280
Arthur, Pres. Chester A., 166
Ashton, Tom, 248
Aspen, Colo., 41
Auraria, Colo., 13
Austin, Robert A. (Bob), 14, 67
Averil, Jim, 31

"Bad Lands," Deadwood, 8
Baggs, Charles (Doc), 37, 87-88
Baldwin, E. J. (Lucky), 15, 50, 54, 211

Baldwin Hotel, San Francisco, 50-51, 53
Baldwin Inn, 53
Baldwin, Verona, 15, 50-54, 211
Barber, Judge Irving L., 209, 251
Barbour, Addie, 67
Barbour, Frances Minerva, 67; *see also* Chase, Frances Minerva
Baring Bros., 130, 137
Bartholomew, George, 210
"Bassett, Amy," 55
Bassett, Charley, 222
Baur, O. P., 141
Bell, Clifton, 70, 84-85, 91
Bell, Horace, 53
Bell, Laura, 29
Bell, Rev. Leonard, 220
Bella Union, San Francisco, 50
Belle Fourche River, 137
Bellmont, Nellie, 66
Bennett, James Gordon, 139
Bennett and Myers ranch, 191
Benton, Jesse James, 216
Bernard, Belle, 14, 211
Berthold, Fort, 139
Big Horn River, 135
Big Plume, 136
Bing Goo tong, 109
Bingham Canyon, Utah, 194
Bishop, Jack, 227
Blackhawk, Colo., 154, 210, 227, 229-30
Black Hills, S.D., 7, 11, 31, 65, 137-38, 210
"Black Prince," 92
Blaine, Jim, 253, 265, 270-72, 274

Blonger, Lou, 80, 89, 93, 97-107, 175, 222
Blonger, Nola, 98
Blonger, Sadie, 98
Blonger, Sam H., 93, 98, 222
Blue Book, New Orleans, 22
Board of Trade Saloon, 229
Bodie, Calif., 79
Bonfils, Fred G., 175-89
Bon Ton dance hall, 27
Boot Hill cemetery, 218
Borah, William E., 193
Boston & Colorado smelter, 230
Bostwick, Henry, 131, 135, 139
Bottom, John T., 186
Boyce, Barney, 14, 67
Bradley, Lieut. James H., 136
Brasier, Pansy, 26
Breese mine, 158
Bridger, Fort, 134
Bridger, Jim, 130, 133-34, 138
Bridges, Jack, 222
Brinker's Collegiate Institute, 69
Broadmoor Hotel, 199, 202-3
Brooks, Billy, 222, 224
Brown, Blanche, 15
Brown, John H., 10-11
Brown Palace Hotel, 47, 71, 173
Brownell St., Georgetown, 28, 226
Bryan, William Jennings, 169
Bucket of Blood, the, 92
Buckskin Joe, 235
Buddhist Church, 285
Buffalo Bill; *see* Cody, William F.
Bull Domingo mine, 158
Bull's Head, the, 217, 219

Burke, Daniel, 67
Burke, Pete, 191
Burlew, Harry E., 48
Burlington & Missouri R.R.; *see* Chicago, Burlington & Quincy R.R.
Burton, Blanche, 29
Bush, W. H. (Billy), 71, 152-73, 176-77
Butler, Hugh, 167
Butte, Mont., 113

Cady, Tom, 72, 87, 90, 92
"Calamity Jane"; *see* Canary, Calamity Jane
California Gang, 89, 267
California Gulch, 27, 229
"California Joe," 224
Canary, "Calamity Jane," 30, 79
Canfield, Richard, 65, 86
"Captain Drew," 224
Carbonate Hall, Leadville, 148-49
Carson City, Nev., 81
Cash on Delivery claim, 191
Casino, the, Saratoga, 50
Cass, Albert A., 70
Casswell, Alexander, 10
"Cattle Kate," 31
Caylor, Jennie, 14, 211
Centennial Park, 266
Central City, Colo., 154, 210, 227-29
Central Overland, California & Pikes Peak Express Co., 13
Central Savings Bank, 68
Chaffee Light Artillery, 112
Chaffee, Sen. Jerome B., 65

Chamberlin's Restaurant, Wash., 85
Chan Hon Fan, 114
Chase, Ed, 3, 14, 22, 64-69, 72, 80, 93, 147, 213
Chase, Frances Minerva, 84
Chase, Helen, 66
Chase & Hunter, 65
Chase, John, 14, 22, 66
Chase, Margaret Jane, 66
Chatillon, Henry, 131, 133
Chatillon, Joe, 131, 133-34
Cheesman Park, 181
"Cherokee Bill," 224
Cherry Creek, 13, 120, 123, 219
Cheyenne, Wyo., 11, 30, 78, 124
Cheyenne-Deadwood trail, 7, 31
Cheyenne Mountain, 199, 202-3
Chicago, Burlington & Quincy R.R., 245, 250
Chicago, Ill., 80
Chicken Coop, the, 71, 92
Children's Hospital, 182
Chilkoot pass, 268
Chin Gee Chow, 113
Chin, James, 109
Chin, Lily, 108; *see also* Look, Lily
Chin Lin Sou, 108
Chin, Willie, 109
Chino Copper Co., 196
Chisholm trail, 216
Chisum trail, 249
Chivington, Col. J. M., 66
Chrysolite mine, 158, 257
Chucovich, Vaso, 69, 80-84
Chung, Louis, 109

Churchill, Mrs. Winston, 124
Cibola Hall, 70
City House, Denver, 141-43, 147-48
City Park, Denver, 265
Civic Benefactors, Court of, 259
Clancy, John, 94
Clarendon Hotel, Leadville, 152, 156
Clark, Etta, 28
Clark, "Windy," 36
Clay, Henry, 65
Clayton, G. W., 64
Clear Creek, 227
Clifford, Minnie, 5, 18, 33-38, 45, 211
Clifford, Tom, 56
Clifton House, 70
Clothilde, Princess, 145
Clough, Johnny, 92
"Cockeyed Frank," 224
Cody, William F. (Buffalo Bill), 37, 131, 138, 140, 220
Coe, Phil, 217, 219
Cohen, Stuyvesant van Rensselaer, 55
Coleman's Place, 77
Coliseum Theater, Leadville, 158
Collier, William Ross (Bill), 119-20
Colorado City, 29, 30, 193
Colorado Midland R.R., 41
Colorado-Philadelphia Reduction Co., 193
Colorado Policy Assn., 80
Colorado School of Mines, 109

Colorado Springs, Colo., 41, 141, 172, 190, 193, 199, 232
Colorado State Historical Society, 134, 169
Colorado State Lottery, 79
Colorado, Territory of, 43
Commercial Hotel, Wray, 271-72
Committee of 303, 94
Comstock lode, 50
Cook, Alpha, 28
Cook, Charles A., 68
Cook, Gen. David J., 112
Cook, Mattie, 28
Cooking Club, 202
Coon Row, Leadville, 28
"Cooney the Fox," 20
Cooper, Joe, 269
Cottage Club, 68, 71
Cox, Harry, 249
Coxey's army, 19
Creede, Colo., 54, 90, 94, 97, 211
Creede, N. C., 90
Creel, George, 280
Cricket Club, 22, 66, 147
Cripple Creek, Colo., 29, 98, 113, 115, 190-203, 267
Cripple Creek Sampling & Ore Co., 193
Cripple Creek Short Line, 193
Criterion Hall, 69
Crooks, Bill, 92, 212
Crow's Breast, 139
Culbertson, Alexander, 136-38
Cummings, Archie; *see* McLaughlin, Archie
Curtis, Gen. Newton M., 5, 6
Custer, General, 220

Dab, Lillie, 243, 260-63, 273
Daingerfield, Edward, 171
Dalaruche, General, 145
Daly, John, 50
Daniel, Rev. H. W., 240
Daniels, Ben, 222
Daniels mansion, 67
Dapron, Louis, 131
Darley, Minnie, 26
Darrow, Clarence, 193
Davenport, "Diamond Lil," 94
Davey, Randall, 203
Davidson, Jo, 203
Davis, "Dangerous Dick," 31
Davis, Herndon, 170
Davis, Richard Harding, 90
Dawson City, Yukon Territory, 268
Deadwood, S.D., 7-11, 30, 65, 79, 138, 210
Dean, Mollie; see Nephue, Mary Ann
De Bars Opera House, 5
de Camp, Leona, 14, 211
Delahunty, John, 86
Delaware College, 244
Demmon Hill, 31
de Murska, Mollie, 26
Dennis, Orville L., 104
Denver Brewing Co., 210, 212
Denver City mine, 158
Denver Club, 38
Denver Exchange, Creede, 91
Denver Gardens; see Olympic Gardens
Denver General Hospital, 84, 283
Denver Hall, 65
Denver Mansions Co., 176
Denver Press Club, 115, 120
Denver Public Library, 163
Denver & Rio Grande R.R., 41, 265
Denver & Rio Grande Western R.R., 133
Denver, Texas & Fort Worth R.R., 41
Denver, Utah & Pacific Construction Co., 159
Deville, Willie, 153
Devol, George, 78
Deyo, Elizabeth C., 28
di Gallotti, Baron Carlos, 142
di Gallotti, Baroness Stephanie, 142-50
di Gallotti, Frederego, 146
Dodge City, Kans., 28, 216, 219, 221-25, 267
Dodge House, 224
Doe, Baby; see Tabor, Baby Doe
Doe, Elizabeth B.; see Tabor, Baby Doe
Doe, William Harvey, 59, 153-68
Doherty, Sam, 209
Dominion Saloon, 269
Drake, John A., 86
Drover's Cottage, 217
Drum, Tommy, 220
Dry Climate Club, 71
Duff, Adolph W., 98
Duffield, Sheriff Glen, 281
Dumont, Clara, 14
Dumont, Eleanor; see "Minnie, the Gambler"
Dumont, Emily, 14
Dumont, Lillian, 14
Dunraven, Earl of, 124

Dupuy, Louis, 227; *see also* Gerard, Adolphus Francis
Durango, Colo., 156, 159-61, 163, 173
"Dutch Henry," 224
"Dutch Jake," 28
Dyea; *see* Skagway, Alaska
Dyer, Phil, 86

Earp, Jim, 222
Earp, Virgil, 222
Earp, Wyatt, 222, 267
Edward, Duke of Kent, 145
El Dorado, San Francisco, 50
Elephant Corral, 143
Ellis, James K., 71
Ellsler, Effie, 26
Ellwood, Col. Isaac, 86
El Paso, Texas, 79, 122
Emmanuele, King Vittorio, 144-46
Empire, Colo., 79
End of the Trail Assn., 203
Estes, Mattie; *see* Deyo, Elizabeth C.
Eulalia, Infanta, 258
Evans, Elizabeth, 176
Exchange Saloon; *see* Murphy's Exchange

Fairmount cemetery, Denver, 274, 283-84
Farley, Blanche, 25
Farmers' Protective Assn., 219
Fashion, the, 15
"Fat Jack," 224
Fay, John E., 94
"Featherlegs, Madame," 31

Featherly, "Con," 71
Feeney, John, 122
Field, Eugene, 38-39, 118
Field, Marshall, 257
First Congregational Church, 45
Fitzgerald, Archie T., 48
"Fitzwilliam, Lord"; *see* Wentworth-Fitzwilliam, Sir William-Thomas-Spencer
Florence, Colo., 194
Ford, Bob, 90-91
Ford Brothers, 65
Forest Queen mine, 98
Forrest, Gen. Nathan B., 6
Fowler, Gene, 117, 123
"Foxy Lil," 24
Foy, Eddie, 20
Francis, Duke of Saxe-Coburg-Saalfield, 145
Frankfort Lottery, 79
Fremont, Gen. John C., 5
French Row, 28
Fulton, Katie, 5, 207-12, 219, 230, 260, 273, 276, 278

Gallotti, Salvatore, 146
Gardiner, Alexander 85
Gardner House, 176
Garfield, Pres. James A., 258
Garland, Sir John Watts, 139
Garry, Tony, 232
Gates, John W. "Bet a Million," 86
Gavin & Austin, 71
Gaylord, Ed, 14, 67, 265
Gee Chow, 110
Gentlemen's Riding and Driving Club, 265

Georgetown, Colo., 28, 78, 85, 154, 210, 225-29, 233

Gerard, Adolphus Francis; *see* Dupuy, Louis

German-American Trust Co., 98

Gibney, W. A., 240

Gleichmann, Charles, 141

Glen Pendry mine, 158

Globe National Bank, 56

Gold Room Saloon, 78

Golden, Colo., 64-65

Golden Eagle Hotel, 25

Goodwin, C. C., 51

Gore Canyon, 129, 133

Gore Pass, 129, 133

Gore Range, 129, 133

Gore, Sir St. George, 129-40

Gould, Anna (Gouldie), 15, 211

Gourney, Lottie, 114

Governor's Guard, 112

Grace Episcopal Church, Colorado Springs, 172

Grand Central Theater, Leadville, 149, 152

Grant, Charley (Pigfoot), 250-53, 270

Grant, Gussie, 14, 211

Grant, Hattie, 29

Grant, Pres. U. S., 257

Grant Street prison, 6

Gratiot Street prison, 6

"Great Eastern," 28

Greeley, Colo., 124-25, 232

Greeley, Horace, 70

Green, Hattie, 208, 215, 278, 284

Green River rendezvous, 139

Greer brothers, 78

Greer, Liz, 29

Gregory Gulch, 108, 111

Gregory, John H., 226, 230

Griffin, Annie, 25

Griffith, D. T., 227

Griffith, George F., 227

Griffiths, William, 56

Grover, Colo., 56

Guard's Hall, 172

Gunnison, Colo., 158

Guth, Anna, 71

Guy, Anna, 14, 211

Haigler, Neb., 245, 248, 254

Hall, "Clubfoot," 87

Hall, Minnie, 14, 20

Hall, Mrs. Ida, 114

Halleck, Gen. H. W., 5

Hallett, Dr. Newt, 6

Hallett, Moses, 68

Hamill, William A., 154

Hamlin, Clarence C., 194

Hamrock, Col. Patrick J., 103-4

Hand, Dora, 224

"Happy Jack," 112

Hardin, Wes, 217

Harlow, Ida M., 68

Harlow, W. J., 68

Harpel, Lou, 26

Harrington, Judge Benjamin F., 163, 167

Hart, Charles; *see* Quantrell, Charles W.

Haskell, Prof. Thomas N., 36-37, 178

Hastings, Beryl, 26

Haunted House resort, 17

Hay, John, 264

Hayden, Clara, 14, 211
Hays, Kans., 216, 219-21
Haywood, W. D. (Big Bill), 115, 193
Healy, John, 25
Heatley, Francis P. (Hub), 14, 65
Heights, the, 37
Henrietta mine, 158
Hibernia mine, 158
Hickey, Chief, 112
Hickey, Dan, 71
Hickok, J. B. (Wild Bill), 8, 78-79, 208, 218-20, 224
Hoffses, Alton E. (Big Al), 67
Hofmann undertaking parlors, 119, 283
Hoggatt, Volney T., 188
Holladay, Ben, 13
Holliday, "Doc," 222-24
Holmes, Jennie, 14, 22
Holy Moses mine, 90
Honore, H. H., 228
Hook, George T., 151
"Hop Alley," 13, 108-16, 276, 278, 281
Hopkin, Robert, 172
Horn Dock, 109
Hostetter, Theodore, 86
Hot Springs, Ark., 240
Hotel de Paris, 227-28
Howard, Mr.; see James, Jesse
Hughes, Charles Evans, 197
Hughes, John J. (Johnny), 14, 82, 93
Hughes, John J., Jr., 68
Hunsicker, C. W., 68

Hunt, W. S., 67
Hunter, George O., 67
Hunter, Sam D., 65

Idaho Springs, Colo., 114
Iliff, John Wesley, 244
Iliff School of Theology, 245
Ingalls, Sen. John J., 166
Inter-ocean Club, 67, 71-72
Ironside dance hall, 192

Jackling, Daniel C., 194-96
Jackson, Gov. Clairborne Fox, 5
James, Frank, 221
James, Jesse, 90, 221
Jefferson City, Mo., 5, 6
Jeff's Place, 94-95
Jerome, Prince Napoleon, 145
Jewell, Belle, 14, 211
Jewell Park, 265
Jiggs' Buffet, 208
Johnson, Hon. "Skunk," 223
Jones, Belle, 25
Jones' Place, 84
Jones, "Texas," 265
Jordan, Jim, 92
Judd, Royal, 284
Jump, Ed, 69
Junction City, Kans., 216-17

Kansas City, Mo., 215, 217, 220, 240
Kansas Pacific R.R., 108, 216-7
Keady, Tom; see Cady, Tom
Kearny, Fort, 139
Kelley, Ed O., 91
Kelly, Etta, 49, 56

Kelly, Jack; *see* Ready, John Dillon
Kennecott Copper Co., 196
Kentucky State Lottery, 79
Kerr, Synne, 25
Keyes, Belle, 29
"Kid Duffy"; *see* Duff, Adolph W.
Kingsley, Charles, 171
Kingsley, Maurice, 172
Kingsley, Rose, 172
Kit Carson, Colo., 218
Klipfel, Louis, 20
"Klondike Liz," 26
Knutsford Hotel, 194
Kong Ping, 113

Ladore Canon, 248
Lady Gay Theater, 224
Laird, Colo., 245, 252, 270, 274
Laird, Hon. James, 245
La Monte, Ada, 29
Landing area, Vicksburg, 80
Lang, Jacob, 47
Lap jacket, 224
Laramie, Fort, 11, 30, 133-34
Laramie National Bank, 68
Laramie River, 133
Laramie, Wyo., 133, 257
Larne, Beatrice, 268
Las Cruces, N.M., 190
Las Vegas, N.M., 12
Lathrop, Mary, 82-84
La Veta apartments, 163
Lay, Mabel, 26
Lead Chief mine, 158
Leadville Club, Denver, 71

Leadville, Colo., 12, 38, 77, 87, 148-49, 154, 174, 224, 229-30, 233, 257
Leavenworth City & Pikes Peak Express, 33, 219
Leavenworth, Fort, 131
Lebfrom, Ernest U. (Blondy), 120-22
Lee Gon, 110
Lee, Rosa, 15, 18, 211
Le Fevre, Frank, 26
Legislative Council, 64
Leiter, Levi Z., 257
Leonard, W. H., 192
Lewis, Emma, 14, 211, 231
Lewis, Eva, 14, 18-19
Lexington Female University, 5
Linnell, Carrie, 28
Little Casino dance hall, 27, 77
Little Cottonwood Creek, 11
Little Missouri River, 137-38
Little Pittsburgh mine, 151, 159
Livingston, Lola, 14, 19
Llewellen, Wellington C., 56
Lloyd, Reuben H., 51
Locke, Charles E., 38
Lomery, Chief James J., 35
Londeau, Annie, 15
London, Belle, 15
Lone Star dance hall, 222
Long's Peak, 211
Look, Lily, 108-9
Look, Pearl, 109
Look Wing Yuen, 108
Loss, Harry, 17, 19
Lost Park, 133
Lott Sing, Leo, 114
Lou Quong, 113

Louisiana Lottery, 80
Lovejoy, Rose, 15, 19
Lovell, Lillis, 54-55, 90, 211
Lovell, Lois, 54-55
Lowe, Joe, 71
Luxembourg, Duchess of, 145
Lyons, Maurice, 56

"Madame Moustache"; *see* "Minnie, the Gambler"
Maid of Erin mine, 158
Majors, Mayme, 29
Mallory, Dwight D., 66
Malloy, Mae, 26
Manhattan, Kans., 159
Mansfield, Billy, 10, 11
Mansion, the, 29
Manton, Joe, 132
Marcy, Capt. R. B., 135
Marie Adelaide; *see* Luxembourg, Duchess of
Marion, George, 67
Marshall, Frank, 92
Marshall, Jim, 71
Martin, John, 67
Masterson, Bat, 91, 222-24
Masterson, Ed, 222
Matchless mine, 158, 174
Mathers, "Mysterious Dave," 222
May, Boone, 10
May Co. store, 121
May, Mollie, 28
Maybray gang, 99
Maynard, Jack, 18
McAndrews, "Hickey," 17
McCall, Jack, 8
McCarren, Sen. Patrick, 86

McCourt, Elizabeth B.; *see* Tabor, Baby Doe
McDaniel, Nellie M., 68
McDaniel, Orville A., 68
McEvoy & Dale, 93, 235
McEvoy, Helen, 14, 72
McGrath, Andy, 94
McIntire, Gov. Albert W., 108
McIntosh, Elias, 65
McKinley, Pres. William, 258
McLaughlin, Archie, 9, 11
McMillan, Mrs. Julie Villiers, 199; *see also* Penrose, Mrs. Spencer
McPherson, Fort, 139
MacNeill, Charles M., 192, 202
Memphis & Mobile R.R., 6
Mercur gold mines, 194
Mercy Hospital, 48
Merrival, Joe, 133
Mershon, Nellie, 114
Middle Park, 78, 133-34
Miles City, Mont., 135
"Minnie, the Gambler," 30, 79
Miramare Hotel, 200
Missoula, Mont., 113
Missouri Club, 92
Missouri Pacific R.R., 41
Moeller, Fannie, 28
Moffat, David H., 202
Moffat Road, 202
Moffat Tunnel, 202
Mohant, Nellie; *see* Bellmont, Nellie
Monte Verde, Lurline, 8; *see also* Vestal, Madame
Montgomery, Paris, 119-20

Moon, Jim, 68, 112; *see also* Wilcoxon, John E.
Morgan, Alice, 152-53
Morgan, James, 71
Morgue, the, 92
Mormon Queen, the, 90
Moustache, Madame, 79
Mowry, Lewis D., 103
Moynahan, Anna, 29
Murat, "Count" Henry, 69
Murat, "Countess" Katerine, 69
Murat, Joachim, 69
Murphy, "Dirty Face," 248, 253, 271
Murphy, Johnny, 92-93, 236
Murphy, "Peg-leg," 271-72
Murphy, "Spud," 30
Murphy's Exchange, 91-92, 235-36, 267-68
Murray, Guiney, 71

Nash, Matilda, 79
Natchez-under-the-hill, 80
National Gallery of Art, 173
National Gold Extraction Co., 193
Navarre, the, 69, 82
Nelson, "Baron," 179
Nelson, Emma, 14, 34
Nephue, Mary Ann, 29
Newman, Edward, 155
Nicholas II, Czar, 258
Nixon, T. C., 222
Nolan, Charles, 208, 268-69, 283
Nolan, Johnny, 192
Nome, Alaska, 54, 267
North Park, 133
North Platte, Neb., 140

Northwest Mounted Police, 268
Nott, Frank W., 265, 274

Occidental Hall, 142-43
Odeon dance hall, 27
Ogilvy, Capt. Lyulph Gilchrist Stanley, 124-26
Ogilvy, David Graham Drummond, 124
Ogilvy, Lord; *see* Ogilvy, Capt. Lyulph Gilchrist Stanley
Olathe, Kans., 215
Olympic Gardens, 207, 210, 212, 273
Ono, T., 282
Oolite mine, 158
Orchard, Harry, 193
Orchard Place, 72, 114
Orleans Club, 91
Oro City, Colo., 172
Overland Park, 263-66, 279
Overland stage line, 217

Pabor, W. E., 36-37
Page, Frankie, 28
Palace Theater, Denver, 66
Palmer House, 257
Palmer Lake, Colo., 70
Palmer, Minnie, 211
Palmer, Mrs. Potter, 228, 257-58
Palmer, Potter, 257
Panhandle Townsite Co., 178
Paradise Alley, 15
Parrish, Maxfield, 199
Paulhan, Louis, 266
Pavilion Club, 71
Pelican and Dives mines, 227
Penrose, Boies, 191-92, 201

Penrose, Dr. Charles B., 195
Penrose, Mrs. Spencer, 201
Penrose, R. A. F., 195
Penrose, Spencer (Spec), 190-
    203
Perry, Carlotta, 164
Persson, Charles, 82
Persson, Pete, 82, 84
Peru, Ind., 240-41, 261
Pikes Peak, 65, 134, 191, 195, 199,
    203, 222, 226-27
Pinkerton Detective Agency, 19
Pioneer dance hall, 27
Platte River, 133, 210, 212, 219
Plymouth Congregational
    Church, 184
Poker Alice, 220
Pomeroy, D. M., 71
Pony Club, 71
Poverty Gulch, 190-91
"Prairie Dog Dave," 224
Preston, Lizzie, 5, 14, 56-58, 154-
    55, 167, 211
Price, Gen. Sterling, 6
Price, Mollie, 28
Progressive Club, 65-66
Proteau, Jeremiah, 131, 137
Pueblo, Colo., 30, 230
Pullman, George W., 228
Purdy, Minnie, 18, 28
Purple, Sallie, 28
Putnam, Marie, 14

Quantrell, Charles W., 9, 209,
    211, 216, 221, 237
Quayle, William, 45
Quincy Club, 71

Rapid City, S.D., 10
Rawhide Butte, 31
Ray Consolidated Copper Co.,
    196
Ready, John Dillon (Handsome
    Jack), 254, 270, 274, 275, 280,
    283-84
Ready, Martha A., 283; *see also*
    Silks, Mattie
Red Book directory, 22
Red Cloud Indian Agency, 6
Red Light dance hall, 27
"Red Stockings," 27
Reid, Frank H., 95-96
Reid, James, 70
Reid, Whitelaw, 264
Republican River trail, 219
Rhodes, Belle, 26
Ricci brothers, 173
Rice Exchange, New Orleans,
    172
Richards, Westley, 132
Richelieu Hotel, 69
Risan, Dalmatia, 80
Rische, August, 151
Riverside cemetery, 55, 113, 118,
    125
Robeson, Erba, 152
Robinson mine, 158
Rock Island R.R., 41
Rock Springs, Wyo., 113
Rockwell, L. C., 157, 161
Rocky Mountain National Park,
    139
Rogers, Clyde, 17
Rogers, Sarah Jane (Jennie), 14,
    18-20, 24-25, 40-49, 211, 275,
    280

Rogers, Will, 203
Ronan, Robert, 71
Rothacker, O. H., 38
Rowan, U. S. Marshal, 94
Running Water, 31
Runyon, Damon, 117
Russell, Fort D. A.; *see* Warren, Fort Francis E.
Ryan, Annie, 14, 56, 211
Ryan, Jim, 56

St. Anne's Infant Asylum, 56
Ste. Genevieve, 6
St. Joseph, Mo., 89, 219
St. Louis, Mo., 132, 138-39, 160, 217
Salt Lake City, Utah, 47
Salzburg, Austria, 144-46
Sampson, Jessie, 18
Samson, C. F., 71
San Antonio, Texas, 87
Sand Creek massacre, 66
Sands district, Chicago, 80
San Francisco, Calif., 11-12, 50, 81, 221, 226
San Luis Valley, 76, 230, 279
Sante Fe, the, 220
Saratoga, N.Y., 64, 66
Schenk, Robert C., 85
Schofield, Gen. John M., 6
Schoonover, Henry, 71
Seattle, Wash., 54, 94
See-Bar-See Land & Cattle Co., 245, 250
Sells-Floto circus, 182
Shafer, "Gyp," 220, 270
Shaw, Bob, 222
Shaw, Judge Lucien, 53

Shea, Arden, 29
Shepard, Bill, 31
Shepard, Tom, 31
Shepherd, William C., 105, 181
Sheridan, Gen. Phil, 139, 220
Sherman Act, 191, 267
Sherman, Sam, 121
Short, Luke, 222
Shotgun Hill cemetery, 91
Siddons, Belle, 3-12, 210; *see also* Vestal, Madame
Silks, George W., 28, 226, 229-30
Silks Hotel, 281
Silks, Martha, 261; *see also* Silks, Mattie
Silks, Mattie, 14, 18, 24, 34, 39, 40, 42-43, 45, 47-49, 53-54, 92-93, 124, 177, 207-86
Silver Plume, Colo., 154, 227
Silver Queen fire dept., 232
"Silverheels," 234-35
Silverheels, Mount, 234
Silverton, Colo., 113
Sioux Indians, 138
Skagway, Alaska, 94-97, 267-68
Skagway Guards, 95
Skiff, F. J. V., 39
Slain, Lulu, 90
"Slanting Annie," 90
Slaughterhouse, the; *see* Murphy's Exchange
Smith, Al, 197
Smith, Bascom, 93
Smith, Daisy, 25
Smith, Jack, 10, 11
Smith, Jefferson Randolph (Soapy), 37, 72, 87-96, 267
Smith, Joseph Emerson, 172

Smith, May, 14, 211
Smith, Tom, 218
Smoky Hill River, 217
Smuggler mine, 158
Snider, Jacob, 227
Snyder, Capt. D. H., 244
Soap Gang, 89, 267
Soapy Smith; *see* Smith, Jefferson Randolph
Sopris, Mayor Richard, 112
Sour Dough Saloon 268
Southern Hotel, St. Louis, 160
Sparks, Cliff, 89, 92
Speer Memorial Hospital, 84
Speer, Robert W., 82, 84, 280
Spring Hill, Kans., 216
Springfield, Ill., 215
Squiresville, Kans., 216
Stackelbeck, Diedrick Franz, 275
Standard Milling & Smelting Co., 193
Stanford, Leland, 64
Stanley, Faye, 14, 211
Stanton, Ruth, 26
"Star Aiden," 29
Star of Blood, 170
Starr, Belle, 28
Steck, Judge Amos, 155, 157, 161-62, 168
Steel Trap, 132, 136
Steunenberg, Gov. Frank, 193
Stevens, Laura, 18
Stewart, J. D., 95
Stewart, Sir William Drummond, 139
Stidger, Willis, 280
Stockdorf, Bertha, 143, 147
Stockdorf, Julius, 141, 143, 149

Stockdorf, Mathilda, 143
Stockton, Robert D. (Bob), 68
Storyville, New Orleans, 22
Strahorn, Robert E., 137
Stratton, W. S., 194
Stuart, C. A., 177
Stubblefield, David, 67
Sughrue brothers, 222
Sullivan Scenic & Decorating Co., 172
Sweet, Gov. William E., 181-84
Swift Creek, 138

Tabor, Augusta, 71, 151-73, 243, 260, 262
Tabor, Baby Doe, 14, 59, 152-74, 176
Tabor, Elizabeth B.; *see* Tabor, Baby Doe
Tabor, Elizabeth Bonduel Lillie, 168
Tabor Grand Opera House, Denver, 25, 33, 37, 70, 84, 92, 114, 120, 156, 158, 170, 173
Tabor, H. A. W., 14, 59, 70-71, 84-85, 92, 111, 151-74, 176, 202, 257, 265
Tabor, Horace Joseph, 169
Tabor, N. Maxcy, 151, 176
Tabor Office Building, 158
Tabor Opera House, Leadville, 152
Tabor, Rose Mary Echo Silver Dollar; *see* Tabor, Silver Dollar
Tabor, Silver Dollar, 169-70, 174
Tammen Curio Co., 177
Tammen, Harry H., 126, 175-89

Tammen, Heye, H.; *see* Tammen, Harry H.
Tammen, Heye Heinrich, 176
Tam O'Shanter mines, 159
Tanner, Charles H., 148-50
"Taos lightning," 70, 80
Tappan's Store, 224
Taylor, Dr. Hugh L., 48
Teapot Dome scandal, 276
Tedmon House, 124
Teller, Sen. Henry M., 160
Terrible mine, 154
Thatcher, Sam, 212
Third Colorado Cavalry, 66
Thom, W. B., 152
Thomas, Lillie, 29
Thompson, Ben, 217
Thompson, Billy, 217
Thompson, "Colonel" W. S. (Billy), 84, 222, 236
Thompson, Wood, 233
Thomson, Corteze D., 54, 92-93, 207-85
Thomson, Martha A.; *see* Silks, Mattie
Thomson, Mrs. C. D.; *see* Silks, Mattie
Thomson's Lake, 270
Thornton, James (Jimmy), 67
Thorp, Russell, 31
"Tid-bit," 29
Tilghman, Billy, 222
Tivoli Club, 91, 93
Tombstone, Ariz., 12, 222
Toner, Will, 209, 271-72
Tongue River, 135-37
Topic Theater, 192
Torrance mine, 159

Torrey's Rough Riders, 126
Tortoni's Restaurant, 15
Tracey, Jim, 71
Trinity Methodist Church, 114
Troy, Joe, 191
Tully, Anna, 25
Turner, Ella, 68
Turner Hall, 143
Turner, William C., 68
Tutt, Charles L., 190

Union, Fort, 136-38
Union Pacific R.R., 30, 79, 126
Utah Copper Co., 194
Utter, "Colorado Charley," 78

Van Cise, Philip S., 102-7, 175
Vanderbilt, Reginald, 86
Van Horn, Mayor M. D., 108
Vastine, Rose, 90
Vaughan, Col. A. J., 137
Venus Alley, Butte, 26
Veragua, Duchess of, 258
Veragua, Duke of, 258
Verandah, The, San Francisco, 50
Vestal, Madame, 3-12, 210
Vicksburg, Miss., 80
Victoria Mary Louisa, Duchess of Kent, 145
Victoria, Queen, 143, 145, 262
Vigilance Committee of 101, 94-96
Vigilantes, 11
Villa, "Pancho," 122
Vindicator mine, 193
Virginia City, Nev., 50
Voges, Gus, 148

Wade, Ben, 29
Wagon Wheel Gap, 90
Waite, Gov. Davis H. (Blood to the Bridles), 93
Wales, Prince of, 158
Walker, Mollie, 29
Warman, Cy, 90-91
Warren, Fort Francis E., 30
Waterloo mine, 158
Waters, A. H. & Co., 14, 231
Watrous Café, 71
Watrous, George, 236
Watrous, Mark, 92
Watson, L. S., 253
Watson's saloon, 11
Webster, C. M., 246-47
Webster, Daniel, 65
Wells, Sady, 29
Wentworth-Fitzwilliam, Sir William-Thomas-Spencer, 130-32
Western Federation of Miners, 193
Westerners, The, 46
Westport, Kans., 131
Wharton, J. E., 63
Wheat, Jessie, 98
White Horse, 268
White, Jack, 70
White, Josephine, 29
White, Lottie, 29
White, Lulu, 23
Whoop-up Canon, 10
Whyte, Lady Maude Josepha, 125
Wilcoxon, John E., 68

Wildcat Creek, 244
Wilde, Oscar, 33-39
Willard Hotel, Wash., 166
Wilson, Annie, 15, 19
Wilson, Bill, 224
Wilson, Clay, 68
Windsor Hotel, Denver, 34, 124-25, 154, 156, 159-60, 164, 167, 170, 176-77
Wister, Owen, 30
Wolcott, Henry, 265
Wolcott, Sen. Edward O., 85-86, 265
Wolfe Hotel, 190
Womack, Bob, 191, 203, 263
Wong, Jim, 115
Wood, Sam, 65
Wood, Stanley, 177
Woods, Jack, 54
Wray, Colo., 209, 245-46, 249-50, 252-53, 270-72, 279
Wright, C. W., 168
Wright, Robert M., 222
Wyoming Stock Growers' Assn., 31

Yee Chow Jung, 113
Yee Chung, 110
Yee Kee, 114
Yellowstone, 135, 137
Young, James, 71
Younger, Bud, 91
Younger, Cole, 91
Yuma, Colo., 250, 253

Zenobia Seminary, 64